U. M. L. L.

Silver

2001

Linings

reread Dec. 2012

Travels around
Northern Ireland

MARTIN FLETCHER

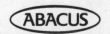

An *Abacus* Book

First published in Great Britain by
Little, Brown and Company in 2000
This edition published by Abacus in 2001

A CIP catalogue record for this book
is available from the British Library.

ISBN 0 349 11251 7

'Claudy', by James Simmons, is reproduced
by kind permission of the Gallery Press

Maps © Neil Hyslop

Typeset in Berkeley by M Rules
Printed and bound in Great Britain
by Clays Ltd, St Ives plc

Abacus
A Division of
Little, Brown and Company (UK)
Brettenham House
Lancaster Place
London WC2E 7EN

www.littlebrown.co.uk

For the good people of Northern Ireland,
in the hope that the bad times are over.

Contents

	Map	viii
	Acknowledgements	xi
1	Garden of Good and Evil	1
2	Rats and Sinking Ships	11
3	Poets and Partridges	37
4	The Magic Kingdom	70
5	Gods, Heroes and Dr Paisley	96
6	Westward Bound	127
7	The Sporting Life	158
8	Bowls and Bullets	191
9	Thugs and Charmers	223
10	Prods, Poachers and Pilgrims	261
	Epilogue	298
	Bibliography	304

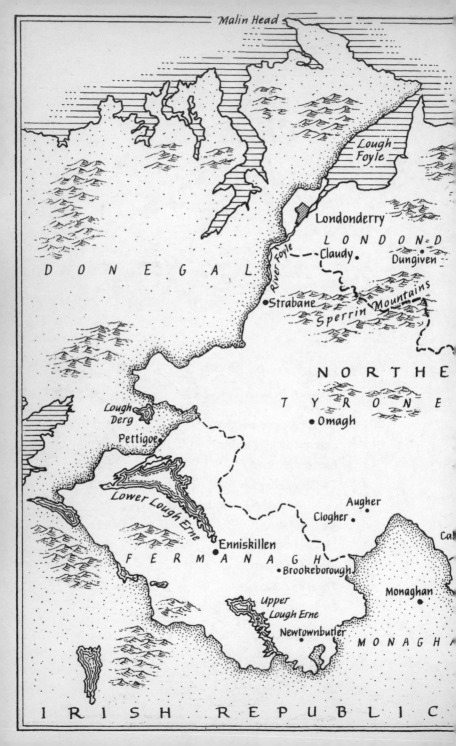

Acknowledgements

There have been hundreds of books written about Northern Ireland's history, its troubles and its paramilitaries. This one is about the people and the place. It cannot ignore the scars of the past thirty years, but I hope it presents a more rounded picture of a province whose beauty, charm and many other virtues are so seldom recorded.

I could not have written *Silver Linings* without the help of Yvonne Murphy, of Belfast's Linen Hall Library, who found answers to all my questions, no matter how obscure, and always did so with great good humour. Andy Wood, Douglas Carson and Robin Masefield – good friends with a wealth of local knowledge – offered invaluable support, advice and enthusiasm, as did my father-in-law, Richard Beney. Many others guided, counselled, fed, accommodated or otherwise helped me. Most feature in the book. Some do not. The latter include Andrew and Heather White, Joe Baird, Crispin Rodwell, Brian Kennaway, Donald Gribben, Mark McCaffrey, Danny Morrison, Austin Hunter and two other fine gentlemen – one from County Antrim and the other a civil servant – who introduced me to some of the rogues I encountered in my travels and must remain nameless.

My agent, Derek Johns of A.P. Watt, gave me great encouragement. At my publishers – Little, Brown – Richard Beswick, the editorial director, Antonia Hodgson, Katy Nicholson and Kate Balmforth were a delight to work with. Ben Preston, then home-news editor and now deputy editor of *The Times*, was very understanding of my periodic absences.

To all the above I am deeply grateful, as I am to my wife, Katy, and my children, Hannah, Barney and Imogen, whom I had to neglect for several months.

It is impossible, of course, to write a book about a place as raw as Northern Ireland without giving offence to someone. I would say only that this book is written in a spirit of affection, and as impartially as I know how, but any comments can be emailed to me at: martinfletcher2@compuserve.com

1
Garden of Good and Evil

In the summer of 1997, after eight happy years in Washington, my employers at *The Times* decided to punish me for some great sin, the exact nature of which I have yet to ascertain. They moved me from the sublime to the ridiculous, from the gleaming, cosmopolitan capital of the free world to dank, dreary, claustrophobic Belfast.

It was a place I knew only from grim headlines and lurid television images, and what little enthusiasm I could muster for this new assignment was rapidly extinguished. The very afternoon that I arrived the Reverend Ian Paisley, Ulster's perennial Doctor No, demonstrated the time-honoured Northern Ireland tradition of the walk-out, on this occasion from the Stormont peace talks.

The next day I watched the funeral of an 18-year-old Catholic girl shot dead by loyalist gunmen as she lay in her Protestant boyfriend's bed. That was quickly followed by the even more barbaric murder of a 16-year-old Catholic boy who was abducted while hitch-hiking, mutilated beyond recognition, and dumped in a water-filled hole used for the disposal of animal carcasses.

It seldom stopped raining. Armed soldiers sped around bleak and cheerless housing estates in slate-grey armoured Land

Rovers. The police stations, courts and other public buildings were grotesque fortresses. I had Unionist leaders shouting down the phone at me for daring to interview Sinn Fein's Gerry Adams, letters from irate readers who claimed to detect a pro- or anti-Unionist bias in my reporting, sharp reprimands from all and sundry for such terrible sins as calling Britain the 'mainland', Londonderry 'Derry', or the people 'Northern Irish'. The BBC provides its reporters with a whole page of guidelines to help them negotiate this terminological minefield.

It is true that the IRA declared a ceasefire within days of my arrival, but there was little excitement because nobody had much confidence that it would last.

In no time at all I found myself sympathising deeply with Reginald Maudling, the former British Cabinet minister still much reviled in Northern Ireland for remarking as he boarded a helicopter after his first trip to the province: 'What a bloody awful country. Give me a large Scotch.'

In a very real sense Northern Ireland – or 'Norn Iron' as the locals call it – is a bloody awful country. Like Pakistan and Bangladesh, it is an artificial entity born – in 1921 – from strife and conflict. More than a third of its inhabitants resent its very existence. During three decades of what were euphemistically called the 'Troubles', one person in 50 was injured and roughly 3,600, or one in 400, killed. More than half the victims were innocent civilians, and many thousands more were kneecapped, beaten or exiled – practices that continue even now. The place is still awash with legal and illegal weapons, not to mention an estimated 20,000 former terrorist prisoners, and there is scarcely a town or village that has not been blighted by violence.

Sectarianism remains pervasive. There are Protestant sports, banks, musical instruments and newspapers – and Catholic ones. Fewer than 14,000 of the province's schoolchildren go to formally integrated schools. Nobody would publicly admit it, but in many areas Protestants still will not sell property to

Catholics, and vice versa. When strangers meet they probe to ascertain the religion of the other from their name, address or where they were educated – and adjust accordingly.

Only in Northern Ireland could a union between a man and a woman of the same colour, nationality and Christian faith be called a 'mixed marriage'.

Like dogs cocking their legs, the two tribes stake out their territory with flags, painted kerbstones and vivid murals on gable ends that glorify their gunmen. Memorials, gravestones and books of condolence are defaced. Great steel 'peace lines' slice housing estates in half to keep feuding Catholic and Protestant 'communities' apart.

Northern Ireland is tiny, and one of the very few places in the world substantially less populated now than it was two centuries ago. It has 1.6 million inhabitants, about the same as Hampshire or Nebraska, and there is just one telephone book for the entire province. It covers a mere 5,267 square miles, roughly the same as Yorkshire or Connecticut. It has nonetheless provided the world with more grim and grisly news over the past 30 years than anywhere else I can think of. But the funny thing was that my wife, Katy, fell in love with it from the moment she and the family sailed up that great sea inlet called Belfast Lough early one fine August morning on the overnight ferry from Liverpool.

We found a large and attractive house in a tranquil village on the south shore of the lough. The children took a little local train four stops up the line to one of the province's excellent grammar schools each day. They did paper rounds in the evenings, and at weekends roamed along the beaches. They were safer, and far freer, than they ever were in Washington.

Neighbours came with gifts of flowers and chocolate cake, invited Katy to coffee, enrolled her in their 'tums and bums' fitness classes, and whisked her off to girls' nights out. Every Wednesday a fish van arrived outside our front door bearing fresh salmon, kippers and smoked haddock. The breads and cheeses were fabulous.

While I was reporting on the tortuous peace negotiations, and on the paramilitary thugs who were creating the headlines, she was meeting the ordinary people of Northern Ireland and finding them warm, generous, intelligent and fun. Most were doing their level best to lead normal, happy, God-fearing lives and were embarrassed by the province's dire international image. While I was frequently reinforcing that image with articles which focused on the negative, Katy was discovering a charming and delightful side of the place that outsiders never hear about.

To start with, Northern Ireland's six counties – Fermanagh, Armagh, Tyrone, Londonderry, Antrim and Down, or FATLAD for short – are astonishingly beautiful. It is a shame about the architecture, which consists largely of plain modern bungalows, but from the Mountains of Mourne to the moors of the Sperrins, from Antrim's spectacular coast and glens to Fermanagh's lakes and rivers, the countryside is empty, remote and lovely.

It is littered with mottes, raths, bawns, crannogs, dolmens, standing stones and other ancient or prehistoric sites. There is no prairie agriculture here because the land is far too boggy – just thousands of small farms with an average size of less than 90 acres. Certainly it rains a lot: 'Gumboots, umbrellas, raincoats etc. are essential unless you want to stay inside reading a book all day,' one guidebook advises. But the compensation is a spectacular lushness capped by Gulf Stream-nurtured palm trees, and wonderful skies embellished by frequent rainbows.

The Troubles caused terrible suffering and destruction. They deterred most visitors except for human rights activists, anthropologists and Irish-American congressmen. They severed the province from the outside world. They greatly retarded social progress – women are still kept firmly in their place, abortion is all but banned, and bars and restaurants are still full of smokers. Dr Paisley fulminated about 'sodomites at Stormont' when Elton John came to give a concert. Protestant fundamentalists even picketed a 1999 production of *Jesus Christ Superstar* at Belfast's Opera House on the grounds that it was blasphemous.

But the Troubles also slowed the modernisation and homogenisation that have rendered so much of Britain and America bland. Since the late 1960s the province has been caught in a time-warp from which it is only now emerging. The pace of life remains slow and an old-world charm survives.

People tend to live in the towns and villages where they, their parents and their grandparents were all raised. There is a strong community spirit, albeit one born of shared adversity. The ordinary crime rate – as opposed to terrorist crimes – is one of the lowest in the industrialised world, and drugs have only recently begun to be a problem. I was often held up by tractors, but there were no traffic jams to speak of. People still drive at an infuriating 45 mph along roads where it's impossible to pass.

McDonald's reached Moscow before it reached Northern Ireland. The giant supermarket chains which spurned the province during the Troubles only began to move in a few years back, meaning the high streets are still full of butchers, bakers, fishmongers, haberdashers, drapers and other attractive little shops that close early on Wednesdays. The province's banks still print their own notes. The calendar is punctuated by events like horse fairs, ploughing championships and cattle markets. People have old-fashioned names like Violet and Irene, Alfred and Albert.

The people may have done terrible things to each other, but they could not be kinder to outsiders – and that includes staunch republicans whose hatred of the British in the abstract rarely extends to Britons individually. I lost count of the people who plied me with home-made scones and cake when I went to interview them.

They indulge in such traditional pastimes as road-bowling in country lanes on Sundays – not to mention poaching, smuggling and poteen-making. They boast an accent for every county, and retain a distinctive dialect. Here 'culchies' (country folk) 'gurn' (complain) about their 'weans' (children), so they do. 'Bout yer?', they'll say by way of greeting. 'Catch yerself on,' they'll tell you if you say something daft. 'Safe home,' they'll tell you when you leave, and you will inevitably be addressed as 'yous', so you will.

As a journalist I was uniquely privileged. There was virtually no one else in the province who could move freely across the sectarian divide, who could walk with equal safety up the Shankill or the Falls, who could interview political leaders and paramilitary godfathers, republican or loyalist. Not the police. Not the Army. Not civil servants. And certainly not the ordinary man in the street.

In the course of my work I met some of the most chilling people I have come across in 18 years of journalism: paramilitary leaders, terrorists, bigots consumed by mindless hatred. But I also met some of the most inspiring: former bombers and gunmen striving to make amends for past misdeeds, victims of terrorism who have managed to forgive, women who have stoically endured the most crushing losses, clergymen and community workers battling the evil in their midst.

The bombs and murders that made the news spawned countless victims' support and anti-terror groups that never did. There is an alphabet soup of paramilitary organisations – the IRA, UDA, UVF, UFF, LVF, INLA, CIRA, RIRA. But there is also an alphabet soup of organisations set up to redress the balance. Nowhere else I have lived has had such an active or well-informed citizenry – the province supports 46 newspapers – or for that matter such a productive and inventive one.

This tiny corner of a very small island has produced an extraordinary number of high achievers. It boasts five Nobel prizewinners – though four won the peace prize and that is obviously easier if you come from a place where there's conflict. It has spawned a president of Israel, two prime ministers of New Zealand, a prime minister of Tasmania and, believe it or not, a Hindu god.

It produced the man who wrote out America's Declaration of Independence, the man who printed it, and several of its signatories. A dozen American presidents – a quarter of the total – were of Ulster stock. It was another Ulsterman, Major General Robert Ross, who burned down the White House in 1814, but not before he had eaten dinner in President Madison's abandoned dining room.

Ulstermen produced America's first daily newspaper, opened its first bank in Baltimore, and supervised the building of New York's first subway. The writers C.S. Lewis and Brian Moore, the poets Seamus Heaney and Louis MacNeice and the actors Kenneth Branagh and Liam Neeson were all reared here, as were the musicians Van Morrison, James Galway and Barry Douglas.

Thanks to the Troubles, Northern Ireland boasts some of the world's leading knee surgeons, pathologists, forensic scientists and manufacturers of bullet-proof vests. The world's first vertical take-off jet and electric railway were built in the province. Harry Ferguson developed the modern tractor and John Dunlop the pneumatic tyre. Sir James Martin produced the ejector seat. Thomas Romney Robinson invented the cup anemometer for measuring wind speed, and Sir James Murray superphosphate fertilisers and Milk of Magnesia.

Northern Ireland rarely fails to commemorate its murders and atrocities, but most of these people remain lamentably uncelebrated.

The province's real golden age spanned the end of the nineteenth-century and the beginning of the twentieth when Belfast – having mushroomed from 20,000 people in 1800 to 200,000 by

1880 – was one of the great industrial hubs of the British Empire. It was the Cape Canaveral of shipbuilding with Harland and Wolff, the world's leading shipyard, producing one magnificent liner after another. The most famous was, of course, the *Titanic*, the biggest and most luxurious ship ever launched. For good measure Belfast also boasted the world's largest ropeworks, linen mill, tobacco factory, gasometer and tea machinery works.

Few traces are left of those glory days, but Belfast City Hall in the middle of Donegall Square is a notable exception. Locals call it 'the wedding cake'. Sir John Betjeman, the late Poet Laureate, described it as 'gorgeous'. It was conceived as a monument to the city's greatness by William Pirrie, a Lord Mayor and head of Harland and Wolff, and his fellow Victorian industrialists. Constructed between 1898 and 1906 for what was, in those days, the massive sum of £360,000, it is quite preposterously magnificent. The building was the last blast of empire, a final flourish of the gilded age, and makes most American state capitols seem quite ordinary.

The City Hall is pretty impressive from the outside. It is a huge, colonnaded edifice built in classical style of Portland stone, ringed by lawns and statues, and crowned with a great, green, 173-foot-high copper dome. In the forecourt is a particularly fine statue of Queen Victoria holding what appears to be a grenade, but just might be an orb.

Here, on 28 September 1912, nearly half-a-million Ulstermen gathered to sign – some in their own blood – a 'Solemn League and Covenant' to use 'all means which may be found necessary to defeat the present conspiracy to set up a Home Rule Parliament in Ireland'. They were determined to remain part of the United Kingdom.

From here, on 8 May 1915, the 36th Ulster Division marched off to France where, the following year, 5,500 of its men were killed or wounded in the first two days of the Battle of the Somme. Their heroics made it politically impossible for the government to shunt Ulster into a self-governing Ireland after the First World War.

It was from here, too, that President Clinton addressed a vast sea of ordinary Protestants and Catholics on a cold November night in 1995. They had turned out in their tens of thousands not just to greet an American president, or to watch him switch on the Christmas-tree lights, but to express their hunger for peace after so much pointless bloodshed. Alas, they had to wait another three years before the warring factions produced the Good Friday accord and the hope of a new beginning.

The interior of the City Hall is yet more opulent – a veritable palace of marble floors, sweeping staircases and magnificent chambers panelled in oak and mahogany. There is a great rotunda with a whispering gallery. There are stained-glass windows and potted palms, Corinthian columns and chandeliers, portraits and statues, exquisite plasterwork and vaulted ceilings. It looks for all the world like the inside of the *Titanic*, which is hardly surprising as it was built by the same craftsmen. Indeed the Lord Mayor's robing room is said to be an exact replica of a first-class cabin, right down to the portholes, mahogany panelling and splendid loo.

In 1997 the Ulster Titanic Society held a dinner in the Great Hall. 'Some of us had a fair bit to drink,' recalled Douglas Carson, the erudite gentleman who organised the event. 'I don't think any would have been at all surprised if this stone *Titanic* had begun to rear up and sink into the lawns.'

Another man had good reason to remember that night. Ian Adamson was Belfast's Lord Mayor at the time, and a 53-year-old bachelor. On impulse he asked Mr Carson's 24-year-old daughter Kerry to dance because, he told me with a chuckle, 'she was the most beautiful person I had ever seen'. He proposed to her on the lawn of Buckingham Palace just before the Queen presented him with an OBE; they married on 15 April 1998, the anniversary of the *Titanic*'s tragic end. They took the *QE2* across the Atlantic for their honeymoon, telephoning the *Belfast Telegraph* from the exact spot where the *Titanic* sank, and stayed at the Waldorf Astoria in New York whose owner perished with the ship.

But I digress. The real point about the City Hall is that it is right in the heart of Belfast, and the roads from Belfast lead to all corners of the province. In short, it is the perfect starting point for a series of journeys to the far corners of this land of tainted beauty, this battleground of good and evil, this shunned but compelling little plot of earth over which the prospect of lasting peace now hangs like one of Northern Ireland's many rainbows – simultaneously real and illusory.

2

Rats and Sinking Ships

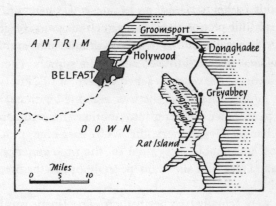

Some imaginative tourist board official once christened Belfast the Hibernian Rio. It lacks the sun, the festive atmosphere, the beaches, the bronzed youth and quite a few other things besides, but you can see the point he was making. The city does have a spectacular setting, as fine as that of any British city. It sits at the head of Belfast Lough, straddling the Lagan River valley and ringed by high hills.

It is where the Lagan meets the lough that I am standing now, on a bitterly cold Saturday morning in November, with Mr Carson, Dr Adamson and their respective wives. To be more precise, we are standing in a patch of industrial wasteland in the docklands no more than a mile east of the City Hall. In the distance there are cranes, old warehouses, once-fine red-brick Victorian buildings that have long since been abandoned and the outline of Belfast's brand new £100 million Odyssey Centre – one of Europe's biggest millennial projects. But right here is just a large expanse of crumbling black tarmac that ends abruptly at the edge of the deep black, salty water. The odd gull wheels overhead, but there is no other sign of life.

We have come on a little pilgrimage, for this is an historic spot. Beneath our feet there was once a great berth surrounded by a vast gantry where thousands of Harland and Wolff employees spent two years building the *Titanic*. It was here, on 31 May 1911, that half the city gathered to watch the world's biggest ship slide into the water with the help of hydraulic rams and 23 tons of tallow, soap and oil smeared across the slipway. The launch took 62 seconds, the vessel reached a speed of 12½ knots by the time she hit the water, and she was festooned with chains and anchors to stop her crashing into another shipyard across the narrow channel. Her owners, the White Star Line, proclaimed her almost unsinkable, a symbol of 'the pre-eminence of the Anglo-Saxon race' and an 'eloquent testimony to the progress of mankind'.

There were actually two berths here. The *Titanic* was built in Slip Three, and her sister ships the *Olympic* and the *Britannic* in Slip Two. The *Britannic* was to have been named the *Gigantic*, but the White Star Line thought again after the *Titanic* sank. At the water's edge there is a large concrete protrusion that may possibly have divided the two slips. At the other end of the tarmac you can just make out the rusting rails that carried the constituent parts of these three great leviathans to the gantries. But there is nothing else, not even a plaque or a marker – just an Ozymandian scene of decay and dereliction.

Had Belfast been an American city, it would have cashed in mightily on the *Titanic*. There would be a *Titanic* museum, a *Titanic* theme park, and souvenir shops selling *Titanic* mugs, *Titanic* models and *Titanic* T-shirts bearing slogans like 'Do You Ever Get That Sinking Feeling?' This is a ship whose 'last supper' menu fetched £19,500 at an auction in 1999, and whose lifeboat nameplates sold for nearly £25,000. A Harland and Wolff gate-keeper told me that tourists turned up almost daily asking where the ship was built.

But there is none of that. There is no Titanic Street, no Titanic pub, no Titanic Towers. There is not a single entry under 'Titanic' in the Yellow Pages. Harland and Wolff sent me a history of the company that devoted just one terse sentence to the most famous ship ever built. After extolling the *Olympic* it noted: 'A sister ship, the *Titanic*, which was built in 1912, sank on her maiden voyage after striking an iceberg in mid-Atlantic.'

The only physical reminder in the entire city is the Titanic Memorial – a rather gloomy statue depicting Thanatos, the Greek Goddess of Death, clutching a black laurel wreath above two mermaids bearing the body of a dead seaman. This once stood in front of the City Hall, in the middle of Donegall Place, but was long ago moved to relative obscurity around the eastern end because it was obstructing the traffic.

This neglect is more than mere oversight. The *Titanic*'s sinking was a terrible blow to the city. It was not just that 15,000 Belfast men helped build the ship, or that Thomas Andrews, the *Titanic*'s designer, and many Belfast crewmen lost their lives. There was also a tremendous sense of damaged pride. The ship-yard's head, Lord Pirrie, was a leading nationalist but its work-force was overwhelmingly Protestant, and at a time when Belfast was fiercely resisting Home Rule for Ireland the *Titanic* was supposed to be a potent symbol of Protestant prowess. 'There was political angst and personal grief and damaged professional pride,' said Mr Carson. 'The shipyard for a generation after that didn't want to be reminded it built the ship that sank.'

One popular myth was that the *Titanic* left Belfast covered in anti-Catholic graffiti, and that the number painted on her hull was '3909 ON' which, reflected in the ocean, read 'NO POPE'. Another probably apocryphal story says that Belfast's Catholics celebrated the news of her sinking by lighting bonfires. What is certainly true is that the *Titanic*'s loss coincided with the start of this once-great city's long and frequently violent decline – a decline from which it only began to emerge in the late 1990s.

As we stood there, the huge, sleek, state-of-the-art twin-hulled superferry that runs between Belfast and Stranraer in Scotland glided soundlessly up the lough. The men who built the *Titanic* less than 90 years ago could never have imagined such a vessel. As for Harland and Wolff, the company is now struggling to survive. At its peak it employed 35,000 men in Belfast and had other yards in Southampton, Liverpool, Glasgow and London. Today it employs just 1,700, building deep-sea oil and gas drilling vessels beneath the two giant yellow cranes – 'Sampson' and 'Goliath' – that are larger than London's Tower Bridge and dominate the Belfast skyline.

It was time for me to move on, eastwards along the lough's southern shore on the dual carriageway towards Bangor. This whisked me past the rows of tiny terraced red-brick houses built for the shipyard workers of east Belfast. Few of the present inhabitants work for Harland and Wolff, but their attitudes remain the same. On almost every gable end are huge, colourful murals depicting armed and hooded loyalist paramilitaries above slogans like 'For God and Ulster' or, with apologies to President Kennedy, 'Ask not what your country can do for you, but what you can do for your country.'

The road took me past Shorts, the world's oldest aircraft man-ufacturers and Northern Ireland's largest private sector employer. The company built the Wright brothers' first six planes, and in 1957 developed the first vertical take-off jet, the SC1.

A few more minutes and I was turning right into Holywood, a town that flourished during the Troubles when the middle classes feared to venture into Belfast. It is full of gift shops, galleries and no fewer than 27 different bistros, wine bars and other eating places. It was where my children went to school, and boasts the only maypole on the island of Ireland. Beyond these two startling claims to fame it is also the home of Noreen Hill, with whom I was soon drinking coffee in her flat at the top of a large Victorian house in a street called My Lady's Mile.

Mrs Hill – one of those truly inspirational women I kept encountering in Northern Ireland – has endured the most terrible hardship without a word of complaint or self-pity. She has lovingly nursed her comatose husband, Ronnie, ever since 1987 when the IRA's Remembrance Day bomb in Enniskillen nearly killed him.

Mr Hill was headmaster of Enniskillen High School at the time. He had just finished teaching a bible class, and when the bomb exploded he was completely buried in masonry except for one gloved hand. He suffered a fractured skull, severe lung damage, and numerous broken bones. He could not talk, but he could write, and on the Monday he was able to ask if a friend, Gordon Wilson, had survived. Mrs Hill has kept the note. 'It was more or less the last communication we had,' she said with a catch in her voice. 'He always thought of others.' At 2 p.m. the next day he slipped into a coma from which he never emerged.

Mr Hill spent five weeks in intensive care in Londonderry, and another four years in hospital in Enniskillen. At that point, after 30 years of being a housewife, Mrs Hill used her government compensation money to buy a residential home for the elderly in Holywood so that she could provide round-the-clock care for him herself.

She lives in her flat at the top of the house, and her husband occupies a back room on the ground floor. He is fed by tube; is taken out of bed for four hours every day; he sleeps and 'wakes', which is to say that his eyes flicker open and his head lolls. Mrs Hill goes in every time she passes, reads to him nightly, and plays him music and audio books. When their grandchildren visit, she puts little presents in his hand for them. For many years she was convinced he was listening because he would yawn and swallow, and says that when she told him of her mother's death a tear ran down his cheek. But he has grown less and less responsive. For a long time she hoped for a miracle, but has now been told that he has heart failure and only a short time left to live.

When we had finished our coffee Mrs Hill took me in to see him. Mr Hill was in bed, his eyes closed, curled up on his side and breathing heavily. His hair was grey, his muscles atrophied. He was 67, though his life had effectively ended at 56. On the wall were pictures of his family and younger self, and a painting of Lough Erne presented to him by his colleagues on his 'retirement' in 1988, one year after the bomb. She patted him, caressed his leg. 'Here's Martin Fletcher. He's come from *The Times*, your favourite paper,' she said cheerily. 'Come on, now. I know you're not asleep.' There was not a flicker of response.

'I don't have a life outside this home,' Mrs Hill admitted, but she feels no self-pity. 'It was my decision to bring Ronnie home. No one forced me into it,' she said. Nor does she feel bitterness towards the bombers: 'Bitterness is a very, very heavy burden to carry. Vengeance is for the Lord. I can leave that to Him.' But she does express sorrow. 'It is sad,' she said. 'Sometimes I go down to Ronnie and think of what he and I could be doing now. I miss him an awful lot. He's here but he can't talk to me. He can't tell me what he's thinking. He can't answer my questions.'

Where does she get her strength, I asked. 'From God,' she replied.*

Holywood marks the beginning of the so-called 'Gold Coast' – a string of villages like Cultra, Craigavad, Helen's Bay and Crawfordsburn that border Belfast Lough and give spectacular

---

* Ronnie Hill died of heart failure on 28 December 2000. He never regained consciousness.

lie to the notion that Northern Ireland is populated entirely by the poor. This is Surrey-by-the-Sea, but with even more BMWs.

Here Belfast's lawyers, businessmen and senior public servants still live in the style to which the English middle-classes once aspired. They buy handsome homes ringed by lush lawns and stupendously thick hedges for the price of a tiny flat in central London. They have no private school fees because the local grammar schools are excellent. They have oodles of disposable income as my son, Barney, was quick to discover. For many weeks (until his teacher caught him) he used to stop at a confectionery shop on his way to school each morning, buy several 25-pence packets of noxious sweets called 'Dweebs' and sell them for double the price to all the boys who were driven to school by their parents.

The denizens of the 'Gold Coast' are not afraid to enjoy themselves. We have friends there who spend every summer at their second homes on America's eastern shore, and who think nothing of jetting off to New York to shop or watch a Broadway show. For rest and relaxation they join the Royal Belfast Golf Club, or the Royal North of Ireland Yacht Club in Cultra (pronounced 'Cult-raw'). They have personal trainers, and boost their tans on the sunbeds of the Elysium health club at the five-star Culloden Hotel.

Any number of prime IRA targets live in heavily protected houses tucked away down these back lanes, but even at the height of the Troubles they were seldom attacked. This is often attributed to the fact that there is only one road back to Belfast and the police could easily have intercepted the bombers. Violence was for the most part something these Gold Coasters watched on television. 'It's as though you're a million miles away,' remarked the estate agent who found us our home. 'It goes on and on and on, but no one bats an eyelid here . . . All we're concerned about is whether there's enough ice in the gin.'

The richest of all the Gold Coasters is the Marchioness of

Dufferin and Ava, who lives on the 3,000-acre walled Clandeboye estate just west of Bangor when not in London. Known as Lindy to her friends, she is an artist, conservationist, benefactor and scion of the Guinnesses – Ireland's 'royal family' or, as they are sometimes known, 'the beerage'.

Clandeboye was essentially the creation of the 1st Marquis, Frederick Temple Hamilton Blackwood, one of those astoundingly accomplished Victorians who served between 1872 and 1896 as Governor General of Canada, Viceroy of India, and British ambassador in St Petersburg, Cairo, Rome and Paris. There is a statue of him outside Belfast City Hall.

The house is stuffed with artefacts he culled from around the world. Lady Dufferin once described Clandeboye as 'an accumulation of objects from all over the empire which evoke the grandeur, romanticism and sense of timeless confidence and comfort that surround that period of history'. According to a book by Harold Nicolson, the 1st Marquis' nephew, those objects include 'the mummified hand of some Egyptian, which from a bandage of stained cerecloth extended a withered digit, complete with a fingernail'. The house allegedly even contains the bed of the King and Queen of Burma, a country the 1st Marquis annexed while Viceroy.

There is a story that during his time in India the 1st Marquis brought a curse upon his family by committing some dreadful sin – looting sacred treasures, perhaps. I have no idea if this is true, but the family has certainly had a pretty rough time of it over the last century.

The 1st Marquis' eldest son was killed in the Boer War, and his next two sons in the First World War – all childless. The fourth and youngest son, Frederick, died in an air crash in 1930. His widow, Brenda, ended up half mad, apparently believing herself to be Queen of the Fairies.

Frederick's son Basil duly became the 4th Marquis. He was a good friend of John Betjeman, who stayed several times at Clandeboye and wrote of his host:

Lord Ava had enormous eyes
And head of a colossal size
He rarely laughed and only spoke
To utter some stupendous joke
Which if it were not understood
Was anyhow considered good.

In 1945 Basil was killed in action in – coincidentally – Burma. His widow Maureen, another Guinness girl, was a great society figure, a staple of the London gossip columns who played practical jokes, hosted annual dinners for the Queen Mother and feuded with her daughters until shortly before her death at the age of 91 in 1998. Their son Sheridan, the 5th Marquis, married Lindy in 1964, but they had no children and he died of Aids in 1988 – the last of a distinctly tragic line.

Naturally, I intended to check the tale of the curse with the Marchioness. I wrote her a very polite letter explaining about this book and asking if I could visit Clandeboye. I even sent her a copy of a previous book I'd written about America, with some of the more flattering reviews. Weeks passed. I heard nothing. Finally I telephoned. 'Lady Dufferin does not want Clandeboye included at this time,' one of her assistants told me sniffily. 'With your permission, Her Ladyship will be adding your book to her library.'

I must confess to feeling a little peeved. I registered a powerful protest a few weeks later by refusing to buy the family Christmas tree from the estate, and opted for a mild trespass instead.

Perhaps the most remarkable and touching thing about the 1st Marquis was his absolute worship of his mother, Helen, who was only 18 when he was born, and widowed shortly after. He named Helen's Bay, the village where we lived, after her. He built a broad tree-lined avenue, more than two miles long and spanned by ornate gothic bridges, to link Clandeboye to the

Helen's Bay beach and railway station (where he had his own private waiting room). Six years before her death from breast cancer in 1867 – the greatest tragedy of his life – he also built a tower in her honour on top of the highest hill on his estate and persuaded such eminent poets as Browning and Tennyson to celebrate this edifice in verse.

By subsequent generations, recalled Harold Nicolson, this tower was 'mentioned only with hushed reverence'. It was 'surrounded with associations which were intangible, awe-inspiring and remote. It checked our gaiety and our excesses with the raised finger of sobriety.'

When first built, the tower was visible for miles around. Today only the topmost turret protrudes from the pine trees that have grown up all around it. If I could not visit Clandeboye, I would at least visit the tower, I decided. That afternoon I set off along a little-known footpath that passes through the back of the estate, then cut up through silent woods of oak and beech planted by the 1st Marquis until finally I reached this Holy of Holies.

It was worth the hike. The tower stands in a little clearing, a great stone folly rearing skywards and topped with romantic battlements and the aforesaid turret. The door was locked, of course, but I already knew from Mr Nicolson's book what was inside. The first floor contains a kitchen, the second a bathroom with a small four-poster bed hung with embroidered curtains, and the third a sitting-room with what must once have been the most stupendous views of loughs and hills and sea. On the walls of the sitting room are hung golden tablets embossed with the Browning and Tennyson poems. Browning's began:

> *Who hears of Helen's Tower may dream perchance*
> *How that great beauty of the Scaean Gate . . .*

Tennyson's read:

> *Helen's Tower here I stand*
> *Dominant over sea and land.*
> *Son's love built me, and I hold*
> *Mother's love in lettered gold.*
> *Would my granite girth were strong*
> *As either love, to last as long.*
> *I would wear my crown entire*
> *To and thro' the Doomsday fire,*
> *And be found of angel eyes*
> *In earth's recurring paradise.*

With Tennyson's poem in particular the 1st Marquis was over-joyed. 'It is very rare in this world that we poor human creatures can make each other supremely happy, but that is what you have made me,' he told the then Poet Laureate in a letter. 'Hundreds of years hence, perhaps, men and women, sons and daughters of my house, will read in what you have written a story that must otherwise have been forgotten.'

A century and a half later I was, in my own humble way, proving him right.

It is nice to write a travel book that allows you to sleep in your own bed at night. Helen's Tower was only a couple of miles distant, but even the furthermost point of the province was less than two hours away. After a leisurely breakfast the next morning I took the ring road around the Victorian seaside resort of Bangor and was soon driving into Groomsport, a pleasant village with a little harbour located just where Belfast Lough widens into the sea.

There is nothing particularly special about Groomsport except that each July it holds a festival to celebrate one of those quirky little adventures which, had it ended happily, might have changed the map of the United States and made this village Ulster's Plymouth, a mecca for every patriotic Yank.

In 1636 a bunch of 140 Presbyterians, feeling religiously oppressed by the Anglican establishment, decided to emulate the exploits of the Pilgrim Fathers 16 years before. They set sail for the New World in a tiny vessel called the *Eagle Wing*, hoping to establish a colony of their own in 'the uncultivated wilds of America'. Unfortunately they reached the middle of the Atlantic where 'the swellings of the sea did rise higher than any mountains we had ever seen on earth, so that in the mid-day they hid the sun from our sight'. The storms 'did break our rudder, with much of our galleon-head, fore-crosstrees and tore our foresail'. In fact they were so severe that 'it was made evident to us that it was not His will that we should go to New England'.

The crew lowered a shipwright over the edge to mend the rudder, turned back, and reached home eight weeks after setting sail with 139 passengers – two having died and one woman having given birth to a child christened, imaginatively, Seaborn. 'That which grieved us most,' wrote one of the leaders of this sorry little expedition, 'was that we were like to be a mocking to the wicked.'

From Groomsport the road turns south down the top of the Ards peninsula which divides Strangford Lough from the Irish Sea. A string of grand homes look out across the sea to the low, flat, almost treeless Copeland Islands a mile or so offshore. A century ago the largest of these had a population of 34, but they were finally abandoned soon after the Second World War. It was a sunny day, and I had not much else to do, so I decided to try and get out to them.

The next little town down the coast is Donaghadee, whose name alone once inspired a Thomas Hardy poem:

> *I've never gone to Donaghadee*
> *That vague far townlet by the sea;*
> *In Donaghadee I shall never be:*
> *Then why do I sing of Donaghadee?*

For two or three centuries this townlet by the sea was actually the gateway to Ireland, the bustling terminal of the only ferry service from Scotland to the north. But it died a sudden death in the mid-nineteenth century when the new Royal Mail steam packets abruptly switched to Larne and the passengers followed suit.

Today Donaghadee is as pretty as its name – a long crescent of old, painted buildings strung out around a harbour with a lighthouse at one end and what appears to be a tiny castle crowning an old Norman mound behind. It is in fact an explosives store built in about 1820 when a new harbour was being constructed. But the town is sleepy beyond measure, and finding a boat to take me to the islands was not hard because there was only one left in the harbour.

It belonged to Quinton Nelson, a friendly soul with the build of a refrigerator. When he was a boy, he told me, Donaghadee was packed with holidaymakers each summer. To keep them amused there used to be 17 boats running excursions to the Copelands and elsewhere, but his was now the only one left and he doubted even he would carry on much longer. 'It's cheaper to go to Spain for a month than here for a week, and you're sure of the sun,' he said. Donaghadee was now full of old people's homes and flats for the elderly and 'I don't think it will ever recover, certainly not to what it was.'

We set off across the becalmed blue-grey water in an old wooden boat which had been in Quinton's family since 1947. The crossing took all of 15 minutes, and our exploration of the islands little more, but it was an eerie experience.

The largest island – some 350 acres – used to support nine farms. The furrows of the fields and their tumbledown walls are still visible. Half-a-century later it boasts just three or four primitive holiday cottages, all shut up for the winter, and is used only for grazing a few sheep and the odd shoot. At this time of year it is inhabited only by ghosts.

Quinton showed me an overgrown graveyard with most of its
stones now broken but two dating back to the 1740s. The only
remotely new one was in memory of Ronnie Ramm, a game-
keeper, 'whose happiest days were spent here on Copeland
Island'.

He showed me the foundations of the old schoolhouse and
the rusted remains of an old treadmill. On the grassy path that
served as the island's 'main road' stood, in splendid isolation, an
old red Edwardian post-box without its door. 'The postman used
to row out, and the sign on the door read "Next Collection:
Weather Permitting",' said Quinton.

From the far side of the island we looked across to its two tiny
neighbours – Mew and Lighthouse Islands. The latter was once
crowned by a coal-fired lighthouse, the remnants of which still
stand. The former has a more modern lighthouse that ceased to
be manned in 1997.

I suddenly realised what made these islands so special. They
had been inhabited well into the twentieth century, but were
utterly untouched by modernity. No car had ever driven on
them; they had never been illuminated by electricity, or tilled
except by hand, or tarmacked over, or dug up to lay sewage or
water pipes. They had never seen a cash register, or witnessed a
credit card transaction.

Their virginity, for want of a better term, is evidently not considered a great attraction. In the old days families would happily
spend whole days on the islands, enjoying their remoteness and
simplicity, Quinton told me as we set off back. 'Nowadays visitors complain after two hours that there's nothing to do. They
like to have shops and cafés and toilets – all the things the island
doesn't have.'

By the time we docked it was lunchtime. I thanked Quinton,
who refused any payment, and headed for Grace Neill's Inn in
the main street which would be much more to the liking of the
modern holidaymaker. Built in 1611, it claims to be Ireland's

oldest pub and consists of two snug little rooms with ceilings made of old ships' timbers plus a whopping new extension at the back which I studiously ignored.

Peter the Great of Russia stayed here, or so the pub claims. So, allegedly, did the composer Franz Liszt – with piano in tow – the poet John Keats and umpteen other luminaries travelling to or from Scotland. On the wall is an ancient black-and-white photograph of Grace Neill herself, a pipe-smoking lady who was given the pub by her father and died in 1916 at the age of 98. Raymond McElroy, the manager, told me that the whiskey, gin and vodka were not the only spirits in the building; Grace Neill still walks around at night, he insisted.

I wouldn't vouch for any of these claims, but I would vouch for the food. I had roast parsnip and carrick-leaf soup with thick wheaten bread and butter, followed by home-made pork and leek sausages with mashed potato and red onion marmalade. For this surprisingly good lunch I had unexpected reason to be grateful to Lady Dufferin: the chef had spent four years as her personal cook at Clandeboye.

From Donaghadee I could have carried right on down to the bottom of the Ards peninsula, past its bays and beaches and rocky strands that vanish at high tides, past its pretty and not-so-pretty coastal villages, past the countless caravan sites – almost exclusively Protestant – to which so many of Belfast's mothers and children traditionally decamp each summer while their husbands stay in town and work.

At the bottom I could have taken a ten-minute ferry ride across the narrow and turbulent mouth of Strangford Lough and carried on to Castle Ward, a sort of Jekyll-and-Hyde house on the lough's southern shore whose two façades, one classical and one gothic, reflect the contrasting architectural tastes of its original owners, Lord and Lady Bangor. Had it been June I would undoubtedly have done so, for that is when Castle Ward becomes Northern Ireland's Glyndebourne – except that tickets are a fraction of the price, and you reach the place through fragrant country lanes not endless London suburbs.

I did none of that; I cut across the lush green farmland of the peninsula on tiny lanes fringed with gorse and blackberry bushes. It took all of ten minutes, and as I came down over the other side I had a tremendous sense of descending into a sea of intense and brilliant light. It was actually the glare of the sun reflecting off the vast blue surface of Strangford Lough with its myriad islands and gentle hills beyond.

The lough is Northern Ireland's version of America's Chesapeake Bay – a sailor's paradise, a great bird sanctuary, a watery cornucopia that produces celebrated oysters, mussels and scallops. It is 150 square kilometres of glorious, serene salt water studded with almost as many islands and ringed by a necklace of small villages. It is the largest sea inlet in the British Isles, and more than 350 million cubic metres of water flow through its narrow mouth with each tide. That is how it got its name. The Vikings called it the 'Strangfjorthr' or 'strong fjord'.

The lane brought me down to the shore just by the walled, wooded estate of Mount Stewart House, the eighteenth-century home of the Londonderry family and one of the jewels of Northern Ireland. Lord Castlereagh, Britain's influential Foreign Secretary during the Napoleonic wars, was born and raised here. After he and Metternich redrew Europe's boundaries at the Congress of Vienna, he somehow managed to bring home the 22 Empire chairs on which the participants had sat. One of George Stubbs' greatest paintings, *The Hambletonian*, hangs in the house and in the 1920s Edith, the 7th Marchioness of Londonderry, created one of Britain's finest gardens here, complete with statues of dodos, dinosaurs, griffins, satyrs and numerous other creatures to entertain her children.

The stories that do not appear in the guide books, and are not related in the guided tours of the house, are of the visits to

Mount Stewart just before the Second World War of Von Ribbentrop, Hitler's foreign minister.

He came by sea-plane, and on one occasion presented Lord Londonderry, who favoured the appeasement of Hitler's Germany, with a biscuit model of a Nazi stormtrooper. On another visit Lady Londonderry took Ribbentrop out on the lough in her boat, the *Uladh*, for a sailing race. She misjudged a tack and her craft was in imminent peril of being rammed by a rival, *Lackagh*, at the very point where Ribbentrop was sitting. Harry Burnett, a member of *Lackagh's* crew, recorded that as the two craft neared 'the strain became too much for this representative of the Nazi master race . . . He threw his arms round his head and bent over double to await the collision and whatever fate may have in store for him.'

In the event *Lackagh* did not ram *Uladh* amidships. Thanks to some adroit last-second helmsmanship, she merely clipped *Uladh's* boom. In light of subsequent events, a direct hit would have been of much more benefit to the human race.

Things have moved on since then. Mount Stewart now belongs to the National Trust. The Londonderrys have all departed save for Edith's now-elderly daughter. Their boathouse, icehouse and the gasworks which fuelled the house are all crumbling away on the lough's shore, and the open-air swimming pool has been filled in, but there are still a few old-timers like Will McAvoy who remember their glory days and Ribbentrop's visits.

Will is a lovely, gentle man in his late seventies, and his family was the last to live on an island in Strangford Lough. He put on his Wellington boots and took me out there. It is called Mid Island, a wooded hillock of about 16 acres that is linked to the shore by a ribbon of causeway at the end of a rutted farm track. The island's only habitation is a long, low, whitewashed cottage surrounded by trees and grass and Veronica bushes and looking too bucolically blissful for words.

Will's grandfather moved into the cottage in the mid-1800s when, according to the 1851 census, the lough had 170 people living on 17 islands. It consists merely of a kitchen and two bedrooms, with a straw barn and a cow byre stuck on to the end, but his three children were all born and raised there, as were Will and his two brothers.

His grandfather acted as a 'shoreherd' for the Montgomery family who owned another big estate in the nearby village of Greyabbey. That meant he kept an eye on how much sand, gravel and seaweed people were taking from the shore. He also grazed a few sheep and cattle, but he and Will's father were really professional 'wildfowlers' who hunted duck, geese and – as Will put it – 'whatever you could put in a hessian sack'.

That is how Will was brought up also. He, his brothers and his father would glide across the water of the lough, often on moonlit nights, in a flat-bottomed boat with a huge muzzle-loaded 'puntgun' mounted like a small cannon on the front. When they found the wildfowl they would let fly with three-quarters of a pound of shot. Will once killed 27 birds with one blast, while his father's record was 36.

They would snare rabbits and hares; they would wade through the shallows on calm summer evenings and spear floun-ders, plaice and skate, or catch mullet in medieval tidal fish-traps constructed by the Cistercian monks of Greyabbey. They kept pigs and ducks. Will's mother baked sodabread and wheaten bread, churned her own butter and made jam from all the blackberries. Every Friday the butcher would arrive at the far end of the causeway, blow a whistle, and Will would be sent over to buy a pound of sausages, a pound of stewing meat and a block of dripping.

The family's seemingly idyllic way of life ended in the 1950s when the government imposed restrictions on the hunting and shooting of wildfowl. Will, who had left school at 14, ended up policing the lough for the National Trust until he retired in

1988 – a classic poacher-turned-gamekeeper. His older brother
lived on in the cottage and died there, like his father and grandparents before him, in 1988. It still lacked electricity. Right to the
end Will's brother used oil-lamps and drew his water from a
well in the garden using a cow-tailed pump. His only concession
to modernity was a black-and-white television powered by a car
battery.

To Will, who now lives on a housing estate in the town of
Newtownards, Mid Island is still home. 'In my heart I've never
left it,' he said as we stood on the island's highest point and sur-
veyed the lough. From his pocket, apropos of nothing in
particular, he pulled two Stone Age flint scrapers that were made
by some of the first inhabitants of Mid Island and picked up centuries later by its last.

There is something else about Will that makes him remarkable: he is one of just a few thousand people left in the north of
Ireland who can still speak Ulster Scots. Debate rages about
whether Ulster Scots, also known as Ullans, is a language or a
dialect, but it is utterly incomprehensible to an Englishman like
me.

It is a derivative of Scots that came over with the first Scottish
settlers in the early 1600s, and survives only in the more rural
areas of the Ards peninsula, County Antrim and Donegal where
they settled most densely. It is a wonderful tongue – earthy,
humorous and full of colourful terms of abuse – and its unoffi-
cial dictionary, *The Hamely Tongue*, is a riveting read.

For example, there is no English word for a man who spends
too much time sitting by the fire, but Will might call him an
'ashypelt'. Ulster Scots speakers have nothing as boring as a marriage registrar; they have a 'buckle-the-beggars'. They don't eat
big meals; they eat 'rozners'.

People are 'carnaptious' not short-tempered, 'engersome' not
irritating, and 'feggogged' not weary. They speak 'blaffum' (nonsense) and act like 'gebberloons' (idiots) when they're 'tapaleerie'

(light-headed). Sometimes they go 'heelsmegairy' (head over heels). I like the insults best. A miser is a 'scrunt', a fool a 'glumph', and a slow, fat person a 'glunterpudden'. These words are linked by lots of 'cannas' and 'cudnas' and 'wudnas', and most sentences seem to end with 'hae'.

When Will was a boy there was no paved road or train down the Ards peninsula, and its inhabitants rarely if ever visited Belfast. It was remote and isolated and Ulster Scots was virtually the native tongue. It was considered uneducated and 'was hammered out of me at school,' said Will, 'but it soon came back'.

More recently, of course, it has acquired the same sort of protected status as the wildfowl of Strangford Lough. It has been recognised by the European Bureau for Lesser Used Languages, whatever that might be. Academics have produced an Ulster Scots grammar book as well as the dictionary. But in the last few years particularly it has enjoyed a revival that can only be described as spectacular. 'It's one of the most dynamic minority language movements in Europe at the moment,' said Philip Robinson, an historian at the Ulster Folk and Transport Museum who is one of the leading authorities on Ulster Scots.

There's a very simple reason for this. Like almost everything else in Northern Ireland Ulster Scots has become – to Will's distress – politicised. Nationalists were strenuously promoting the Irish language, so Unionists seized on Ulster Scots. Any concessions to Irish had to be matched, they insisted, by concessions to their 'language'.

The new inter-governmental body on the Irish language established under the 1997 Good Friday peace accord was thus expanded to cover Ulster Scots as well. Northern Ireland's new assembly had to recognise both languages, and employ an Ulster Scots speaker to record debates even though hardly anybody ever spoke it. Wags even invented Ulster Scots versions of key political phrases: 'Oorsels Worlane' (Sinn Fein), 'Nee yell-hee-mij' (No Surrender) and 'A'll winnae mak road' (I will not give way).

As Will and I drove into Greyabbey I spotted one more manifestation of this phenomenon. 'Welcome to Greyabbey, formerly Greba', said the road sign. The street names were the same. 'School Lane, formerly Schuil Loanen', read one; 'North Street, formerly Hard Breid Raa', read another.

Despite the road signs – and the painted kerbstones – Greyabbey is an attractive old village with a glut of antique shops. Beyond the Wildfowler pub was the entrance to Greyabbey House, and Will took me up the long, curving drive to meet Bill Montgomery, the eleventh generation of his family to live in what is now a splendid, 50-roomed, late-Georgian pile since James I dispatched one of his forebears to help settle Ulster in 1607.

Down through the centuries the first sons have alternately been christened Hugh or William, and still are. One member of the family – William 'the rebel General' – captured Quebec for the American colonialists during their War of Independence and consequently had the capital of Alabama named after him.

A charming, humorous, rather aristocratic man who represents Sothebys in Ireland, the present Mr Montgomery ushered Will and me inside even though we'd arrived completely unannounced, and he and his wonderfully hospitable wife Daphne subsequently became good friends. He readily showed us round the house, particularly the gothic dining room added by the daughter of the Bangors of two-faced Castle Ward when she married into the family. If her mother could have a whole gothic façade, she could at least have a gothic dining room.

In Mr Montgomery's office was a framed pronouncement dated November 1885: 'All former permission to boat or draw seaweed off the shores or islands at Greyabbey, the property of Hugh Montgomery Esq., is hereby withdrawn.' Seaweed was a valuable fertiliser in those days, and it was part of Will's grandfather's job to protect it. The pronouncement set out a new set of rules governing its collection: none to be gathered before the morning bell, none to be gathered between May and January, none to be sold. The bigger your holding the more you could take, but you paid two shillings an acre and two shillings a horse.

But what really caught my attention was an old, leather-bound book containing the tragic letters home of young Hugh Bernard Montgomery, Bill's great-great-great-uncle. He was a captain in the Third Guards who actually fought against Napoleon Bonaparte ('Boney') in the Battle of Waterloo, and his letters include his first-hand account of that momentous event.

The battle, he wrote to his sister on 21 June 1815, was 'one of the bloodiest that has been fought for some time, and you may see by the return of the killed and wounded how much we have suffered, but the victory was so complete and decisive as to rec-ompense us for any loss. In fact we have almost destroyed the French army composed of all the oldest and best soldiers.'

His own brigade, he told his mother in another letter:

> . . . defended the wood and farmhouse of Hougoumont
> where the action commenced, and bore the brunt of it
> during the day. It was warm work, the French fought like
> devils, but could make no impression on us. At the time I
> gave it up for lost and was certain we would have all been
> taken. They brought up an immense force, and got a
> good deal into the rear of our flanks, but were soon
> driven back by fresh troops. There never was such a
> complete rout. Everything fell into our hands . . .

The dashing young Captain Montgomery did not escape unscathed:

> My wound is but a trifle [he told his sister], but
> unhappily it is in just the same place as my last one,
> except this being in front of the ankle. I had two other

blows, one in the calf of the same leg from a spent ball, which hurt me considerably, but only cut the skin. From the third I had a most miraculous escape. I had my sword against my left arm when it was struck by a ball, which very nearly passed through it and a steel scabbard. It sunk completely in and bent both sword and scabbard double.

We were engaged from twelve to nine at night. I left the field about half past seven. I am so very slightly wounded that I expect to join in a few days. Though I have been so lucky in respect to wounds, my bad luck otherwise sticks to me. I have a woeful tale to tell.

The day of the battle our baggage, which we had not seen for some days, was ordered to the rear. After it had got about seven miles from this, a set of cowards made a false alarm that the French were in full pursuit and that they would all be taken prisoners. My servant, being as great a coward and a greater fool than any, threw away all my baggage that he might fly the faster, by which means here I am without a single stitch to my back.

Sadly the loss of his baggage did not prove the worst of Captain Montgomery's misfortunes. He did not rest his leg; the wound did not heal. The rest of the letters chart his journey from Brussels to Paris to London, where his leg became alarmingly swollen and inflamed with, one presumes, gangrene. In one of his last letters he wrote that the doctor had prescribed 'two more purgatives for tonight and tomorrow, and an aromatic strengthening draught to help expel the enemy who had had himself strongly entrenched. But he is giving way, and we will soon be able to drive him from his stronghold.'

Unfortunately, before the enemy was expelled the captain died.

I would like to have lingered in Greyabbey and explored a bit. In the grounds of the house there are still the crumbling remains of the Cistercian abbey founded in 1193 by Affreca, the wife of John de Courcy, to give thanks for her deliverance from a stormy sea crossing after visiting her father, the king of the Isle of Man. On its roofless walls are memorials to numerous past Montgomerys – 'Sir James by pirates shot and thereof dead and . . . by them i' the sea solemnly buried,' reads one. Next to the abbey, in a graveyard stiff with tombstones, is the grave of a minister hanged for supporting an eighteenth-century revolt against British rule in Ireland.

But I had another mission to undertake. It was to search for rats. Not just any old rats, you understand, but great big black monster rats.

Let me backtrack. A few months earlier some friends had inveigled the Fletcher family on to a charter boat for a day's cruise around Strangford Lough. Our crew were a genial pair of middle-aged, chain-smoking, whiskey-drinking yarn-spinners named Paul and Stuart. As the *John Blamey* wove its way between the various islands Paul pointed to one distant tree-clad hillock standing all by itself way out in the middle of the lough.

'That,' he announced proudly, 'is Rat Island.'

A century ago, he informed us, a ship had sunk nearby and its rats had swum ashore. There they spawned and thrived, living off birds and birds' eggs, each generation growing bigger and blacker until the island was positively crawling with the beasts.

'Last time I was down there I counted twenty of them – massive things, the large ones about the size of a Jack Russell terrier,' he said. 'The only way I'll go on to that island is with a shotgun.'

'I've seen four or five of them, each one bigger than a cat,' Stuart confirmed.

Back home I telephoned Davy Andrews, a warden for the National Trust which manages the lough's wildlife. There were rats on many of the islands, he said. Where they'd grown so

numerous that they threatened nesting birds, the Trust occasionally tried to exterminate them. He'd heard stories of packs of
rats being spotted swimming between the islands, and did not
dismiss the Rat Island story out of hand. Thus were sown the
seeds of the Great Ratcatching Expedition.

My wife, Katy, was strangely reluctant to come along, but
graciously agreed to drive down the children – Hannah,
Barney and Imogen. Armed with hockey-sticks, penknives and
one rusty sheath-knife, we duly presented ourselves at the
end of a wooden jetty late that afternoon where Stuart, Paul
and Paul's 12-year-old son Jonathan collected us in the *John
Blamey*.

It was getting cold, but the blue water was still sparkling
beneath the wintry sun. On both sides of the lough the long, low
hills were draped in a patchwork quilt of tiny green, brown and
golden fields. Once again we glided between the islands, the
occasional ruined cottage the only sign they were ever inhabited,
until an expanse of open water was all that lay between
Dunnyneill Island, alias Rat Island, and ourselves.

It was quite unlike the other low, bare islands. It was a tree-
covered dome with a seaweed and shingle skirt once used,
according to local legend, to bury victims of the plague. Only a
long strand projecting northwards like a handle spoiled its otherwise perfect symmetry. As we approached, Stuart shut off the
engine and weighed anchor while Paul, the self-appointed Chief
Ratcatcher, precariously lowered his considerable bulk into a
tiny rowing-boat and ferried all of us save Stuart to the shore.

It has to be said that the shingle beach was not aquiver with
great black rats the size of dogs. To be strictly accurate there was
not a single one in sight, but Paul's enthusiasm was undimmed.
We lined up, and off we marched in confident pursuit of our
quarry.

We climbed up the hill, and down the hill, fighting our way
through dense undergrowth previously untrampled by any

human being. We walked right around its base, protected by fluorescent orange life-jackets and with hockey-sticks to hand. We found giant marooned jellyfish with multi-coloured innards and fearsome tentacles; we found the bones of dead birds, and a half-eaten dogfish that Paul seized on as irrefutable proof of a ratty presence. We followed umpteen trails of flattened grass that Paul unequivocally declared to be rat runs, though none actually led us to a hole. In short, we found everything save the mega-rodents that we had come for.

The Great Ratcatching Expedition was not entirely in vain, however. In the deepening dusk we trudged to the end of the strand to exhaust every possibility. There on the rocks, to the children's delight, we found not a rat but a furry white seal pup that watched us with big black round eyes as we stood enraptured just feet away.

Village lights began to twinkle on the dark hillsides of the distant shores. On the horizon, this being November, occasional fireworks exploded soundlessly into brilliant sprays of transitory colour. A large yellow moon had risen over the water to the east, and in the golden path it cast upon the water we could see the bobbing head of a bull seal apparently unperturbed by our proximity to its pup. For that brief moment it seemed we were not in Northern Ireland at all, but some fantastical children's world.

3

Poets and Partridges

Head directly north from the City Hall into Belfast's main shopping area and you have to go by foot. Thanks to the Troubles, and the constant threat of car bombs, the area was one of the first in the United Kingdom to be pedestrianised. The advantage is that if you lift your eyes you can savour those small flourishes of prime Victorian architecture that you'd never even notice from a car.

Take the splendidly ornate old building on the corner of Donegall Square and Donegall Place that was once the Robinson and Cleaver department store. The lines of stone faces peering down at me from just above the first- and second-floor windows on this chilly January morning are those of its favourite customers, including Queen Victoria, various European princes and the Maharajah of Cooch Behar to whom it sent the finest

Irish linen. At one point the store accounted for a third of all the parcels posted from Belfast.

Head on up Royal Avenue and you'll notice that above the usual array of shop fronts – C&A, Body Shop, Boots – the tops and window-ledges of the buildings are all exactly the same height. This is the result of a decree that no building should be higher than the City Hall's dome. Adorning another fine old Victorian building, that now houses a Tesco supermarket, are stone figures depicting the ancient high kings of Ireland.

It being nearly lunch-time I turned right up Castle Lane, past street vendors hawking six gents' hankies or a Teletubby necklace for £1, and into Ann Street. There I ducked into Pottinger's Entry, one of the narrow alleys where you invariably find a colourful pub. This one has the Morning Star – an old coaching house where the Dublin–to–Belfast mail coach finished its journey. It is where Henry Joy McCracken, a leader of the United Irishmen's 1798 insurrection against English rule in Ireland, was allegedly brought in a desperate effort to revive him after he was hanged.

Admire the wonderful Victorian pub sign and the lovely wrought-ironwork that supports it. Look for the statue of a winged lion perched above the entrance door. Sit with your pint at the old mahogany bar. Except for the inevitable television the place is a veritable museum – right down to the cloth-capped old-timers who mingle with the yuppies.

The menu is heavily tilted towards local produce – wild pheasant, roast venison, oysters and mussels from Strangford Lough, Portavogie prawns, goujons of crocodile . . . well, perhaps the latter came from further afield. For £3.50 I had all the hot Irish stew that I could eat and resumed my walk somewhat more revived by my visit to the Morning Star than poor old Henry Joy McCracken.

Back in Ann Street I almost immediately passed the Glasgow Rangers supporters' shop – concrete evidence of today's disunited

Irishmen. In the absence of any major football clubs in Northern
Ireland, literally thousands of fans take the ferry across to
Glasgow every Saturday for what is a de facto extension of the
province's tribal warfare. Protestants support Rangers. Catholics
support Celtic. The ferries will take one set of fans or the other,
but never both together. Northern Ireland boasts no fewer than
220 of Rangers' 550 supporters' clubs, and one of its biggest
sporting events of the year is the Rangers v. Celtic game over the
sea in Scotland.

At the end of Ann Street I turned left into Victoria Street and
there was the Albert Memorial, a 113-foot tilting clock tower
that is Belfast's equivalent of the Leaning Tower of Pisa. Beyond
the tower you can see the ferry terminal and the start of the
docks where the Lagan meets the lough. Where else can ferries
glide so close into the heart of a city?

The docks themselves once bustled with bands of foreign
seamen, and with burly dock-hands who lived in rows of tiny
terraced houses in what was known as Sailortown. Vessels of
every description put in here, though to Belfast's great credit,
slave ships were banned. As recently as 1938 the travel writer
Eric Newby left here on a four-masted sailing ship to fetch grain
from Australia. Belfast had not impressed him. It was 'a strange
city, like a studio set for a Hitchcock thriller and equally
deserted. The rain shone on the cobblestones and the wind
howled down the dismal thoroughfares,' he wrote in *The Last
Grain Race*. 'I was glad to be leaving the miles of grey streets and
squalor and filth that had beset the ship during her weeks in
port.'

Today the area has been physically severed from the city by a
motorway flyover. The old warehouses and terraced homes have
long since been demolished, and are now being replaced by
smart new offices, yuppie waterfront apartments and urban land-
scaping. There are few dockers left, and still fewer foreign
seamen, because modern container ships require very few of

either. Once one of imperial Britain's most cosmopolitan cities – it has streets named after almost every city of the empire – Belfast had, by the late twentieth century, become a place where a black face or foreign accent was sufficiently rare to excite comment.

But there are still relics of Sailortown's colourful past. The tiny pubs somehow still survive. There is the splendid Victorian Customs House, and the equally elegant Harbour Office. And then there is the Sinclair Seamen's Church, a distinctly unorthodox place of worship erected by the family of a local ships' victualler in 1857 to 'watch over the spiritual interest of seamen frequenting the port'.

The church looks ordinary enough from the outside, except for its tall Venetian-style campanile. Inside it is anything but. The pulpit is a bowsprit flanked by port and starboard lights, the font is a binnacle or ship's compass. Flags painted on the floor by the door say 'welcome' in semaphore. A solid brass ship's wheel and a fine old capstan stand before the altar. There is a ship's bell that is rung at the start of every service, the windows are shaped like portholes, and even the collection boxes are miniature lifeboats.

Inside I found John Beattie, a church elder, and Ailsa Campbell, a committee member who helps keep the place ship-shape. They were only too happy to show me round, and even produced tea and buttered scones which we ate in front of the altar.

This amiable pair were very proud of their nautical church, and with good reason, but I couldn't help feeling it had been left a little stranded by the changing times. Each day someone tours the ships in port to spread the word, they said. A few seamen still visited the church, but it was not like the old days. The crews were smaller, they slept on board, the ships turned around in no time. The church deeds insist that 50 seats be reserved for visiting seamen each Sunday, but it was an awful long time since they were last filled.

The next morning I became a motorist again, and headed north past the church on a 10-lane motorway that bears testimony to the huge amounts of taxpayers' money that successive governments have poured into Northern Ireland over the past 30 years. It would have done credit to Los Angeles had it lasted more than a few miles, but where Cave Hill tapered away on my left it split. The main road veered westwards towards Londonderry. I swung right into 'something of which Ulster can be really proud'.

That is how the BBC described the Rathcoole housing estate when it was being built in the 1950s. Indeed it was seen then as a veritable utopia, a garden city overlooking Belfast Lough with open green hills as a backdrop. The more ambitious of Belfast's working classes – Protestant and Catholic – abandoned their two-up, two-down inner city slums with outside loos and moved in en masse.

Today Rathcoole is no longer a place of which Ulster boasts. Catholics initially comprised about 30 per cent of the estate's population, but as the Troubles escalated in 1971 they were driven out. Those who fled included Bobby Sands, the IRA man who later starved himself to death in the Maze prison during the 1981 hunger strikes.

The better-off Protestants bought private homes and moved out as well, leaving behind the elderly, the unemployed and the undesirables. Rathcoole once boasted of being the world's largest Protestant housing estate, with a population of 17,000, but only about 9,000 now remain. Whole blocks of flats have been demolished. Only one of its three secondary schools remains open. Just a handful of Catholics, mostly elderly, remain – and 'they keep very quiet', said Mark Langhammer, a burly and admirably forthright local councillor who showed me round.

The estate still has four churches, not to mention a fundamentalist mega-church just beyond its boundary. 'Fear Not Tomorrow – God is Already There', proclaimed a large sign at the entrance to the estate. But one sensed that the men of God were heavily outnumbered by the men of violence. Red, white and blue appeared to be the statutory colours for kerbstones and lamp-posts, and there were murals of loyalist gunmen everywhere – not just on the gable ends of houses, but right in the heart of the estate's wretched, litter-strewn shopping parade.

That initial impression was quickly confirmed when Mark introduced me to four women drinking tea in a centre I had better not identify. They were reticent at first, but slowly opened up. The paramilitaries ran everything, they said; they were just like the Mafia. The Ulster Defence Association and the Ulster Volunteer Force had divided the estate between them, and they were as 'scummy' as each other. 'It's all racketeering and money.'

The paramilitaries got their recruits young. One of the women said that her nine-year-old son was already scrawling paramilitary slogans across his school exercise books. Another admitted that one of her three teenage children had joined, but had subsequently been beaten up and fled the estate. As mothers, they lived in constant fear of a knock on the door and the paramilitaries 'sorting out' their sons with a beating, a shooting or a broken limb.

Their dilemma was that the police did nothing about petty crime. No officers lived on the estate any more because even the lowliest constable was so well paid, and even if they did they would be 'put out' by the paramilitaries. That meant you had to turn to the paramilitaries themselves to deal with troublemakers: 'You go to the man in the Alpha,' they all said.

The man they were referring to was a loyalist paramilitary who came close to assassinating Gerry Adams in 1984. The Alpha was an old cinema in the heart of Rathcoole that is now a drinking club where members of the UDA hang out. The loyalist paramilitaries run plenty of illegal drinking clubs or 'shebeens', but this one appeared above board. On the outside wall is a plaque erected by the UDA's South East Antrim Brigade 'to the memory of the officers and members of our organisation who were murdered by the enemies of Ulster and to those who paid the supreme sacrifice whilst on active service during the present conflict'.

Mark offered to buy me a drink there. We went in through a steel cage protecting the entrance. Inside was a large, plush, windowless, split-level lounge with a pool table in the middle, a small stage, and a bar in one corner. It was still early, but a couple of dozen men were sitting around drinking. Mark knew one of them and we joined his group. They did not volunteer conversation, particularly when they saw my notebook.

'What happened to the cinema?' I asked.

'It burned down,' replied a man in a baseball cap and turned-up collar.

'How?' I asked.

'It just burned down. These things happen,' he said in a manner designed to convey that he knew much more than he was saying.

'We're hard men. We're known as hard men,' another interjected.

'What makes you hard men?' I asked.

'We don't like people robbing old folk, joyriding, things like that,' he replied.

'Isn't that the job of the police?' I ventured.

'We get in first. We make sure they don't do it again. If the police get them they just get a fine or something like that.'

'What if you get the wrong person?'

'That's tough,' he replied. 'But we don't. We know.'

Mark had to get back to work, but he wanted to show me that Rathcoole was not all bad and not entirely hopeless. He took me to a cluster of four high-rises that used to be known as 'Beirut'. They'd recently been ringed by high red railings. You could now enter only through a smart new reception lodge, complete with potted plants, from which concierges monitored the entire complex around the clock with the help of 30 security cameras. It was more reminiscent of Chelsea than Rathcoole, but had transformed the place.

The vandals, thugs and drug-dealers had moved out, and for the first time in memory there was a waiting list for flats. Amongst those wanting to move in, said Mark, were paramilitary leaders for whom the flats offered protection from reprisals.

I drove on, but not very far. Somewhere a little beyond Rathcoole – and for security reasons I cannot be more precise – was the ideal place for viewing the arsenals of these paramilitaries. It is an old factory housing the Forensic Science Agency, and if anyone ever wanted to establish a Museum of the Troubles this would provide the bulk of the exhibits.

After three decades on the front line of a terrorist war, the Agency has become a world leader in its field – so successful in fact that the IRA paid it the back-handed compliment of blowing up its former premises in south Belfast with a monster van bomb containing 3,000 lb of explosives in 1992. I first visited it in the wake of the 1998 Omagh bombing when it had achieved the daunting feat of reconstructing the bomb's timer power unit after sifting through 30 tonnes of debris. But what had really impressed me was the Agency's extraordinary collection of every conceivable sort of terrorist device, so I asked for a quick tour.

The head of the explosives section, who must also remain anonymous for security reasons, showed me drawers full of detonators, wires and metal fragments displaying the scars caused by different types of bombs. There were timers and circuit boards illustrating the telltale handiwork of the province's principal bombmakers. Using actual examples retrieved from the field, he traced the rapid development of the IRA's home-made mortars from primitive devices consisting of tin cans attached to broom handles and fired from shotguns, right up to the lethal Mark 10 fired at Downing Street in 1991 and 200-lb 'barrack busters' made from outsize propane gas cylinders that were lobbed over the walls of fortified security bases.

Republicans specialised in bombs and mortars. The loyalists' paramount need was guns, and the Agency's firearms section boasts an equally impressive array of home-made weapons – not to mention a chilling armoury of manufactured guns including a Russian DShK with armour-piercing bullets capable of bringing down helicopters.

The head of that section showed me everything from converted starter-pistols and nautical flare projectors adapted to fire .22 bullets, to home-made machine guns fashioned from exhaust tubes and steel rods. Some of these firearms were made in garden sheds, others in the machine shops of well-known Belfast companies. Some were so simple that even I could have made them, but no less lethal for that. Others displayed engineering skills which even the section head acknowledged were 'superb'. Once again the people of Northern Ireland have proved themselves incredibly resourceful – but if only that inventiveness had been put to more constructive use . . .

With its domestic work happily now running down, the Agency's explosives section in particular is actively marketing its unique expertise in trouble spots around the world. Northern Ireland has been 'a microcosm of terrorist activity', says one of its promotional leaflets. 'No other region has experienced terrorist explosive and device development on such a scale. The knowledge and expertise gained has established the laboratory at the forefront of forensic explosives investigation.'

There was a time when the north shore of Belfast Lough beyond Rathcoole was mostly country punctuated by occasional towns and villages. Today it is one unbroken ribbon of development for 10 or 20 miles out of Belfast. Tyre depots and nursing homes have filled the gaps between handsome old waterfront villas. The University of Ulster and new mid-market housing estates have devoured green fields. Whiteabbey now turns seamlessly into Jordanstown which turns seamlessly into Greenisland which turns seamlessly into Carrickfergus, and so on up the coast, all but obliterating its colourful past.

Whiteabbey, for example, is where Anthony Trollope once lived while he worked for the Post Office. It was here that he finished his first Barsetshire novel, *The Warden*, and started *Barchester Towers*. 'Though the North of Ireland is not the choicest permanent residence, it has some charms for the tourist,' he wrote to a friend. Those charms no longer include the house where he lodged, which was knocked down to make way for an elementary school.

Carrickfergus, Northern Ireland's oldest town, was a place of considerable importance centuries before Belfast even existed. On the harbour wall, next to a faded green plaque marking the Queen's visit in 1961, is a shiny blue plaque commemorating the 1690 landing of Protestant King William to take on Catholic James II – a landing whose consequences continue to reverberate more than three centuries later.

Beyond the inevitable McDonald's and Co-op supermarket the town's huge castle juts boldly out into Belfast Lough. Since the Norman knight John de Courcy built the castle in the late twelfth century it has been attacked and sacked umpteen times, and was in continuous military use until 1928. On one occasion, in 1760, French naval forces besieged the castle, and the garrison, having exhausted its ammunition, resorted to firing its buttons.

Carrickfergus is now on the tourist trail. It is a perennial winner of Ulster's best-kept town competition, and presents the prettiest of faces to casual day-trippers, but in the estates behind the town the fighting continues.

I will remember Carrickfergus primarily as the place where, during the province-wide anarchy that followed the banning of the Orange Order's Drumcree parade in the summer of 1998, loyalist paramilitaries engaged in what can only be described as

'ethnic cleansing'. Working-class Protestants burned and intimidated their Catholic neighbours out of the housing estate on the
hill behind the town and declared it a 'Taig-free zone'. In an
underpass beneath the loughshore road, I spotted graffiti consisting of rifle sights and the letters 'A.T.A.T. – All Taigs Are
Targets'.

As a boy, the Restoration dramatist William Congreve lived in
the castle while his father was a serving soldier there in the late
seventeenth century. Carrickfergus was also the childhood home
of the poet Louis MacNeice, whose 'Bagpipe Music' is one of
those poems that makes you really want to learn it by heart:

> It's no go the Yogi-Man, it's no go Blavatsky
> All we want is a bank balance, and a bit of skirt in a taxi . . .

MacNeice's father was rector of St Nicholas's church in the early
1900s. Initially the family lived in a tall, thin house on the waterfront almost opposite the castle, then moved into a large
Victorian rectory with a graveyard right behind it. MacNeice's
childhood experiences influenced much of his later poetry and
one of his poems is actually named after the town:

> I was born in Belfast between the mountain and the gantries
> To the hooting of the lost sirens and the clang of trams
> Thence to smoky Carrick in County Antrim
> Where the bottle-neck harbour collects the mud which jams
>
> The little boats beneath the Norman castle,
> The pier shining with lumps of crystal salt;
> The Scotch Quarter was a line of residential houses
> But the Irish quarter was a slum for the blind and halt.

In another he recalls 'one shining glimpse of a boat so big it was
named *Titanic*' as she sailed out of the 'wrinkled lough'.

But as in Trollope's Whiteabbey, I searched in vain for any acknowledgement of Carrickfergus's most famous son. I found the tall, thin house; it is sadly dilapidated, with pigeons flying in and out of the broken top-floor windows, but the rectory has long since been demolished to make way for an old people's home. There was not even a blue plaque to mark the spot.

Worse was to come. The next village up the shore – though now consumed by Carrickfergus – is Bonnybefore. The parents of Andrew Jackson, America's seventh president, emigrated from here to the Carolinas just in time for him to be born on American soil in 1767. The council has done up an old thatched and whitewashed cottage near the waterfront as the Andrew Jackson visitor centre, and a very good job it has done. It is not the actual Jackson homestead, alas: that stood 100 yards away, and was demolished to make way for the railway line.

This sorry sequence reached its climax a couple of miles further on in the ancient parish of Kilroot where yet another literary giant, Jonathan Swift, was the Anglican prebend from 1694 to 1696. He loathed the place because it was full of prickly Presbyterians, but it was here that he supposedly conceived *A Tale of a Tub* while skimming stones across the water. It is said that the view across the lough to the faraway Copeland Islands gave him the idea for the flying island of Laputa in *Gulliver's Travels*, and that Belfast's Cave Hill, which resembles a sleeping giant, was the inspiration for Gulliver.

Where Swift's thatched oval-shaped cottage once stood, there is now a monstrous power station that blights the whole of Belfast Lough.

Beyond Kilroot you finally reach open country, or so it appears. In fact you are driving over a large industrial enterprise. A thousand feet below is a great honeycomb of subterranean passages formed by one of only three salt mines in the British Isles.

I telephoned the Irish Salt Mining and Exploration Company

and asked if I could visit. Of course, said the company adminis-
trator. The salt was the residue of an ancient landlocked sea, he
explained in his spartan office on the lough shore. This mine
was opened in 1965 and its network of criss-crossing passages
now stretches two miles underground. It is capable of producing
up to half-a-million tonnes of salt annually, which is loaded
straight on to cargo ships from the company's own jetty and
taken to England, Scotland and the eastern coast of America to
de-ice roads.

A young mine surveyor fitted me out with bright orange overalls and a miner's hat and we drove in a Land Rover into what
appeared to be an old warehouse. At the far end we entered a
tunnel that ran down into the bowels of the earth and a warren
of caverns linked by passages wide enough for a three-lane road.
As we drove in, an interminable conveyor belt was carrying
crushed salt out.

It was a warm, dark, silent world. When you switched off the
headlights it was pitch black. Any sense of direction soon vanished in this featureless labyrinth, and a stranger like myself
would have been lost within minutes. But it was not uninhab-
ited. Occasionally we passed another Land Rover or old
maintenance buildings. There was a canteen and a mechanics'
shop – or more accurately a mechanics' cave. At the furthermost
point we found yellow diggers loading mounds of brown rubble
into 30-tonne dump trucks. The surveyor picked up a rock.
Taste it, he said. It was pure salt turned brown by impurities.

We ended up at what might have been the set for a Hollywood
science-fiction movie. It was a vast, rumbling crushing plant
running the length of a huge cavern illuminated by arc lights.
High at the far end the dump trucks were emptying their loads
into the first of four great crushing machines, one below the
other, which ground the rocks into a gritty powder that was
whisked away on the conveyor belt at a rate of 300 tonnes per
hour. It was an awesome demonstration of brute power, a sight

that lingered in the mind long after we emerged blinking into the watery light and fresh sea air of this late January afternoon.

It was the building of the railway from Belfast in the 1860s that first triggered the development along this coast, but the consequences were not all bad. Early the next morning, where the lough broadens into the Irish Sea a few miles beyond Kilroot, I came down over a hill into the pretty little town of Whitehead with its broad promenade and a jetty from which a few boys were fishing in the wintry sun.

Whitehead exists because of the railway, not the other way round. To put passengers' bottoms on its carriage seats, the Belfast and Northern Counties Railway Company offered free tickets for 10 years to anybody who built homes in what was in those days a tiny village. The offer evidently worked and the result is a little-known repository of fine late Victorian and early Edwardian architecture, albeit surrounded by some pretty ghastly newer stuff.

The railway company also sought to lure day-trippers out from Belfast. It built a golf course and a tea house in Whitehead, but its real masterpiece was a long-forgotten feat of engineering called the Gobbins that I'd been told about by a friend.

Beyond Whitehead the coast turns sharply northwards up a narrow peninsula called Islandmagee once noted for what one might charitably describe as its backwardness. It produced Ireland's last convicted witches – they were pilloried in Carrickfergus in 1711 for 'putting the evil eye' on some poor woman and giving her fits. One of the witches lost an eye from the rotten eggs and cabbage stalks. An 1830s Ordnance Survey report said of Islandmagee's inhabitants: 'Their drunkenness and intemperance is everywhere proverbial.' The women 'drink raw spirits in such quantities as would astonish any native', while 'the farmers drink on all occasions to excess'.

The peninsula is tilted so that it rises to sheer cliffs some 250 feet high on its seaward edge. I drove up a small lane through lush green fields to the top of these cliffs, and savoured the magnificent view across the deep blue channel to the snow-capped mountains of Scotland 30 or 40 miles to the east. I tried to forget that in the 1640s Protestants from Carrickfergus drove Catholics over these cliffs to their deaths – an atrocity which makes those of the Troubles seem relatively mild.

I soon found the narrow break in the cliffs I was looking for, and clambered down a grassy track to a rocky little beach backed by a tumbling waterfall. At the north end of the beach some stone steps led up to a hole cut through a jutting rock stack. By the side of the hole the name 'The Gobbins' was chiselled into the rock face. This was the start of what was in its heyday a spectacular one and a half mile walkway along the very face of the cliffs.

Designed by Berkeley Deane Wise, the railway company's chief engineer, the path was blasted from sheer basalt, led through tunnels, past caves and out to sea stacks. It spanned chasms on fragile steel or suspension bridges, climbing as high as 70 feet above the raging sea at some points and dropping as low as 25 feet at others. It was opened in 1902 and became an instant success. The Edwardian middle classes flocked out from Belfast, paying sixpence each for the thrill of walking the Gobbins – unless they produced the return half of a railway ticket, in which case they walked it free. Members of the British Association for the Advancement of Science paid a visit, and one declared: 'There is . . . nothing like the Gobbins path anywhere in the world.'

The Gobbins' decline began when it was closed during the Second World War. Its iron bridges and railings began to rust and erode for lack of maintenance, and by the 1950s it was barely walkable. A sign now warns that it is defunct and dangerous, but there was nobody around so I ducked through the hole, known as Wise's Eye, and followed the crumbling ribbon of path around the rocky outcrop. For a couple of hundred yards I climbed up steps and down steps as I worked along the cliff face past rusting iron posts and twisted railings. The path abruptly ended where a long-vanished bridge once spanned the boiling water. Beyond I could see that odd stretches of the walkway still survived, but I somehow doubted they would ever be walked again.

There was nothing else to detain me in Islandmagee. I rejoined the main road north and was soon rolling into the port of Larne with its own special way of greeting visitors. 'Welcome to loyalist Larne', read the graffiti on an abandoned railway bridge across the road. 'No Surrender' and 'God Save Our Queen' read graffiti painted in even larger letters on the road surface right outside a primary school. It is always easy for travellers to determine the allegiance of the towns and villages they are passing through. If it is not patently obvious from the graffiti, flags and kerbstones, then they can tell from whether the newsagents advertise the pro-Unionist *News Letter* or the nationalist *Irish News*.

I passed a disused quarry, a cement works, abandoned warehouses. To my right, beyond the ferry terminal, was a large power station as ugly and obtrusive as that on Belfast Lough. I had never liked Larne. I had always associated it with out-and-out sectarianism. The one time I'd visited it for work was to write about a young Catholic woman with four small children who suffered a fractured skull when loyalist paramilitary thugs broke into her house at 2.45 one morning and beat her senseless. When she returned from hospital she received a 'Get Well' card inscribed: 'Get out of Larne while you can.' She and her children took the 10 p.m. ferry to Scotland that night and have lived in England ever since.

The family of Mark Twain (born Samuel Langhorne Clemens) lived in the area before wisely deciding to exchange the delights of Larne for those of Hannibal, Missouri. I mention that only because this chapter has assumed a literary flavour. Larne also produced Amanda McKittrick Ros, the wife of the stationmaster who was crowned the 'world's worst novelist' by London's literary critics.

Alliteration was Mrs Ros's particular forte. She wrote a string of novels with titles like *Irene Iddesleigh*, *Delina Delaney* and *Helen Huddleson*, not to mention such poetic gems as 'Poems of Puncture' and 'Fumes of Fomentation'. She treated her critics with disdain, dismissing them as 'claycrabs of corruption', and 'hogwashing hooligans'. She did nothing as prosaic as 'die'; in 1939 this lovely lady joined 'the boundless battalion of the breathless'.

I had intended to drive straight through Larne, but a sign pointing off the main road to the Ulster-American Memorial caught my eye. I drove a few hundred yards down a nondescript residential street and there, in the middle of a small municipal park, was a rather fine statue of a family of emigrants about to set sail for the New World.

The father is holding his arm protectively around his wife, who clutches a bible. Their son is carrying his shoes to preserve the leather. The inscription on the pedestal dedicates the memorial to 'all those first Ulster emigrants who sailed from Larne in May 1717 upon the "Friends Goodwill" bound for Boston. They were to be the first of many.' Beneath that is a quotation: 'There is no other race in the United States that can produce a roll of honour so long and so shining in distinction, and who shall deny our claim to have done more, much more, than any others to make the United States?' I don't know who said that, but it was hard to disagree.

The family of another American president, Andrew Johnson, came from Larne. There is no statue of him, however, and no Johnson ancestral home preserved. He was the only American president besides Bill Clinton to have been impeached. 'We don't really talk about him,' a woman in Larne's historical centre had very candidly informed me on the telephone.

It is extraordinary how beauty and ugliness exist side by side in Northern Ireland. Within minutes of leaving Larne I was heading north up the Antrim coast road that William Thackeray – to continue the literary theme – described in his *Irish Sketch Book* of 1842 as 'one of the most noble and gallant works of art that is to be seen in any country'. It is a route that should by rights be packed with tourists, but is actually almost empty.

The narrow ribbon of road hugs the shore between towering limestone cliffs and steep wooded hills on one side, and a wonderful expanse of flat blue waters on the other. It passes through picturesque fishing villages with tiny harbours where Antrim's nine glens run down to the sea. Clouds were by now scudding across the sky, trailing short sharp showers in their wake, but this merely enhanced the natural drama. Shafts of sunlight illuminated the vivid greens of the hills one minute and the deep blues of the sea the next. Rainbows appeared for a few minutes and then vanished, as did the distant view of Scotland.

Before the coast road was built in the 1830s, the inhabitants of this remote area were so cut off from the rest of Ireland that they sailed to Scotland across the Sea of Moyle – as the channel is known hereabouts – to buy and sell. Today it remains sufficiently remote to still have old red telephone-boxes, and mobile telephones work only intermittently.

About 10 miles north of Larne I passed through the pretty village of Glenarm which straddles the Glenarm River where it joins the sea. Here is the ancestral home of the Earls of Antrim, a romantic old castle with pepperpot towers hidden behind high walls and containing, within its estate, the first of a series of bizarre graves that I was to discover in my travels around Northern Ireland.

It is that of the 11th Earl, who was known as 'The Buzzard' by his family. His favourite spot was on top of a hill nearly three miles up the glen behind the castle – the only one of the nine

Antrim glens that is privately owned and not bisected by a public road. The Buzzard not only demanded to be buried on this hilltop, but asked to be buried upright so that he could continue to enjoy the distant view of Scotland. The pallbearers staggered up there in 1918, but were allegedly so exhausted that they inserted the coffin upside down.

The 14th Earl and his son, Viscount Dunluce, once took me up to see the grave, and it was a steep climb even for the Viscount's Jeep. The grave was marked by six large rocks laid out in the shape of a cross, and there really was a spectacular view back down the hidden glen to the sea, but if it was solitude the Buzzard craved he must have been sorely disappointed.

His wife, Queen Victoria's lady-in-waiting, was later buried next to him – though horizontally. After the Buzzard's son, the 12th Earl, was buried up there in 1936 a small chapel was erected and the graves walled in. It is now standard practice for family members to be buried on the hilltop, their coffins transported on horse-drawn carts, and the present Earl and his son have every intention of continuing the tradition.

I didn't stop in Glenarm on this occasion. I had a date in Carnlough, a couple of miles further up the coast, with a friend of a friend named Francine O'Neill whose family have owned the town's ivy-covered Londonderry Arms Hotel for the past half-century. She had kindly agreed to show me around, and I had found her just in time. Francine, a lawyer, was shortly to marry an American general and set up home in Baltimore.

The hotel was built as a coaching inn in 1848 by the Marchioness of Londonderry, Francine explained as we lunched off mounds of prawns and home-made wheaten bread with butter. When the Marchioness died in 1865 it passed to her grandson, and when he died it passed to Sir Winston Churchill, his second cousin.

A picture of the great man hangs above one of the hotel's fireplaces, but there is no record of him ever having visited his property and Francine's family prefers to celebrate a horse instead. On the wall of the hotel's Arkle bar hangs a shoe that the famous racehorse wore when winning the Cheltenham Gold Cup in 1965. In fact, Francine's father so admired Arkle that he kept hairs from the horse's tail in the hotel safe.

The Marchioness inherited much of the Antrim coast and a considerable fortune from her mother, the Countess of Antrim, in 1834. She married yet more money in the form of Lord Charles Stewart, Britain's ambassador to Austria, and was 'given away' at her wedding by the Duke of Wellington. Her admirers included Czar Alexander I of Russia.

Evidently concerned about her tenants' lot, the Marchioness built Carnlough's attractive little harbour, and just outside the hotel the road is spanned by an elegant arched bridge. Across this ran a railway line, three-quarters of a mile long, that she commissioned to carry limestone from the town's quarries to the harbour where it was loaded on to ships for Glasgow.

We hopped into Francine's Mercedes and drove a short way up into the hills to see what was apparently the Marchioness's idea of a famine relief measure. Called Garron Tower, it is a huge, square castellated mansion ringed by lush green lawn and eucalyptus trees, backed by sheer gorse-covered cliffs and with a breathtaking view across the sea to Ayrshire. No expense was spared – even the stable block was designed by Charles Lanyon, the celebrated architect.

The Marchioness commissioned the mansion in 1848, at the height of the Great Famine. She used it for just a few weeks every summer, throwing glittering parties for Europe's aristocracy in what she called her 'little bathing lodge'. She died in 1865 and left the place to her three-year-old grandson; but he showed no interest when he came of age, and Garron Tower became first a hotel and more recently a Catholic school.

The bursar let us in. The place has been completely institutionalised. The only remnants of Garron Tower's short-lived grandeur were the staff dining room's lavishly carved double wooden doors and the equally magnificent carved fireplace depicting Hermes giving the Arts and Sciences to Man.

Outside, Francine showed me one other reminder of the wilful Marchioness. She led me up a path through the rhododendron bushes and there, looking out towards the sea, was a huge tomb-stone marking the grave of Her Ladyship's favourite dog bearing verse even worse than that of Amanda McKittrick Ros:

> *Here Urisk lies and let the truth be told*
> *This faithful dog was blind, infirm and old.*
> *Deaf to all else, his mistress's voice he knew,*
> *Blind though he was, his step to her was true;*
> *So strong an instinct by affection fed*
> *Endured till Urisk's vital spirit fled.*

Poetry was obviously not the Marchioness's strong point. Back down at the coast road, Francine showed me a massive block of limestone called the Famine Stone on which Her Ladyship had this inscription chiselled:

Frances Anne Vane, Marchioness of Londonderry, being connected with this province by the double ties of birth and marriage, and being desirous to hand down to posterity an imperishable memorial of Ireland's affliction and England's generosity in the year 1846–47, unparalleled in the annals of human suffering, hath engraved this stone.

> *Fair tablet fashioned by the Almighty's Hand*
> *To guard these confines of the Sea and Land*
> *No longer shall thou meet the stranger's sight*
> *A polished surface of unmeaning white*
> *But bid him ponder on the days of yore*

When Plague and Famine stalked along the shore
And pale Aerne veiled her drooping head
Like Rachel weeping for her children dead.
Tell him that to assuage these pangs and fears
Britannia gave her bounty with her tears
And bear this record though in phrases rude
Of England's love and Ireland's gratitude.

The memorial actually proved far from 'imperishable'. Ireland lost a quarter of its population to starvation or forced emigration during the famine. The locals here did not feel any 'gratitude' for England's 'generosity'. The lines they found most offensive have long since been defaced, and now the inscription is barely legible.

Francine and I drove on through Glenariff, with its broad and sandy beach, and Cushendall with its little old shops and central sandstone tower built as a 'place of confinement for idlers and rioters'. Beyond Cushendall we turned inland and followed a tumbling peat-brown river up Glenaan past tiny fields, primitive cottages with chickens in their yards, and the stone shells of long-abandoned hovels. These glens would have been more populated 150 years ago than they are today, and soon we were up on wild, desolate moors where even at the height of summer you would encounter only the occasional turf cutter amidst the purple heather.

At a tiny crossroads we turned right and were soon following another swollen river back down another of the glens, Glendun, towards the sea. There was no traffic except for the odd tractor, no sign of life apart from a couple of old men with leathery faces beneath inevitable cloth caps. Towards the bottom of the glen, Francine parked the car beside a wood and led me up to a little enclosure surrounded by an old stone wall. There was a large boulder snared in the roots of an ancient tree with a little altar built in front of it. This was a Mass Rock where Catholics would come furtively to worship when the penal laws forbade them from practising their religion in the early eighteenth century. Each summer the local priest still conducts a service here, and it would be hard to imagine a more peaceful setting.

The latter-day church, St Patrick's, was just a few hundred yards down the lane. By now it was raining hard, but we sloshed through the graveyard to see yet another curiosity known as the sweetheart's stone which lies flat on the ground amid the other upright tombstones. Etched on its surface is a crude picture of a ship with two anchors and the hand-carved words: 'Charles McAlaster burrying place. Here lies the boddy of John his son. Died March 1803 aged 18 years. Your ship Love is mored head and starn for a fulldiew.'

The story is that John McAlaster joined the Navy during the Napoleonic wars to earn the money to get married. A 'Fulldieu' or 'full due' was a sailor's wages after a long voyage. Unfortunately he died when he fell from the rigging. His fiancée spent an entire night carving the picture of the ship and was found dead by the stone the next morning.

Suitably moved, Francine and I drove into the village of Cushendun with its Cornish-style cottages erected by Lord Cushendun as a memorial to his Penzance-born wife. There we stopped for a drink in McBride's – the smallest pub in Ireland before it built an extension in the mid-1990s and so lost its biggest selling point. I could see the landlord's dilemma. It would not have been easy to accommodate coach parties in the one original room – it was no bigger than a very small garage, and half of that was taken up by the bar.

There was one more place I wanted to see in Cushendun to complete my literary tour of the Antrim Coast. We crossed the River Dun on a lovely old stone bridge just before it joined the sea, and followed a track around a headland to where the sea sucked and gurgled amid lonely stacks of rock. The track led

into a tunnel. Unfortunately there was a locked gate at the far
end, but we could just see the roof of the house beyond.
Called the Cave House, it is surrounded by cliffs, accessible
only through the tunnel and fully visible only from the sea.
Today it is a Catholic retreat, but earlier this century it
belonged to the wife of John Masefield, the former Poet
Laureate, who came here for his honeymoon and subsequent
summer holidays.

Shortly before his wedding Masefield wrote to a friend:

> *In County Antrim near the sea*
> *How very happy I shall be . . .*
> *Our married life will be begun*
> *Within the walls of Cushendun.*

He added: 'I hope it will be fine on the sea, for seasickness on a
honeymoon seems a hellish prospect.'

This is the same John Masefield who wrote 'Sea Fever':

> *I must go down to the seas again, to the lonely sea and the*
> *   sky,*
> *And all I ask is a tall ship, and a star to steer her by,*
> *And the wheel's kick and the wind's song and the white sail's*
> *   shaking,*
> *And a grey mist on the sea's face, and a grey dawn breaking.*

Perhaps by the time he wrote 'Sea Fever' he'd had enough of
married life.

It was late afternoon, and Francine had to go, so she drove me
back to Carnlough where I picked up my own car. I had hoped
to reach Ballycastle, on the north coast, by nightfall, but there
was one more thing I wanted to do before leaving. As we drove
down from Garron Tower earlier in the day, Francine had
pointed to a track leading back up into the hills behind the

coast. Up there was the 'Hidden Village' of Galboly, she'd told me. It was abandoned long ago, but a Cistercian monk, Brother Veder O'Kane, still lived there in the ruins. She'd once seen him hitching by the road and given him a lift.

I drove up the track until it petered out at an old farmhouse, where I left the car and walked up a muddy path for another half-mile to the base of some near-vertical cliffs. There indeed were the remains of an old village, with the same magnificent view across the Sea of Moyle far below. I counted the shells of half-a-dozen stone cottages, most with trees now growing out of them but a couple still with vestiges of roof. An alarmed sheep ran out as I peered through an old window. Just one cottage still had a proper slate roof, glass in its windows and a gate to its garden. There was no light on inside, or smoke from the chimney, but the back door opened just as I approached and out came Brother Veder. Whether he or I was the more startled it was hard to say.

He was a gaunt, middle-aged man wearing a black woolly hat, thick glasses, anorak and Wellington boots. He was not the hostile recluse that I had feared – but nor was he eager to be interviewed. He had his evening chores to do, he said, and I could talk to him while he did them if I wanted. With that he picked up a white plastic bucket that he very obviously used as a toilet and walked up to the foot of the cliff to empty it. There was no sewerage system up here, he explained. There was no mains water or electricity. Someone had offered him a mobile telephone as a Christmas present, but he'd said no.

We returned to the cottage to fetch his washing, and in the half-light trudged up to a small burn where he spent the next 10 minutes washing his clothes in the icy water. The village used to have about 50 inhabitants, he said, but one by one they died or left to find work in towns. There was just one man left when he arrived 30 years ago, but he had died within two months. Did he get lonely, I asked? People are much lonelier in cities, he replied.

Why did he choose to live out here by himself? 'To be in touch,' he replied cryptically. His company was stoats, weasels, foxes and rabbits.

It was a peculiar, almost surreal conversation. Brother Veder was clearly an intelligent man, but quite determined not to talk about himself. In fact I found myself being quizzed. What was the national flower of England, he asked? What was its Latin name? From roses we moved on to snowdrops, and whether the snowdrop appeared in Samuel Johnson's first English dictionary, and when that dictionary was published. We filled a couple of plastic milk containers with water, and returned to his cottage.

He didn't invite me in. To have asked to have seen his cottage was out of the question. He was not unfriendly, just very private. We shook hands, he pointed out a short cut to my car and I set off in the dark. The sky had cleared, the stars were out, and as I squelched across a muddy field all I could see in that great dome of blackness was a lighthouse flashing on the distant Scottish coast.

The most spectacular part of the entire coast road lies just north of Cushendun. The main road actually cuts straight across to Ballycastle, but this is a little by-road that goes right around the north-east corner of the island of Ireland. My children know it well. Indeed they will never forget it – or let me forget it.

One evening the previous summer I had persuaded them to cycle round it. It looked flat enough on the map, and not too long. We duly set off from Cushendun and had cycled all of half a mile before the first downpour began. That coincided with the first great hill. For the next three hours we pushed our bikes up mountain-sides in pouring rain, coasted briefly down the other side and then repeated the process as the occasional passing motorist tittered from the comfort of his car.

In vain did I try to distract my grumpy offspring with the odd glimpse through the cloud of the Mull of Kintyre just 13 miles across the water. In vain did I try to lift their spirits with hearty renditions of the Paul McCartney song. They were resolutely, determinedly fed up. As they repeatedly reminded me, they could have been at home – dry, warm and eating supper in front of 'The Simpsons'. Some 15 or 20 miles later, when we finally rejoined the main road and found a pub, I was duly punished. As they sat and demolished comic-strip portions of sausages and chips, I had to hitch-hike back to Cushendun to fetch the car.

It was too late now to retrace that route once more, so I took the fast road across to Ballycastle and found a bed-and-breakfast for the night. I had to be up early the next morning to catch the ferry to Rathlin Island, a formidable L-shaped chunk of battered rock from whose meagre soil and surrounding waters 1,000 people somehow managed to eke a living in the nineteenth century. Today it supports just 106, but is the last inhabited island off the coast of Northern Ireland.

Ballycastle's great claim to fame is that Guglielmo Marconi found the first commercial use for his newly invented radio transmitter here in 1898. At the behest of Lloyds of London, the Italian genius established a wireless link to Rathlin Island so that the islanders could send reports on passing ships. Until then communications from the island had been distinctly unreliable; they consisted of flags which could not be seen in poor weather, or carrier-pigeons that were regularly devoured by hawks.

Something happened to the weather overnight; when I awoke in the morning the wind was howling and the temperature had plummeted. To the east of Ballycastle the great bald dome of Knocklayd mountain was white with snow. Along the empty seafront, walls of coiled waves were thundering in from the north Atlantic and smashing on to the forlorn beach amid billowing clouds of icy spray. There was no way the ferry could set out for Rathlin Island in this, I thought. Even Marconi's radio signals would have been daunted by such a crossing.

I was wrong, of course. Fortified with a large 'Ulster Fry' breakfast I bundled up and headed for the harbour, stopping with commendable foresight on the way to buy a £1 woolly hat. I just had time to admire the large rock erected in Marconi's memory by the citizens of Ballycastle before boarding the alarmingly small Caledonian McBrain ferry, the MV *Canna*. 'Will I be able to get back tomorrow?' I asked a burly crewman. 'Och, I canna guarantee it,' he replied. 'At this time of the year we take it day by day.'

As the steel car ramp rose to cut off my escape route, I found myself facing a gang of heavily armed men in camouflage gear with an assortment of dogs straining at their leashes. The IRA? A UVF invasion of Rathlin Island? Actually, nothing more sinister than a shooting party. They were not English toffs in tweeds and wellies but a good-natured bunch of friends from County Tyrone – builders, joiners and small businessmen out for a good day's sport and an even better night's 'craic' – the Irish term for banter. In no time I was invited to join them.

It was a 45-minute crossing, and the ferry heaved and bucked like a foaming stallion in the blue-grey swell. Somewhere in the watery depths below was the wreck of the cruiser *Drake*, torpedoed by the Germans during the First World War and now the home of conger eels. In front of us Rathlin's fortress-like cliffs reared from the sea, and from a distance we could see what looked like a huge plume of smoke rising vertically into the sky from a small cleft in the rock face. As we drew closer it turned out not to be smoke at all, but a waterfall being forced upwards by the sheer force of the wind. 'It's been trying to get down there for the last three days,' joked Seamus McAleese, the shoot's cheery organiser.

In the angle of the 'L' was Church Bay, where the cliffs ran down to a small harbour surrounded by a cluster of cottages. Into that harbour we in peril on the sea were soon mercifully delivered. We dropped our bags in the island's old manor house, newly converted into a bed-and-breakfast by the National Trust, and gathered at the island's one and only bar – McCuaig's – for a restorative dram before the fun began.

On the face of it Rathlin is an unlikely place to have a shoot. The west or 'upper' end of the seven-mile long island is a celebrated bird reserve whose craggy cliffs play host each spring and summer to approximately 5,000 puffins, 28,000 razorbills and 40,000 guillemots.

At the 'lower' end, however, the farmers are practical souls who were quite happy to earn a little extra income by letting Seamus, a natural entrepreneur, release 7,000 partridge and pheasants on to their land in 1998. The result is one of the most scenic, challenging and unorthodox shoots in the British Isles.

Duly fortified, the shooters and beaters piled into an American Vietnam-era military truck and an equally ancient Land Rover. These laboured up tiny lanes on to the top of the island where they disgorged us into a barren, treeless landscape of boggy fields, tumble-down stone walls and gorse-covered hills raked by an icy, gale-force wind.

In the seventeenth century both Scotland and Ireland laid claim to Rathlin, and from here you could see why. Ten miles to the south lay the rugged, sunlit North Antrim coast, its hills dusted by snow. Thirteen miles to the east was Scotland's Mull of Kintyre, its equally rugged contours starkly visible in the crystal-clear light. To the north, beyond Rathlin's East Lighthouse, the open blue Atlantic stretched away to the horizon with not a vessel in sight. Not many places in the world offer such a panorama.

Seamus's technique was simple. He lined up the seven sportsmen below a succession of steep escarpments while the beaters drove the pheasants and partridge towards the edges. The wind propelled the birds high into the sky like feathered bullets against a blinding sun as the gunmen unleashed copious volleys of lead shot in their direction.

Some were good shots, others execrable, but in such conditions even a top marksman would have been sorely tested. Seamus waived the conventional limit on how many birds the party could bag, but there was no chance of it reaching any such limit anyway. Some birds did crash into the bogs and gorse, to be retrieved by eager dogs, but the great majority easily outwitted this particular bunch.

Thus the day sped past until, by way of a grand finale, Seamus led his men down to a narrow, boulder-strewn beach beneath another great cliff face. 'This,' he proudly announced, 'is the Cliff Drive, and will soon be known throughout the British Isles.' Minutes later the first birds shot over the clifftop and wheeled and dipped and veered sharply left or right as they spotted the firing squad and churning waves below them. Surf and shotguns combined in a magnificently noisy crescendo as partridges and pheasants flew the gauntlet. Some crashed into rocks; others plunged into the surging foam from which even the dogs hesitated to retrieve them. Many pulled off miraculous escapes.

Late in the afternoon, frozen but exhilarated and with 71 birds between them, the weary party trooped back to McCuaig's bar where scalding soup and piles of sandwiches awaited them.

I headed back to the manor house, anxious for a hot bath, but fell into conversation with a strong-minded young woman named Charlene who single-handedly runs the place for the National Trust. Almost immediately I sensed her disapproval. Shooting was not what Rathlin Island was about at all, she told me forcefully. It was not about running around with guns in military vehicles on Saturdays, but a place where most people came to get away from such things.

I reserved judgment on the shooting, but I could not quibble with her assessment of the island. In just the few hours I'd spent there I could already see that it was a throwback to an earlier, simpler and more tranquil age. Indeed the place only got proper water, sewerage and electricity services in the early 1990s.

There is no crime, except for the odd high-jinks when day-trippers visit in the summer, and no policeman. There is no traffic, except for tractors and the occasional old jalopy, and no more than two or three road signs on the entire island. One primary school serves the island's Catholic and Protestant children – all seven of them. There is a Catholic Church and a Protestant one, but the islanders are all buried in the same grave-yard. The cemetery also contains the graves of four servicemen whose bodies were washed ashore during the First World War – 'Known Unto God', says the inscription on their tombstones.

Rathlin Island is probably the only place in the entire province that was utterly unaffected by the Troubles. Even if it had kerbstones, which it does not, nobody would think of paint-ing them. Indeed, it becomes a refuge each July for those desperate to escape the tensions of the loyalist marching season on the mainland.

There are two nurses but no doctor. Pregnant women have to leave the island two weeks before they're due, and no baby has been born there for 40 years. There is one telephone box, one post-box, one fire engine, one bar and one tiny shop. The islanders mostly telephone the shops in Ballycastle and have their groceries sent over on the ferry. On Wednesdays they send petrol cans on the ferry to have them filled on the other side. If the ferry can't run for more than three consecutive days, the RAF flies in the essential supplies.

Three or four millennia ago Rathlin led the world in the pro-duction of stone axe heads, but was put out of business by the advent of copper. It never really discovered another industry apart from small-scale farming and fishing. The islanders don't seem unduly bothered. They are not concerned with careers and pensions and the prices of their property; they live on Rathlin because they want to, and find what work they can. The ferry is now the biggest employer, followed by the bar. Most of the islanders have several jobs. The postman, for example, is also a farmer, a fireman, a coast-guard and part-owner of the bar.

There is also a strong sense of community. By way of entertainment the islanders regularly stage plays, quizzes, ceilidhs and, in the summer, home-made yacht and raft races. There is a monthly newsletter called *Island News* produced by Alison Hurst, a West Country woman who has made Rathlin her home after falling in love with the place in the early 1980s. 'I only like to publish good news. I don't do scandal,' she told me.

The bar is the islanders' meeting place, and it was there that we all convened for dinner shortly after 8 p.m. to find half the island had already arrived – perhaps because the priest had been unable to cross from the mainland for Saturday evening Mass. It turned into one of those long, convivial and very Irish evenings. Drinks appeared unordered. Umpteen 'kitties' were exhausted and replenished. Complete strangers quickly became old friends. Packie O'Neill, one of the shooters, showed himself to be considerably more accurate with a snooker cue than a shotgun by winning the bar's pool tournament. Midnight came and went with no sign of the bar closing. Nobody seemed remotely concerned about being breathalysed in the unlikely event of their ever deciding to leave.

I slipped away at 1.30 a.m. when the party was still going strong. Outside the wind was still howling, and the distant lights of Ballycastle twinkled in the freezing blackness. I staggered back to my bed at the manor house just in time – or so it seemed – to be woken for breakfast by Charlene.

I had definite plans for the day. I would go to the bird reserve and steel myself to peer over the top of the vertical cliffs to the turbulent sea below. I would admire the 150 acres of 'bonsai' fir trees that the forestry service had planted many years before in one of its more spectacularly unsuccessful experiments. I would then round off my visit, before catching the afternoon ferry home, by visiting the cave where Robert the Bruce took refuge in 1306 after his defeat by the English at Perth and watched a spider repeatedly trying to spin a web. Inspired by that display of arachnoid perseverance, he returned home and won the Scottish throne at the Battle of Bannockburn.

My plans did not outlast my sausage, egg and bacon. Outside the gale raged on and the waves were crashing over the harbour wall. From the dining-room window we could see the 9 a.m. ferry boldly preparing to depart. Take it, advised Charlene, or you could be here for days. The cave was only accessible by boat in any case, she belatedly informed me. Forsaking the charms of Rathlin Island, and fearing for my liver if I stayed much longer, I hurriedly packed my bag, sprinted down to the harbour and splashed aboard.

4

The Magic Kingdom

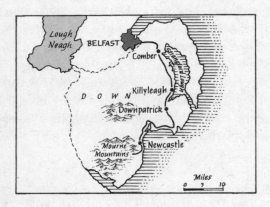

In 1888 in May Street, not a 100 yards east of the Belfast City Hall, a man called John Boyd Dunlop revolutionised modern life when he developed the first successful pneumatic tyre.

Dunlop, a vet with a long white beard, had a nine-year-old son who was tired of jolting along cobbled streets on a tricycle with solid rubber tyres, so he fixed air-filled tubes covered with canvas to the wheels. They seemed to work and Dunlop applied for a patent. Initially the public guffawed at his 'sausage tyres', but soon changed its mind when they proved much faster. He formed a company to exploit his invention, which happily coincided with the advent of the motor car, and made a fortune. Within half-a-century the Dunlop Rubber Company was a giant worldwide business with 93,000 employees.

I knew the Ulster History Circle had erected a blue plaque in his honour in May Street, but on this damp, dark winter's evening I searched for it in vain. I was finally stopped by a passer-by so old he probably remembered Mr Dunlop personally. 'Wot yer looking fer?' he asked. I told him. 'Cum 'ere,' he said, and took me back down the street to a small car park behind a row of billboards. There was the plaque, fixed to a side wall and completely hidden from the street by a giant Smirnoff vodka poster.

'Who could see that?' the old man snorted in disgust. 'You never see the good stuff in this place. It's all the bad things they show you. It's just troubles, troubles, troubles.'

I'd found a kindred spirit.

I carried on to the far end of May Street, past the monstrously fortified High Court, past the newly refurbished Victorian building that houses St George's fruit and vegetable market, to the banks of the cleaned-up Lagan River where Belfast old and new stand face to face.

On my right was the back of Friendly Street, a curving and unbroken row of public-sector houses with a name almost as inappropriate as that of nearby Joy Street. This is the nationalist Markets area of Belfast, scene of numerous bloody republican feuds and of murderous attacks on policemen.

On my left, however, was the Waterfront Hall – a circular, glass-walled, state-of-the-art concert centre that stands as a proud symbol of the city's spectacular recent renaissance. It was opened by Prince Charles in 1997, and already a Hilton Hotel, a British Telecom office block and numerous costly riverside condominiums have sprung up around it.

The Waterfront Hall was my destination for the evening. I joined the sober-suited burghers of Belfast as they poured into this brilliant bubble of light. Soon I was sitting high in the gods, watching a stocky, bearded figure perform a Prokofiev Sonata on a silver flute on the stage below me. The capacity audience sat rapt, mesmerised by the brilliance of the world's pre-eminent flautist – a man raised in a back-street ghetto barely a mile from where we were sitting.

James Galway is a perfect riposte to those who believe that nothing good comes from Northern Ireland. He was born in 1939 in a tiny terraced house with one cold tap and an outside toilet in Carnalea Street, just north of the city centre. His father was a riveter at Harland and Wolff – when there was work. Young Jimmy began with the penny-whistle, graduated to the flute, and by the age of nine was playing for a flute band in Orange Order parades.

At 14 he left school to work in a piano shop, and there he would doubtless have stayed had John Francis of the Royal College of Music not visited Belfast with the London Harpsichord Ensemble. Jimmy's flute teacher arranged for him to play before the great man, and in no time he was studying at the Royal College while living in Mr Francis's splendid St John's Wood home. He never looked back.

I'd arranged to meet Mr Galway the following morning at the upmarket guest house where he was staying. I found him in his shirt and braces having breakfast with his American wife, Jeanne. Though now in his early sixties, he still has a distinct Belfast accent and the impish air of the urchin who played end-less pranks in Carnalea Street like tying doorknockers together. 'We did lots of terrible things,' he chuckled. 'We couldn't be rec-ommended as role models for anything.'

I suppose I'd expected Mr Galway to wax lyrical about his youth, but not a bit of it. He'd had a happy childhood, he said, but felt no nostalgia for Belfast and certainly didn't consider it home. He was raised in a completely Protestant neighbourhood where, he now realises, sectarianism was rife. He remembered going to the wedding of a fellow employee at the piano shop, realising it was a Catholic church, and thinking, 'I'm going to be damned to hell and never come back.'

Music was simply a means of entertainment in the absence of

diversions like television. 'We didn't see it as important. It was just what you did. It was something that gave life a better quality.' A particular reason for pursuing it was that he suffered from an eye condition that made reading difficult.

Mr Galway now lives in a house with 16 rooms near Lucerne, in Switzerland, and says that every time he passes the fuse-box he marvels at how far he's come. As a boy he swapped a stamp for some electrical device with a chum named Billy Chambers and managed to fuse the entire street.

Today he returns to Belfast only because it has two great concert halls – the Waterfront and the Ulster Hall – and to see an old childhood friend named John Lyttle whom he met on the swings. He has no family left here. He doesn't revisit old haunts like Carnalea Street because they've all been demolished. He looks and sounds like an Ulster Prod, but certainly no longer thinks like one. As a practising Christian who has long since shed the convictions of his youth, he no longer has any time for Northern Ireland's bigotry. He considered the Troubles 'ridiculous', believes it is high time Ireland was reunited, and insists the people have to put the past behind them.

'Someone has to tell them life is better if you don't hate people,' he said. 'Hating occupies part of your mind. If you hate this guy or that guy every day they are renting space in your head and not even paying for it. It hurts you more than it hurts them because you can think about them all day and send daggers through the air and they're not even aware of it. It's you that's hurting yourself.'

That is not a lesson which has yet been absorbed in old red-brick, working-class East Belfast that begins on the far side of the Lagan. One afternoon a few days later I resumed my journey, crossing the Albert Bridge behind the Waterfront and entering a world of tiny terraced homes, painted kerbstones and loyalist paramilitary murals with Harland and Wolff's two giant yellow cranes as the ever-present backdrop. The only time I ever felt in danger in Northern Ireland was in this urban warren during the riots that engulfed the province after the blocking of the Orange Order's Drumcree parade in 1998.

It was a warm July evening. Mobs were on the rampage, roused by the beat of the Lambeg drum and fortified with alcohol. They were stringing barricades across the roads, setting fires and hijacking the few vehicles whose drivers were foolish enough to be out. I suddenly realised that my exit routes were being swiftly sealed off, and I escaped only by dint of two or three rapid U-turns and some high-speed jinks through the maze of back streets. From the relative safety of the deserted Belfast–to–Bangor dual-carriageway, I looked back and saw columns of black smoke billowing skywards from a dozen different blazes. Was this really a part of the United Kingdom, I asked myself?

On this grey February day, all was quiet as I returned in search of a road called Hyndford Street. This proved, at least in appearance, completely indistinguishable from any of its neighbours. In fact it is the street's utter ordinariness, its total lack of pretension, its lack of anything at all to uplift or inspire the soul, that makes the little brass plate on No. 125 all the more remarkable. 'Singer-songwriter Van Morrison Lived Here From 1945–1961,' it says.

You could see why affluent Cyprus Avenue – a broad avenue lined with tall trees and elegant villas half a mile further eastwards – so impressed the young George Ivan Morrison that years later it became the subject of one of his most famous songs. To a kid from a tiny two-up, two-down house with an outside loo in Hyndford Street, it must have seemed another world. And so it would have remained had his father, a Harland and Wolff electrician, not had what was considered a rather eccentric passion in 1950s Belfast.

Mr Morrison Snr. collected American blues and jazz records. He thus sowed the seeds that turned his son into one of the world's great songwriters instead of another unemployed shipyard worker or loyalist paramilitary. Today Van the Man could buy Cyprus Avenue in its entirety, including the comfortable middle-class home of that rabble-rouser Ian Paisley.

The door of No. 125 was ajar. I knocked on it, but there was no answer. The curtains twitched next door and an elderly lady came out to see if she could help. 'Leslie's car's here. He must be around,' she said. I asked if she remembered Van Morrison. 'Oh yes,' she replied. 'He was a very quiet and shy boy. He hardly spoke coming back from school. He hung his head, he was that shy. It's funny to think he could go up and perform in front of thousands of people.'

Her name was Ethel Bleakley, and she couldn't have been friendlier. She invited me into her tiny sitting room. She had lived there 45 years, she said, and her late husband had worked at Harland and Wolff with Van's father. The shipyard and Shorts the aircraft builders were the only jobs around in those days. Her own son was only two years younger than Van, but they never played because Van was only interested in his music. 'As a wee boy he didn't play wee boy's games. He wasn't interested in football.'

She remembered Van forming a 'skiffle' group with improvised instruments and practising in the back yard. She remembered him learning to play the trumpet – she probably meant the saxophone – and keeping her awake at night by practising. I suggested that people would nowadays pay a fortune for such a personal concert, but Ethel was unimpressed. 'I don't think he's that good, to tell you the truth. He's not my idea of a singer, but he's done really, really well and for that he deserves credit. His mother was a good singer. I used to hear Violet singing through the wall.'

Van's parents left his childhood home years ago when he bought them a house in a posher part of East Belfast. The last time Ethel had seen Van was at his father's funeral in 1990. He never came back to Hyndford Street.

I thanked Ethel and prepared to leave. Lots of people came to look at the plaque, she told me on her doorstep. They came from America, Canada and all over, and they all wanted to be photographed in front of it. 'An Australian couple knocked on the door and asked Leslie if they could come in. Of course, he said, but then they asked to look round the house and see the bedrooms and he says, "Listen, this isn't a show house!"'

Leslie was apparently a single middle-aged man, and seemingly no great fan of Van's either. No. 125 has had three or four owners since the Morrisons left, and he probably had no idea he was buying a shrine. His door was still ajar, but I decided to leave the poor fellow in peace.

Astonishingly this tiny corner of East Belfast produced another man who made an even bigger impact on the world, selling more than 100 million books as one of the twentieth century's most distinguished Christian intellectuals. On a dull post-war block of flats in Dundela Avenue, not five minutes from Hyndford Street, there is a plaque that reads: 'C.S. Lewis 1898–1963 Author and Christian Apologist Born on This Site'. Around the corner, outside the local library, is a statue erected on the centenary of Lewis's birth that shows Digory Kirke, his fictional alter ego, entering the kingdom of Narnia through the magic wardrobe.

Lewis's father was a Belfast solicitor, and the family soon moved from Dundela Avenue to a huge, rambling house called 'Little Lea' in Circular Road in the more affluent suburbs of East Belfast. It still stands. 'I am a product of long corridors, empty sunlit rooms, upstairs indoor silences, attics explored in solitude, distant noises of gurgling cisterns and pipes, the noise of wind under the tiles,' Lewis wrote later. 'Also endless books. My father bought all the books he read and never got rid of any of them.'

His mother died in the house when he was nine and he was sent to boarding school in England, but he returned every holiday and in the summer he and his brother would roam the

Holywood hills that rise out of Belfast beyond Circular Road and run across the top of County Down.

I often used to take a back road home to Helen's Bay across these hills. From the top there is the most fantastic view across the gorgeous rolling countryside of County Down to the mysterious, magical silhouettes of the Mourne Mountains some 30 miles to the south.

Lewis obviously felt the same sense of exhilaration at this view of a 'different world', as he called it in his autobiography. 'Having seen it, blame me if you can for being a romantic. For here is the thing itself, utterly irresistible, the way to the world's end, the land of longing, the breaking and blessing of hearts.' Heaven, he once said, was 'Oxford lifted and placed in the middle of the County Down.'

As for the Mourne Mountains, he described them as:

. . . steep and compact and pointed and toothed and jagged. They seem to have nothing to do with the little hills and cottages that divide you from them. And sometimes they are blue, sometimes violet; but quite often they look transparent – as if huge sheets of gauze had been cut into mountainous shapes and hung up there so that you could see through them the light of the invisible sea at their backs.

The Mournes clearly made a huge impression on young Jack, as he was known. It is widely believed that they were the inspiration for his magic kingdom of Narnia. They were also my distant destination on this particular journey.

On the other side of the Holywood hills, I drove down through Dundonald to the neat little town of Comber at the north-east tip of Strangford Lough.

Comber once produced a famous whiskey, but the distillery closed more than fifty years ago. It produced Thomas Andrews, the *Titanic*'s designer who went down with his ship, and his brother, John Andrews, who became Northern Ireland's Prime Minister in 1941. Soon after his elevation Mr Andrews asked for a meeting with Sir Winston Churchill. Downing Street resisted, gently pointing out that there was a war on. Mr Andrews persisted and was finally granted 15 minutes. After 45 minutes an exasperated Churchill emerged into his private office demanding: 'Will someone pray tell me who, or what, is Comber?'

The town also produced Major-General Sir Robert Rollo Gillespie. In Comber's pretty town square there are three memorials. The smallest commemorates five local members of the security forces 'who gave their lives in defence of their country' – i.e. fighting the IRA. The medium-size one honours the dead of the two World Wars. The third is a magnificent tall column topped by a statue of the General, who was an eighteenth-century Superman.

He was born in a house on the square in 1766, joined the cavalry at 17, eloped, and killed a member of the Dublin gentry in a duel but was acquitted of murder. He went to Jamaica and was shipwrecked in a hurricane, but reached land in an open boat. Attacked by eight brigands, he killed six and chased away the others. He later commanded troops in Java, Bengal, Nepal and elsewhere. He was hauled into a besieged fort at Vellore on a rope. It was too good to last, alas. In 1814 he was shot through the heart while attacking the fort of Kalunga in the Himalayas. Inscribed on the column are his famous last words – 'One more shot for the honour of Down'.

Comber no longer produces heroes of such epic stature, but it still produces characters like Noel Spence. With his twin brother, Roy, Noel builds Santa's grottoes for department stores during the day, but at night he runs a private 66-seat cinema in the garden of his bungalow.

It's called 'The Tudor'. You can rent it for about £30 an evening and order any film you want, but Noel's real passion is for 1950s black-and-white American science horror films made for the teenage drive-in movie market. He has built a 'fraternity' of about thirty co-enthusiasts – policemen, doctors, accountants – who gather each Sunday night to watch such masterpieces as *The Thing That Couldn't Die*, *The Screaming Skull* or *Attack of the Giant Blood Leeches*. 'It's like our secret other life,' he jokes. There is no admission price: 'I pay them to come,' he laughs. But you do have to prove your love of the genre by naming, for example, the American title of *The City of the Dead*.

I'd heard of the cinema but never been there, so I telephoned Mr Spence to see if I could visit. He generously waived the admission test and gave me detailed instructions. Take the main road a mile out of Comber, turn right at the bus stop, go up the hill till you see a sign for a riding school and past the school you'll see the cinema.

It had turned into a foul, pitch-black evening with my windscreen wipers fighting a losing battle against the lashing rain. There was not another car out, and I was half expecting to catch some gruesome extra-terrestrial in my headlights. The road became a lane, which became a tiny track that led deep into the inky-dark countryside but there, suddenly, was this tiny Fifties-style cinema, with two or three cars outside and the title of that night's movie – *The Astounding She Monster* – in lights above the old swing doors.

'It was an old hen house,' explained Noel, a friendly, balding man in his fifties with flyaway hair. It is far from that now. It is a perfect miniature cinema, a period piece lovingly reconstructed from the salvaged fittings of closed-down flea-pits. The red velvet seats came from the Limavady Regal, the footlights from the Portaferry Picture House, the showcase for 'Coming Attractions' from the Tonic in Bangor, and the seashell wall-lights from the Aurora in Rostrevor. The cinema's name sign came from the Tudor in Bangor, which showed its last film in 1962 and then hung a notice on the door that read simply: 'Closed due to lack of people.'

It was into old flea-pits like those that Noel, playing truant from school, would sneak as a boy. It was there that he fell in love with these ghoulish offerings from across the Atlantic. Roughly five hundred were made before they turned 'bloody and gory and tasteless', and by dint of building his own cinema in 1974 he's been able to watch them more times than he can count.

'They're part of my being,' he explained with delightful self-deprecation. 'I say the lines inside myself. As soon as one's run, I just want to watch it all over again. It's the ingenuousness and the enthusiasm and the inventiveness of them.' At that moment Roy arrived. 'Trainspotters would think we're daft, just as we'd think they're daft,' Roy suggested. 'It's everyone to their own.'

Noel slipped into the projectionist's room. The lights dimmed, and *The Astounding She Monster* began before an all-male audience of precisely four including the Spence twins.

I won't bore you with the plot. Suffice to say that the film was wonderfully, gloriously dreadful. It wasn't mediocre – it was terrible – the flimsiest plot, the corniest script, the hammiest acting and the most clichéd melodrama that I've ever had the good fortune to watch. There was not a drop of actual blood, not one chaste kiss, not a single swear word, but I loved every minute of it. 'Excellent,' cried Roy as the final credits rolled, his eyes still watering from laughter.

Before I ventured out into that vile night again, Roy told me a little secret. Had I noticed that the She Monster never once turned her back to the camera, he asked? That was because she ripped the back of her shimmering, skin-tight dress while rehearsing and the producers couldn't afford to mend it.

*

The next morning I continued southwards past the Castle Espie wildfowl reserve on Strangford Lough which plays host each winter to almost the entire world population of Light-Bellied Brent goose – about 12,000 of the creatures. There are not many living things that would choose to spend a wet, grey winter in Northern Ireland, let alone travel 3,000 perilous miles from the Canadian Arctic for such a dubious pleasure, but these birds have been doing it for the past 10,000 years and evidently find the lough's abundant supply of long, thin eel-grass quite irresistible.

I had not driven more than another 10 miles down the rolling country road when a fantastic, fairy-tale edifice with battlements, high walls and great round pointed towers loomed out of the mist in front of me – a cross between a Loire château and a Rhine schloss towering over the rooftops of the village of Killyleagh.

I'd seen Killyleagh Castle before, of course, but this time I'd telephoned ahead to ask if I could visit. Of course, replied Colonel Denys Rowan-Hamilton, the owner. At 10.30 a.m. I drove up Killyleagh's neat but humble high street, through the gatehouse arch and into a great walled courtyard with towers at each corner and an expanse of vivid green lawn running up to the castle itself.

I half expected a liveried manservant to open the front door, but I was greeted by the tall, courtly, silver-haired figure of the Colonel wearing the opposite of his Sunday best. He ushered me into a cavernous hall and up a grand panelled staircase to the library where he introduced me to his equally tall silver-haired wife Wanda.

The Colonel is no Johnny-come-lately to Ulster's landed gentry. Killyleagh Castle has been owned by his family since about 1620, the year the Pilgrim Fathers set sail for America. In fact the Hamiltons have been around almost as long as their friends the Montgomerys of Greyabbey across the lough. He and his wife live all alone in two or three rooms of their splendid home, except at weekends when any or all of their seven children and 20 grandchildren are likely to invade. Troubles or no Troubles, the only trouble they've ever experienced has been drunken youths from the village using their courtyard as a race-track in the middle of the night.

Mrs Rowan-Hamilton brought coffee and home-made short-bread. We sank into comfortable old chairs pummelled into shape by a thousand bottoms, and as she quietly knitted he recounted a history of the castle as colourful as its appearance.

Its oldest parts date back to about 1180 – one of a series of castles built by John de Courcy, he said. This man de Courcy, I was soon to discover, built almost everything of any antiquity in Ulster.

Early in the seventeenth century James Hamilton, dispatched from Scotland by James I to settle Ulster and secure his kingdom's western flank, procured Killyleagh from a local chieftain named Conn O'Neill – allegedly in return for helping to secure O'Neill's release from prison. Hamilton and his son, the 1st Earl of Clanbrassil, went on to amass vast tracts of land but that, said the colonel, was 'the apogee of the family's fortunes'.

The 1st Earl's dim-witted son married Lady Alice Moore, daughter of the Earl of Drogheda. The scheming Lady Alice soon discovered not only that her husband was impotent, but that her father-in-law had bequeathed the entire estate to five cousins unless she produced a male heir. She broke into the 'muniment room' where the family documents were held, tore up the will and persuaded her husband to write a new one leaving the estate to her. His mother warned him that he'd be dead within three months if he signed such a document, but he did and he was – poisoned by his wife.

The Hamilton cousins naturally contested the new will. It was a battle of Dickensian proportions that lasted decades until one day a family retainer entered the castle's 'muniment room' and found the discarded wrapping of the original will. On it was a complete first draft on which the 1st Earl had spilled some ink; unwilling to waste scarce paper, he had had it made into an envelope for the second draft.

The Hamilton cousins had all died by then, but the last had had the foresight to make a will decreeing that if the lawsuit was ever won, one half of the estate should go to his daughter Anne and the other to his nephew Gawn. Unfortunately the courts interpreted his words absolutely literally. Gawn got the castle, Anne the gatehouse and the courtyard. Even the village was divided, with the Dufferin Arms on the north side of the High Street and the Hamilton Arms on the south side.

That bizarre division lasted more than a century, during which time Anne's family built a Georgian manor in the court-yard. It was the 1st Marquis of Dufferin and Ava, our old friend from Clandeboye, who finally put matters right in 1847. By then his estate had absorbed Anne's half through marriage, but with a characteristically generous flourish he returned it to the Hamiltons, declaring: 'I will not keep a man from his own front door.' He even tore down the manor.

The 1st Marquis asked just one thing in return – that the Hamiltons should pay his family one golden rose and one golden spur on alternate years. 'We paid it until 1914. After that the Hamilton side said we'd paid enough,' the Colonel chuckled. The Dufferins evidently thought otherwise. The Colonel recalled with amusement how the first time he met Maureen, the previous Marchioness, 'she came in, looked me straight in the eye and said, "You're behind with the rent!"'

The Colonel took me on a tour. We went through elegant unheated reception rooms, down rows of empty bedrooms, through sculleries and a dusty snooker room. We ascended the grand central staircase, clattered down the wooden back-stairs of the servants' quarters, and finally climbed the spiral stone stairs of the north-east tower until we emerged on to the battlements themselves. Below us was the village, and beyond lay Strangford Lough stretched out beneath the low grey sky.

I had taken the story of the will with a slight pinch of salt, but the Colonel now pointed out where Gawn had had to build an entry through the north wall to give himself access to his property. To the south a beautiful garden sloping down to a swimming pool, tennis court and pond was bisected with mathematical precision by the remains of an old dividing wall. On frosty days, said the Colonel, you could still see a line in the grass showing where the courtyard lawn was cut in two.

As we returned to the library we passed the bust of Archibald Hamilton, the Colonel's great-great-great-grandfather, whose life made even Sir Rollo Gillespie's seem a little grey and who is affectionately known within the family as 'the Rebel'.

He was sent down from Cambridge, joined the United Irishmen's late eighteenth-century opposition to British rule, and was condemned to death. According to Harold Nicolson, who was a relative of the Rowan-Hamiltons as well as the Dufferins, 'the Rebel' then escaped from Dublin's Newgate jail, was befriended by Robespierre in Paris and given rooms in the Palais Royal. When Robespierre fell he rowed up the Seine in a Thames wherry boat, sailed to Philadelphia and settled in Wilmington, Delaware, where he had several illegitimate children. Overcome by boredom, he successfully petitioned for a royal pardon and returned to Killyleagh. At 74 he challenged an MP who accused him of treachery to a duel. He died on 1 November 1834, 'in charity with all mankind and wishing Ireland and the whole world happiness and free institutions'.

As I left the castle after taking my leave of the Rowan-Hamiltons, I noticed a large boulder to the right of the gatehouse bearing a plaque in honour of another local man. 'Sir Hans Sloane 1660–1753,' it read, 'Physician, Botanist and Bibliophile whose extensive collections formed the nucleus of the British Museum.' I bet young Hans, growing up in Killyleagh, never thought he'd give his name to a famous London square, let alone to a whole breed of smart young, bepearled London women.

To Edward Hinks, vicar of Killyleagh for 40 years from 1826, there is no memorial, though his bust did stand for many decades in the entrance of the Cairo Museum in Egypt. This unassuming man never visited Egypt, and lived far from any libraries, but from plaster casts of ancient stones he unravelled the mysteries of hieroglyphic and cuneiform scripts.

From Killyleagh it was only a few more rural miles to Downpatrick at the foot of Strangford Lough. This ancient and attractive town is dominated by a lovely old cathedral where Saint Patrick is allegedly buried. A large granite stone engraved with a Celtic cross and the word 'Patric' commemorates the man who brought Christianity to Ireland in the fifth century, and whose annual feast day is now celebrated from New Zealand to New York. Unfortunately nobody can pinpoint exactly where he lies.

Downpatrick also has some fine old Georgian streets, and a beautiful setting in a cradle of hills, but the real reason for stopping there was to meet Danny Morgan and Cecil Telford in the Roundhouse pub at lunchtime.

Danny is a plumber, and Cecil a school bus-driver, but they also happen to be chairman and secretary respectively of the Down District Skittles Association. Cecil, moreover, has been the individual Down Skittles champion for three consecutive years. Indeed one could almost say he is the world champion because Down Skittles is not like your common-or-garden game of skittles as played in England. It is one of those traditional sports with obscure origins and its own unique rules that is played only in south County Down.

The association has 34 eight-man teams from 34 pubs. Matches are played on long summer evenings in the pubs' car parks or on the lanes outside, and the *Down Recorder* devotes a page to the sport each week. It was now February, and raining outside, but Danny and Cecil happily agreed to stage an exhibition match amid the beer kegs in the pub's backyard which doubles as the Saul Hibs team's home ground.

The five skittles or 'pegs' are pieces of brightly painted broom handle chopped into three-inch lengths. Four of these 'pegs' are placed around the circumference of a circle painted on the concrete with the help of a 24-inch bicycle wheel. The fifth is placed in the middle, and each is worth between one and five points.

The thrower has to stand 27 feet from the centre of the ring, and uses nothing as bland as a ball. His weapon is a round yew log nine inches long and three inches in diameter, soaked in water for extra weight and durability. The log can hit the ground before a line drawn just in front of the circle, and the winner is the man who first scores exactly 41 points. Score 42 points or more, and your tally returns to 32.

This particular match was no contest. Even in the midst of winter Cecil was in devastating form; it took him barely 12 throws to amass the 41 points, and we scurried gratefully back into the warmth of the bar. What's the secret? I asked him. 'Two pints of Tennants to start off with,' he replied with a grin. And where did all the yew logs come from? Cecil and Danny both hesitated. 'You find yew trees in churchyards,' said Cecil quietly. 'There aren't too many left around here now,' confessed Danny.

As I left Downpatrick that afternoon my eye was caught by one of those brown signs denoting sites of interest, pointing down a narrow lane. 'Struell Wells', it said, and because I was in no hurry I turned off. The lane took me deep into the countryside, past an elegant old farmhouse, until I reached one of those remarkable places that would have been spoiled by tourists anywhere but Ireland, yet here has been virtually forgotten.

In a secluded little valley, ringed by gorse-covered hills, half-a-dozen old stone structures stood on a sward of lush green grass. 'Struell Wells – Healing Wells', said a notice. I wandered round. There was the shell of a church; there was a small round stone building with steps leading down to a ferny 'drinking' well, and another containing an 'eye' well. At the far end were two stone bathing houses, one for men and one for women. The men's had an ante-room with bare stone benches for undressing, and an inner room with a sunken stone tank into which flowed ice-cold water from the underground stream that supplied the other structures. The women's was much the same, but had lost its roof.

There was nobody else there, and complete silence except for the distant lowing of cows. It was tremendously atmospheric. The place felt – and was – ancient. There was a chapel recorded on the site in 1306, and it was a place of pilgrimage in the middle ages. In one of the wells, according to the sign, St Patrick "was known to have spent the great part of the night stark naked, singing psalms and spiritual songs'. I did not feel remotely tempted to follow suit – certainly not in February. Did I drink from the well and wash my eyes? Well, yes, I did. Call it superstition, but you never know.

It was at this point in my journey that a certain Mr Ernest Sandford intervened. I don't know who he was, but a quarter of a century ago he had the brilliant idea of writing to more than a hundred Women's Institutes across the province in search of information. The result is a wonderful but little-known guide book called *Discover Northern Ireland* that is packed full of arcane facts about obscure places. The book also achieves the remarkable feat of failing to make a single mention of the Troubles which at that time were at their peak.

It was while flicking through this book that I came across an entry that read: 'St John's Point, 3km S. of Killough, with lighthouse and ruins of a 10th century church, is reached by a rugged coastal walk passing en route a corbelled pigsty protected as an ancient monument.'

I wasn't particularly interested in the church or lighthouse, but where else in the world would you find a listed pigsty? I made some inquiries and was put in touch with Professor Ronnie Buchanan, a former Director of Irish Studies at Queen's University in Belfast, who had discovered this amazing structure while researching for a Ph.D. in the 1950s. In fact he had discovered several in the coastal area immediately south-east of Downpatrick, and had written an erudite 22-page article on them in the 1956 *Ulster Journal of Archaeology*. He was, he modestly confessed, 'the world authority' on corbelled pigsties.

These dated back to the late eighteenth or early nineteenth centuries, he told me. They were elaborate structures whose roofs were 'corbelled' – constructed from ascending layers of flat stones that overlapped till they met in the middle. Mere shacks wouldn't do because pigs were a valuable commodity in those days, and had to be kept warm and cosseted. The one mentioned in Mr Sandford's book was the finest surviving example, and he told me how to find it. Drive east from Killough towards Minerstown, look for the ruins of a village called Murphystown and in the middle of those ruins you will find the pigsty, he said.

Killough, a thriving herring port in Victorian times, was a lovely old seaside town with a silted-up harbour and broad, tree-lined main street of brightly painted houses. It was the sort of place you go to as a child for long summer holidays and remember with great nostalgia in middle age. The trouble was that it had two roads leading along the coast to Minerstown, and soon I was quite lost.

For 30 minutes I drove around looking for some porcine mansion of indeterminate size and shape. I hesitated to ask locals the way to a pigsty, but I was eventually obliged to do just that and was rewarded with looks of bemusement and amusement. I was about to give up when I spotted some ruined cottages on a low hill set back from the road that I took to be Murphystown. The only problem was that between me and them was a long narrow field, every inch of which had been churned into deep mud by a large herd of cows. Crossing it was out of the question, but I had not come this far to be thwarted. I fought my way through a thicket of brambles at one end of the quagmire, went up to my calves in a stream and ripped my jacket ducking through a barbed-wire fence, but finally reached my goal.

The former residents of Murphystown obviously thought more of their pigs than they did of themselves. The pigsty was the only complete building still standing amid the ruins, and a very splendid pigsty it was too. It was squat and square, with impressive dry-stone walls and a pyramid-shaped stone roof tall enough for me to stand up inside. It was, moreover, a pigsty with a view. From the low doorway I could look out across the magnificent silky blue sweep of Dundrum Bay to the majestic Mourne Mountains beyond. Yes, I thought. Were I a pig, this is where I'd want to live.

The Mournes, and food, beckoned. I squelched back to the car and sped round the top of Dundrum Bay. The sea was becalmed, but on a single tempestuous January morning in 1843 it devoured no fewer than 74 local fishermen. I was coasting down to the town of Newcastle – where, as the old song says, 'The Mountains of Mourne sweep down to the sea' – when all of a sudden a great derelict, three-storey Georgian-style mansion appeared on the top of a hill in front of me. I was tired and hungry, but once again my curiosity prevailed.

There was a gatehouse off to my right, and a long drive which I followed up the hill. I noticed a newish bungalow built in the mansion's shadow, and was greeted by the friendliest of ladies before I could even knock on the door. 'You want to look round?' she asked before I'd said a word. Obviously I wasn't the first.

The house was called Mount Panther, she told me. It was built in the 1700s, lived in by a succession of families, extended and remodelled. Her father-in-law, a farmer called Paddy Fitzpatrick, bought it in 1930 and her late husband, Seamus, inherited it. Early one Saturday evening, when Mrs Fitzpatrick was in her curlers and bathing her children, Princess Margaret and Lord Snowdon came up the drive – rather as I had – and asked to look round.

'We lived in it until 1962 or 1963, but my husband was a farmer and we couldn't afford to keep it up,' said Mrs Fitzpatrick. They auctioned the furniture and moved into the bungalow. 'It went downhill very fast after that. It's just gone to rack and ruin.' In the late 1980s the roof was removed because it was about to collapse.

I wandered over. It was one of the saddest, most poignant places I'd ever seen. The garden had reverted to nature, the broad front steps had vanished beneath the undergrowth, the first- and second-floor ceilings had collapsed. Through the warped and twisted window frames you could still make out the fine blue-and-white plasterwork of the ballroom, the wooden shutters in the library and the tiled walls of the kitchen, but it was amazing how fast it had deteriorated. The windows were eyeless sockets, no longer capable of surveying the wonderful panorama of undulating countryside for which this site had undoubtedly been chosen.

Another great edifice was my destination for the night, and it took me only a few more minutes to reach it. At first sight Newcastle's vast red-brick Slieve Donard Hotel looks like a cross between a Victorian mental institution and a particularly grim, third-rate English public school. But mental institutions tend not to be flanked by the sea on one side, a gorgeous clump of mountains on another and one of the world's top ten golf courses – the Royal County Down – on the third. They tend not to win four stars for service, or have interiors of oak and mahogany, blazing fires and crystal chandeliers. They tend not to be the sort of place to which my family will happily come to meet me as they did this Saturday night.

The Slieve Donard was built in the late nineteenth century by the Belfast and County Down Railway Company to provide a particularly grand attraction at the end of its line. The hotel was the last word in Victorian grandeur and luxury, and for just £3.10s guests could procure first-class rail travel from Belfast, dinner on the evening of arrival and full board and lodging for a week.

Charlie Chaplin stayed here in 1921, though not to take advantage of the special offer. He was hiding himself away after divorcing his wife, only to learn that his true love, Hetty Kelly, had died in the meantime. The hotel has not been slow to exploit the fact: it has named its bar Chaplin's Bar, adorned it with pictures of the famous comedian, and framed the relevant page from the hotel register. Sandwiched between the signatures of Miss Montgomery from Co. Dublin and Captain L. Scott-Taggart from Belfast is that of 'Charles Chaplin, New York City'.

In 1948 the railways were nationalised and the hotel became part of the Ulster Transport Authority. By the 1960s it was cheaper to fly off on package holidays to Spain where it seldom rained and the sea was actually swimmable. By the 1970s the Troubles were in full swing and the Slieve Donard was bombed at least four times, which had the entirely understandable effect of deterring visitors. At one particularly low point the financial director of the Hastings Hotel Group, which bought the pile in 1971, renamed it The Titanic because it looked like sinking the entire company.

The Slieve Donard could have ended up like Mount Panther, but happily its owners went for broke. They sank millions of pounds into the place, restored it to its former glory and it is now thriving – the only hotel I have ever stayed in where the plugs in the basins work, the windows actually open so that you don't risk dying of asphyxiation in your sleep, and the bathrooms are equipped with yellow rubber ducks.

My children spent most of the night in the swimming pool,

but breakfast was the real highlight. This was served in a sun-filled, oak-panelled dining room the size of the *Titanic*'s. The buffet table was the length of a cricket pitch, and laden with silver drums full of bacon, sausages, eggs, mushrooms, tomatoes and potato bread. Moreover, the waiters and waitresses passed every test Mrs Fletcher and her children could contrive.

The butter came in pats, not horrible little sachets. The marmalade arrived in a bowl, not tiny globs of plastic. My wife successfully demanded wheaten bread instead of toasted white cardboard. My daughter Imogen ordered honey, which arrived in a little silver bowl. My son Barney ate at least 169 sausages without a murmur of complaint from the management. I made a mental note to include the Slieve Donard in my next book – a guide to hotels where you can walk in off the street and eat a huge free breakfast because nobody asks for your room number.

My bloated family were curiously reluctant to accompany me on the final leg of this particular journey, which was to climb Slieve Donard, the highest of the peaks. As they returned to Belfast, I drove a few miles further south along the narrow ribbon of road which is all that divides the steep mountainsides from the deep blue water of the sea.

I met Dawson Stelfox, my guide for the day, at Bloody Bridge, site of one of the myriad massacres that lend Irish history its peculiar charm. Dawson is a wiry, athletic fellow in his early forties, a genial Belfast architect who not only knows every nook and cranny of the Mourne Mountains but in 1993 gained the distinction of becoming the first Irishman ever to climb Mount Everest. I was dressed in jeans and sneakers. He was clad, rather ominously, in boots and Gore-Tex. He slung a rucksack across his back, and off we set for Narnia.

It was a cold but sunny day, there was not another soul in sight, and it really did seem as if we were entering some storybook world far, far removed from the dangerous streets of Belfast.

We followed a trail called the Brandy Pad that eighteenth-century smugglers used to bring in spirits, wines and silks from France. We scattered a few sheep as we climbed. On precarious stepping stones we criss-crossed the Bloody Bridge River as it tumbled back down towards the sea. We made a brief detour into an ancient granite quarry – an eerie place with dripping walls and skeletal huts that once provided Liverpool, London and other English cities with their kerbstones. After 90 minutes and a final squelch across the Bog of Donard, we reached a gap in the mountains and the great stone wall that encloses the magic kingdom.

The wall is 22 miles long, 8 feet high and wide enough to walk on. Like a miniature version of the Great Wall of China, it loops over mountain tops and plunges down valleys as it recedes into the distance. Dullards insist that the wall was built to enclose the catchment area of the Silent Valley Reservoir which supplies distant Belfast with its water, but you and I know better.

What it really encloses is a child's wonderland – a great bowl of grass and heather ringed by smooth round peaks with mysterious names like Slievelamagan and Slieve Commedagh. Here is a gaping black chasm called the Devil's Coachroad. There is a great granite outcrop called Hare's Castle. To the north is a fearsome natural amphitheatre called the Pot of Legawherry. A silver sea glistened through gaps in the yellow-brown mountains to the south, and to the west mist swirled around the rest of the roughly fifty peaks that constitute 'the Mournes'. There are no roads, no buildings, no sign of habitation. This is the preserve not of humans but of foxes, ravens and peregrine falcons, of wicked witches and noble lions, and of who knows what besides.

Dawson stopped in the shelter of the wall and performed some magic of his own: he conjured hot coffee from his backpack. He's been exploring the Mourne Mountains since he was a boy, he told me, but he never tired of them. It was true they had no yeti, and the highest peak was a mere 2,796 feet compared with Everest's 29,021, but 'every time you come up they're different,' he said. 'They're never static. The weather changes, the seasons change, the colours change. You can have a gentle hill walk, or one of the most difficult rock climbs in the United Kingdom.'

The top of Slieve Donard was off to our right, and only another 1,000 feet up, but to reach it we had to traverse a particularly fine example of that peculiarly Irish phenomenon – the vertical bog. The footing was treacherous. An icy wind was by now whipping across the mountainside. For Dawson it was probably a mere 'dander', as they say in Northern Ireland, but for me it was a long, hard slog.

As we climbed he regaled me with the tale of his final ascent of Everest. That, too, involved a climb of about 1,000 feet, but it took him 12 hours and his exhausted companion was forced to turn back. When he finally reached the summit late in the afternoon he could see all the other snowcapped, sunlit Himalayan peaks breaking through the clouds. He did not plant a flag, however, because even there – 5,000 miles away and on top of the world – he could not escape the politics of his homeland. It was an all-Ireland expedition and Dawson knew he would have caused offence to somebody, somewhere, whether he planted the Union Jack, the Irish tricolour or both.

I thought I had devised the perfect ending for this chapter. Slieve Donard is not only the highest point in Northern Ireland, affording a magnificent view across rolling farmland to the Sperrin Mountains on the far side of Lough Neagh. It is also about the only point in the British Isles from which, on a clear day, you can see all their constituent parts – Northern Ireland, the Republic of Ireland, England, Scotland and Wales.

It was with a considerable sense of anticipation, therefore, that I staggered up the last few feet, braced myself against a hurricane-force wind and turned my eyes south-eastwards towards Snowdonia. Nothing – just a thick sea mist.

I swivelled eastwards towards Scafell in the Lake District, then northwards towards Scotland. Again nothing – not even the Isle of Man midway across the Irish Sea.

Even the Republic, a mere 15 miles southwards across Carlingford Lough, had vanished in the haze. In fact all we could really see were the rest of the Mourne Mountains – a fairytale landscape of peaks and valleys that looked more than ever like an enchanted little kingdom in the sky.

5

Gods, Heroes and Dr Paisley

It is lunchtime, it is snowing, and in front of the City Hall a great bear of a man wearing a blue beret and long black coat with upturned collar is bellowing into a loudspeaker.

'God's love,' the man roars at the largely indifferent passers-by, 'has no ending.'

'God's love has no-o-o finish, no-o-o conclusion,' he thunders against the noise of passing buses.

'God goes on loving so that whomsoever believeth in him should not perish, should not be damned, should not be in Hell, but have Everr Larrsting LIFE!'

With that triumphant peroration a dozen anorak-clad souls grouped around this striking figure burst into a song led by 'Brother Fred' on the accordion. 'Take me back to the old-fashioned meetings,' they sing with impressive gusto. 'Lead me on in that old-fashioned way . . .'

Some drivers honk in protest as they pass this little gospel meeting. Others wind down their windows and shout insults. A few policemen hover discreetly on the fringes, and the group is flanked by two highly alert bodyguards who are poised to whip the guns from beneath their jackets at the very first sign of danger. This particular preacher is not some madcap nobody; it is Ian Paisley MP, MEP, member of Northern Ireland's Assembly, Leader of the Democratic Unionist Party and Moderator of the Free Presbyterian Church of Ulster. This is the man to whom, at the time of his ordination, a prominent evangelist asked God to give 'a tongue like an old cow' so it would be 'as sharp as a file in the heart of the enemies of the King'.

'You brought the snow,' he bellows at me as the 'open air' ends – in Northern Ireland the noun 'meeting' has been dropped. He extends a great paw to shake my hand; he comes here most Fridays, he explains with a chuckle, to 'exercise my civil and religious liberties'.

I have a real problem with Dr Paisley. I deplore the politician. No single public figure has done more to inflame sectarian hatred in Northern Ireland, to widen the province's divisions or to wreck successive efforts to achieve peace through compromise. In the face of an immensely complex historical conundrum requiring bold and imaginative leadership, he has endlessly inflamed the fears and prejudices of ordinary Ulstermen with his simplistic absolutism and dead-end cries of 'No Surrender', 'Not an Inch' and 'Never, Never, Never'. He has offered no positive solution to the province's woes, just endless defiance in the face of threats real and imaginary to his beloved Protestant Ulster. In his absence Northern Ireland would surely have found a way out of its nightmare long ago.

And yet, like many other journalists, I find myself quite fascinated by this larger-than-life figure. In private Dr Paisley is warm, funny and rather charming. Though now in his mid-seventies, he has the energy of a 20-year-old. He is by far the most compelling public speaker in Northern Ireland, and probably the United Kingdom, and has been a giant presence on the province's political scene since the 1960s. Indeed, his political profile has been so high that it is often forgotten that he has also built an entire Church from scratch.

The Free Presbyterian Church began in 1951 when the young fiery preacher and some fellow fundamentalists accused the official Irish Presbyterian Church of apostasy and backsliding. They stuck rigidly to the word of the bible; they decried drinking, smoking, homosexuality and miscegenation – though the latter was hardly a problem in all-white Northern Ireland. They barred women from office, and expected them to cover their heads in church. Above all they rejected any accommodation whatsoever with Roman Catholicism and by extension, of course, the predominantly Catholic Irish Republic.

Dr Paisley's Free Presbyterians 'tithed' 10 per cent of their income, and whatever else they could spare. They proselytised, spread and multiplied, and now boast more than 100 churches as far afield as Australia, Canada and America. Dr Paisley's son Kyle is minister of a Free Presbyterian church in East Anglia.

The spiritual heart of this organisation is the Martyrs' Memorial, a 2,000-seat mega-church in East Belfast's Ravenhill Road where Dr Paisley delivers hell-and-damnation sermons each Sunday from a throne-like pulpit flanked by the Ulster flag and Union Jack. There is no choir – he long ago disbanded it for being troublesome. The hymnbook is somewhat unorthodox; Hymn 757, for example, begins: 'Our Fathers knew thee, Rome of old/And evil is thy fame;/Thy fond embrace, the galling chain/Thy kiss the blazing flame.' The religious martyrs the church honours are people like Thomas Cranmer, Nicholas Ridley and William Tyndale, and it is hard to escape the conclusion that Dr Paisley includes himself amongst their number.

The church's corridors and inner sanctums are liberally hung with portraits of the good doctor. On tables are stacked copies of *The Revivalist* magazine and *The Battle Standard* newspaper, both edited by Ian R.K. Paisley. They contain articles with headlines like 'Rome's Infiltration of Evangelicalism', or 'Another Bishop in Abuse Scandal', and advertisements for such riveting publications as *Sermons with Startling Titles* by you-know-who.

Attached to the main church is the £1.4 million Paisley Jubilee Complex which, a brochure informs me, Dr Paisley had 'very reluctantly' agreed to have named after him. The complex was opened in 1997 by Bob Jones IV, grandson of the founder of the fundamentalist Bob Jones University in North Carolina which is unique for many reasons, not least the fact that it once awarded Dr Paisley an honorary degree.

The complex contains meeting rooms, a library and a marriage chapel, but I was particularly struck by the dozen engraved windows in the Jubilee Hall upstairs. These were donated by Dr Paisley and tell the story of his life – his birthplace, the hall where he preached his first sermon, the Crumlin Road Prison where he was twice imprisoned for civil disobedience, the British and European Parliaments and so on.

Dr Paisley granted me a few minutes of his time. I had planned some aggressive questioning, but found him infuriatingly disarming. Had he ever been challenged for the post of moderator? 'I've been challenged, but the challenger didn't succeed,' he replied with a loud chuckle. Would the church survive his passing? 'Oh yes. It will fare much better because God will send them a young Joshua,' he responded with a grin. How could a man of God preach such hatred and division? 'I don't preach hatred and division,' he protested with evident indignation. 'If you're in a burning house and I pull you out by the hairs of your head, you could say I didn't do it lovingly but I got you out. I believe the Roman Catholic Church is the anti-Christ. It's my duty to save people from the deceptions of the Roman

Catholic Church. I'm a Protestant, and I'm teaching nothing different from what my forefathers preached.'

When he faced his Maker, I wondered, would he really be able to say he'd left the world a better place? 'When I leave the world I will leave behind a loyal people who were transformed because I brought them the gospel,' he retorted. 'That's the greatest contribution you could leave behind. I have no regrets at all about my stand. I don't think anybody who's a campaigner in the way that I'm a campaigner is going to get the plaudits of the world . . . If God had not been with me, no doubt I would have been destroyed.'

But just when you conclude that the man has an absurdly inflated sense of his own worth, he goes and pricks his pomposity himself. He recalled preaching his first sermon in Sixemilecross in County Tyrone when he was still a teenager. 'It lasted two and three-quarter minutes,' he told me with a great belly laugh. 'I sat down in total confusion. I needed to be taught a good lesson not to be proud.'

Dr Paisley and his bodyguards piled into a sleek new Vauxhall and sped off into the midday traffic. I retrieved my car from a nearby multi-storey and headed off in pursuit of other larger-than-life characters – including one who really was deified by his followers.

I drove south down Belfast's so-called 'Golden Mile' of nightclubs, pubs and restaurants – a description justified only if you compare the area with what it was at the height of the Troubles. I drove past the entrance to Belfast's lovely Botanical Gardens and the statue of Lord Kelvin, the eminent Victorian physicist who made the first scientific calculation of the earth's age, gave his name to a temperature scale and was instrumental in developing the first transatlantic telegraph cable. 'He elucidated the laws of nature for the service of man,' says the inscription.

Beyond the old buildings of Queen's University with their mullioned windows and manicured lawns I drove through affluent, leafy South Belfast, one of the only really mixed areas of the city where even the protective walls of the police stations have been prettified. After one brief flash of countryside, I reached the market town of Lisburn in the Lagan River valley.

Lisburn serves as the Army's headquarters. The Thiepval barracks are a virtual town within a town, and harder to get into than Fort Knox since the IRA managed to explode two car bombs inside them in 1996. However, the soldier I'd come to see was not in the barracks but standing on a pedestal in the town's pretty Market Square. He was brandishing a sword above his head with one hand and wielding a gun in the other, though passers-by were paying him no notice whatsoever. 'To Brigadier General John Nicholson who led the assault at Delhi on 23rd September 1857 and fell in the hour of victory, mortally wounded at the age of 35,' reads the inscription, but that does not begin to do justice to the man.

Nicholson was raised in Lisburn, one of five brothers. Aged 16, he joined the Bengal Infantry, sailed for India and was soon fighting in the Afghanistan War. He was captured by tribesmen and held for six months before being rescued. In the Khyber Pass he spotted the naked, mutilated body of a European on a hillside and found that it was his younger brother Alexander.

Nicholson, a giant of a man, rose rapidly through the ranks. He served in this war and that, in Kashmir and the Punjab, suppressing the natives and imposing the law. His reputation grew until, in 1849, a certain Hindu devotee decided that he was the incarnation of Brahma. To the horror of their modest idol, the sect grew and flourished. The more the people worshipped 'Nikalsain' the more he flogged them, but they took their punishment like martyrs and repeated the offence. He imprisoned them until they promised to desist, but nothing deterred the 'Nikalsainis'.

When the Indian Mutiny broke out Nicholson charged around the Punjab 'overawing the people and disarming tainted native regiments', according to one account. In one instance he spent more than twenty hours on horseback chasing 700 mutineers for 70 miles. 'When the day's work was finished 120 were slain, 150 taken prisoner – 40 of whom were afterwards blown from the guns.'

Having suppressed the Punjab, he left for Delhi where he personally led 5,000 men in a dawn assault on a city held by 50,000. They breached the wall and flooded in, but Nicholson was shot through the lung by a sniper. Back at camp he found himself in the bed next to another of his brothers, Charles, who had lost a foot in the same battle. Charles survived, but Nicholson died.

Following his death, one 'Nikalsaini' declared there was no point in living and slit his throat. Others converted to Christianity so that they could worship Nicholson's God. The East India Company granted his mother a pension of £500 a year in honour of his gallantry, which was some consolation for the poor lady. By the time she died at the ripe old age of 88, four of her five sons had perished in India and the fifth had died at home when he was just 14.

From the statue I wandered up to Lisburn's Christ Church Cathedral at the top end of the square. It is actually no bigger or grander than an average church, but it does have a marvellous marble memorial to Nicholson showing British soldiers clambering inside the breached walls of Delhi over a jumble of stones, dead bodies and upended cannon. 'The grave of Brigadier John Nicholson is beneath the fortress which he died to take,' says the inscription. 'He had an iron mind and frame, a terrible courage, an indomitable will, a form seemed made for an army to behold, a heart to meet a crisis of an empire . . . He was a tower of strength, the type of the conquering race.'

There is one curious thing about the memorial: Nicholson himself is not depicted. His mother, who erected it, was apparently anxious to give the 'Nikalsainis' no further encouragement.

Another statue greeted me as I drove into Hillsborough, just a few miles south of Lisburn. This one was of the 4th Marquess of Downshire brandishing not a gun or a sword but a walking stick. He was looking across the road towards what is, by Northern Ireland's standards, a particularly fine church with a double drive in a broad avenue of trees. The 1st Marquess built it in the vain hope that it would be adopted as the diocesan cathedral.

Hillsborough is one of the prettiest little towns in the province and would hardly look out of place in the Cotswolds. It is also the only town of its size without a bookie or chip-shop. The high street winds up past brightly coloured houses, gentrified pubs and smart little shops to a fine square bordered on one side by the magnificent wrought-iron railings of Hillsborough Castle.

The castle is probably the only one in the British Isles that is guarded far more heavily today than it was when it was built back in the eighteenth century. There is a very good reason for this. It is now the official residence of the Secretary of State for Northern Ireland, and the place where all visiting VVIPs (and some mere VIPs) usually stay.

Mo Mowlam was the Secretary of State during most of my time in Northern Ireland. I had known her since the late 1980s when she was a new MP and I was a young reporter at the House of Commons. We used to play football together in the MPs' annual match against the Lobby. A couple of times she invited my wife and me to Hillsborough, and while I know better than to write about her private dinners I do have her dispensation to write about the castle.

It is actually more of an elegant country house than a castle. Its beautiful grounds boast a gigantic rhododendron bush the size of a small hill that is apparently in the *Guinness Book of Records*, though I couldn't find it in my edition. The fireplace in the State Entrance Hall is flanked by two full-size silver spades used for planting ceremonial trees, and to judge by the plethora of tiny plaques covering the handles the Royal Family has done little else in recent decades.

In the adjoining Candlestick Hall is one of the world's great autograph books, otherwise known as the castle's visitors book. 'Thank you for your gracious hospitality in this beautiful place,' Hillary Clinton wrote across one entire page. 'Tony Blair', read another entry, and in the address column the Prime Minister had helpfully written '10, Downing Street'. The Duke of Edinburgh had simply written 'Philip', omitting the 'Buckingham Palace'. There was even a paw-print from Lucy, the guide dog of the blind Cabinet minister David Blunkett.

The whole place is stuffed with signed photos of royals and prime ministers, portraits of lords and ladies, and valuable antiques. The dining-room table is longer than a stretch limousine. There is a 'Throne Room' with two gilded thrones used for investitures and other grand occasions. Look carefully at the paintings on the wall and you will see that the artist responsible for the portrait of Lord Wakehurst, a former governor general of Northern Ireland, has mischievously depicted him in a state of sexual arousal. Upstairs there is the Queen's bedroom and, separated by an ante-room, the Duke's bedroom.

Never having been in one of the Queen's bedrooms before, I was naturally curious. While the Duke's room has two single beds, hers has one enormous double with yards of matching material rising to form a majesterial backdrop. His room is blues and reds, hers soft pinks with prints of roses on the wall. He gets *Country Life* magazine, she gets *Harpers and Queen*. The Queen also gets a boudoir, and while I would like to report that she has a particularly magnificent loo I'm afraid I can't. This particular 'throne' is a plain white china job with a wooden seat just like yours or mine.

The 4th Marquess greeted me as I drove into Hillsborough. The 3rd, who died in 1845 when he fell off his horse during an apoplectic fit, bade me farewell from the top of a tall Doric column that stands in a farmer's boggy field just south of the town. But it was Lord Arthur Hill, the 5th's younger brother, to whom I really warmed. His parents prevented him from marrying his sweetheart. The story goes that when the lady he did marry died young he heard someone sing a heart-rending song: 'In the gloaming, Oh my darling, think not bitterly of me/Though I stole away in silence, left you lonely, set you free . . .' He guessed that his first love must have written it, traced her through the publishers and married her to live happily ever after.

I had an appointment in the little farming town of Dromara – seven pretty, rolling miles south of Hillsborough. It was with a former policeman for whom the Troubles have had an unexpected silver lining. Kenneth Stanford is founder and chairman of Highmark, one of the world's leading producers of bulletproof clothing.

The son and grandson of policemen, Mr Stanford was himself a former Chief Inspector in the RUC and has lived a truly charmed life. The first Protestant killed in the Troubles died on the very spot in riot-torn West Belfast where Mr Stanford had been standing just minutes earlier. The first policeman to die was standing right in front of Mr Stanford when he was shot.

That was in 1969. By the mid-1970s all RUC officers had to wear body armour. It was so heavy that in 1978 Mr Stanford walked into a butcher's shop in central Belfast and had his weighed. It tipped the scales at 32 lb, which is an awful lot to carry around for eight hours every day.

Mr Stanford was also an Olympic and Commonwealth pistol shooter who had been involved in testing the body armour. He decided to develop his own, using a newly developed synthetic fibre called Kevlar. His first order came from the Irish Garda while he was shooting in the 1980 Moscow Olympics – some consolation for coming eighteenth. He won another order from the Turkish air force after refusing to let his potential customers shoot at a waistcoat while he was wearing it and insisting that a dummy be used instead. In the event, the gunman missed the waistcoat and hit the dummy in the neck.

Mr Stanford left the police to go into full-time business in 1983, two years before his family would have completed an unbroken century of service. He now has 80 workers in three factories and an annual turnover of several million pounds. He supplies most of Britain's police forces, United Nations personnel and security forces in trouble-spots as far apart as Malaysia, Pakistan, Croatia and the Middle East. The one force that will not buy from him is the RUC – 'It's sour grapes, spite and a bit of envy,' he said before zipping off in his sleek new Porsche.

An underling took me round the factory. I was particularly taken with the 'stabbing machine' used for testing 'stab-proof waistcoats' made of 'knitted wire'. My guide gave me a demonstration. He attached a dagger to a 4.2 kg weight suspended about four feet above a sample of that knitted wire and released the trigger. The dagger plunged downwards and slashed straight through the wire into the tin of plasticine below. Whoops!

From Dromara I could have followed the tourist board's brown road signs southwards through 'Brontë Country' where the Rev. Patrick Brontë, father of the novelist sisters Charlotte, Emily and Anne, was raised. However, the Rev. Brontë left for Cambridge as a young man and never returned, so the attractions of Brontë country seemed distinctly limited. Indeed the most interesting – and tragic – fact about him was that he suffered almost exactly the same fate as John Nicholson's poor mother. When he died at the age of 84 in 1861, he had outlived all his six children.

It struck me that the brown road signs should really have pointed a few miles westwards to the town of Banbridge, birthplace of another of those truly remarkable men produced by this small patch of earth.

Captain Francis Crozier was born in 1796 and joined the Navy at 14. By his early thirties he had made three voyages to the Arctic with Captain Parry. In 1845 he set sail in command of HMS *Terror* on an expedition led by Sir John Franklin in HMS *Erebus* to discover the North West Passage between Greenland and Northern Canada. Crozier persevered despite Franklin's death, and the expedition succeeded, but he never returned to tell of his triumph. Four years later the ships were found abandoned near Montreal Island where the entire party had died of cold and starvation.

The westernmost point of King William's Island is named Cape Crozier in his memory, and more than 2,000 miles away in Banbridge there is a splendid monument to the man. It stands in the middle of what must once have been a pretty if rather irregular town square, but is now a busy road junction with a bewildering array of traffic lights. A statue of the captain crowns a tall and elaborate pedestal flanked by four stone polar bears.

I dodged the cars to reach this marooned little island and read the inscriptions in the fading light. On two sides were stone carvings of the *Terror* and *Erebus* trapped between Arctic icebergs. On the third side the inscription read: 'To perpetuate the remembrance of talent, enterprise and worth combined in the character and evidenced in the life of Captain Francis Rawdon Moira Crozier RN FRS.'

It was the words on the fourth side that I found particularly moving:

> Although there remained no survivors of the expedition
> enough has been shewn that to it is justly due the honour
> of the discovery of the long sought for North West
> Passage and that Captain Crozier having survived his
> chief perished with the remainder of the party after he
> had bravely led them to the coast of America. He was
> born at Banbridge September 1796 but of the place or
> time of his death no man knoweth unto this day.

If Captain Crozier was not deterred by ice, I was not going to be deterred by darkness. There was one other remarkable son of Ulster whose birthplace I wanted to find before retiring for the night. I drove up through the 'cut' – a gash slashed through a steep hill in the very heart of Banbridge to make life easier for Dublin–to–Belfast stage-coaches. There I turned right and followed a country road a few more miles westward till I came to the village of Scarva which stands on a dribble of brackish water that was once the first canal in the British Isles. Completed in 1741, the canal linked Lough Neagh to the sea below Newry and flourished for more than a century until the advent of the railway put it out of business.

I stopped at a pub called the Park Inn to ask directions. There were half-a-dozen locals sitting at the bar. Could anyone tell me the way to Druminargal House, I asked in a rather proper English accent. 'Whar?' they chorused in broad Ulster. The place where Charles Lucas was born, I replied. 'Hae?' they retorted. The man who was awarded the first ever Victoria Cross, I told them.

Deep in their memories something stirred. Yes, they said. Come to think of it, they had heard of such a fellow. Suddenly the hunt was on. A portable pay-phone was set up on the bar; a woman was dispatched to find a telephone directory. Calls went out to local historians, schoolteachers and members of the British Legion until finally we came up trumps. Cross the canal, I was told by a disembodied voice on the other end of the line. Turn left to Poyntzpass and go on till you come to a sharp right-hand bend with a chevron sign and begin climbing a hill. The house is soon after that on the right. With cries of 'good luck' from my new friends I went out into what was by now a pitch-black night.

I found the chevron sign and began climbing the hill. Spotting an old gateway in the beam of my headlights, I followed a long, pitted drive up to a large, dilapidated and rather ghostly grey house surrounded by trees. There were no lights on. I rang the bell, and as I stood there in the darkness I tried to imagine what it must have been like for a mere 14-year-old setting off from a home like this in 1848 to join the Navy as Lucas did.

Four years later he was a ship's mate fighting in the Burma War. Six years after that he found himself on a wooden paddle sloop called the HMS *Hecla* as she attacked the Russian fortress of Bomarsund in the faraway Baltic. The Russian gunners managed to land a shell right on the ship's deck. As the rest of the crew flung themselves flat Lucas walked over, picked up the shell and calmly threw it overboard. Seconds later it exploded with a deafening roar, drenching the ship's company. He was immediately promoted to the rank of Acting Lieutenant, and three years later Queen Victoria personally awarded him the first ever Victoria Cross.

Nobody answered the bell so I left, but a few days later I ascertained the name of the owner – a semi-retired farmer named Bill McLean. I telephoned and asked if he lived in the house of the first Victoria Cross winner. He sounded a delightful fellow, but obviously shared my inability to remember names.

'Yes,' he said. 'Lewis lived here eight years. He joined up at eighteen and joined some old war they were fighting against Russia. He was on the deck of the ship and this bomb lit at his feet. Lewis picked it up and threw it overboard and it exploded as it was thrown, and the captain said if it wasn't for him there wouldn't have been a single one of them left. Queen Elizabeth made a special thing for him and he was presented it by Queen Elizabeth. Then he married the daughter of the captain and rose to be a very famous man and now I'm living in his house!'

This was something I was discovering in my travels around Northern Ireland. History was a very malleable commodity.

A few minutes after leaving the house the lights of Poyntzpass appeared before me. It was a village I knew, a place which one night in March 1998 witnessed an act as cowardly as Lucas's was brave.

Up till then Poyntzpass had been untouched by the Troubles. It was a remote, tranquil, well-kept little community in the rolling green hills of County Armagh where there were no loyalists and republicans, just Catholics and Protestants who had achieved the rare feat in this divided province of living happily and harmoniously together.

That night there was a sheep sale taking place in the village. Seven people were having a drink in the front room of the tiny Railway Bar just off the main street. They included Philip Allen, a Protestant, and his best friend Damian Trainor, a Catholic who was to be best man at Mr Allen's wedding.

The bar was an easy target. It was unprotected, and the several country lanes leading out of the village offered an easy escape route. At about 9 p.m. a stolen white Ford Escort drew up outside. Two masked men with hand-guns got out, burst through the bar's front door and shouted: 'On the floor, you bastards!' The gunmen then opened fire on the helpless customers and fled.

A priest administered the last rites to Damian as he lay on the floor, and prayed with Philip who died in the operating theatre of Newry hospital shortly afterwards. Four days later the entire village and hundreds of outsiders, Protestant and Catholic, turned out for their funerals. The funerals of those killed in sectarian atrocities in Northern Ireland are not just about consigning the dead to their Maker; they are one of the very few means by which the vast majority of decent, law-abiding people can express their horror.

The gunmen, members of the Loyalist Volunteer Force who wanted to wreck the peace process, came from Captain Crozier's home town of Banbridge. A few weeks later one of them was savagely murdered by his LVF colleagues in the Maze prison for cooperating with the police. It was hard to feel too sorry for him.

By coincidence I arrived to find there was another evening sheep sale on. Both sides of the street were lined with jeeps and trailers, and there was a powerful smell of livestock. I parked, walked into the small building surrounded by animal pens where the sale was taking place, and immediately regretted it.

The place was packed with ruddy-faced farmers in cloth caps, overalls and Wellington boots standing on tiered benches encircling a central pen. Every one of them fell silent at the sight of a complete stranger, and patent townie, entering their midst. It was the auctioneer who broke the silence. 'He must be from the "broo",' he said, and the farmers erupted in laughter. The 'broo' is the 'bureau' or social security department, and they clearly believed I'd come to check which of the locally unemployed were making a bit of money on the side.

I couldn't just turn and leave. I made my way up rather sheepishly – if you'll excuse the pun – to one of the backmost benches and watched the auction recommence. It took a few minutes for my blushes to disappear, and a few more to attune my ears to the auctioneer's broad Ulster spiel, but then I became quite fascinated.

Before that night one sheep had always looked to me much like another, but now an infinite variety was paraded before me – big and little, clean and dirty, black-faced and white-faced, horned and unhorned, mangy and magnificently hirsute. Some emitted high-pitched bleats and others gravelly baas. They came and went with bewildering speed, and if counting sheep really was a cure for sleeplessness every farmer there would have been snoring within minutes. Some were sold for a few pounds only, and others for more than £40. For a mere £2 I could have bought three particularly scrawny little lambs, but I wasn't certain that Katy would have appreciated them.

I left before I scratched my head and inadvertently found myself the proud owner of an obstreperous old ram. Outside I could hear men talking in the Railway Bar across the road. I thought of going in, but decided I'd had enough of being stared at for one evening. I'd also been in once before, a few months after the killings, when the bar was completely deserted except for Bernadette Canavan, the elderly landlady. Signs of the attack were still painfully apparent; she pointed out the chipped tiles on the floor and the bullet-scarred door through which she had crawled to safety. I could think of happier places to have a drink.

The next morning I resumed my journey at Newry and that little bump sticking down from the bottom of Northern Ireland called South Armagh. Had those who partitioned Ireland in 1921 left that bump in the south – as they originally intended – they would have prevented no end of grief.

A rough circle with a diameter of about twenty miles and population of 25,000, South Armagh is the heartland of militant republicanism. It was dubbed 'bandit country' early in the Troubles, and the label stuck. More than 160 soldiers, policemen and members of the Ulster Defence Regiment were killed here, not to mention about eighty civilians and thirty members of the IRA or the Irish National Liberation Army. According to one study it suffered 1,255 bombs, 1,158 gun attacks and 378 murders during those 30-odd years.

It is hard to believe that South Armagh is part of the United Kingdom. Even today the police are flown in from outside and huddle inside heavily fortified bases in a few key towns. The Army mount heavily armed foot patrols, and man the hill-top observation posts. Little happens without the Army watching, but ceasefire or no ceasefire, peace process or no peace process, it is still the republican gunmen who control the low ground. The police require military protection even to serve a routine summons on someone, and will on occasion approach houses across fields lest the lanes or drives are booby-trapped.

Newry itself is a bustling, thriving town with some fine buildings strung out along both sides of the old canal. I'm sure it is
full of warm and decent people, but I'm afraid I shall remember
it for other reasons.

Its recent history is best summed up by its entry in the index
of a journalist's bible called *Northern Ireland: A Chronology of the
Troubles*. It reads: 'Newry, Co. Down: riots p. 12; soldiers shoot
three p. 40; bombs pp. 55, 65; PIRA attacks security forces pp.
100–101; Miami Showband murders p. 103; UDR captain killed
p. 128; four killed at checkpoint p. 184; nine killed p. 184; three
RUC men shot p. 200.' Those are only the edited highlights;
they do not include countless lesser attacks, or the particularly
horrific murder in 1999 of an IRA defector named Eamon
Collins.

Collins was a man of extreme courage or extraordinary reck-
lessness depending on your point of view. As an IRA man he was
responsible for at least five murders. He subsequently turned on
his former comrades-in-arms, repeatedly denouncing the IRA in
print and on camera. He even testified for the defence when
Thomas 'Slab' Murphy from neighbouring South Armagh unsuc-
cessfully sued *The Sunday Times* for calling him an IRA
commander. But rather than flee to England and take a new
identity, Collins defiantly chose to remain living with his wife
and four children right in the heart of Newry's staunchly republican Barcroft estate.

His car was petrol-bombed. An old family home he was renovating was burned. On the morning of 27 January 1999, he got
up at 4.30 to paint out some distinctly prescient graffiti on a wall
facing his home – 'Eamon Collins British Agent 1984–1999', it
read. While it was still dark, he went for a walk along a nearby
country lane. His body was found soon after dawn. He had been
repeatedly stabbed and cudgelled to death and then run over; his
injuries were so appalling that the police advised his widow not
to view the body. Two days later neighbours watched in cold

silence as his tiny funeral cortege went past their homes. 'He committed the cardinal sin. He named names,' one told me.

I had no particular desire to linger in Newry. I drove a couple of miles on to Bessbrook, a model village built in the mid-nineteenth century by a Quaker linen manufacturer named John Grubb Richardson. There is still no pub in its two large squares because Richardson believed alcohol was the root cause of poverty and crime, but the neighbouring village of Camlough compensates with six.

Mr Richardson also intended that Bessbrook should have no police, but it has ended up with a huge Army base, nicknamed 'Fort Apache', and what is commonly described as Europe's busiest helipad. The villagers are given free double-glazing by the government, and free chimney-sweepings courtesy of the helicopters. It was in Bessbrook that 23-year-old Stephen Restorick, the last British soldier shot in Northern Ireland, was killed by an IRA sniper in 1997.

I'd arranged to meet an aggrieved young Protestant named Willie Frazer here. Willie is in his late thirties, married with two children, and owns a couple of bars. He is also vice-chairman of a group called Families Acting for Innocent Relatives, set up in late 1998 to highlight the suffering of Protestants in South Armagh at a time when IRA prisoners were being freed en masse and Sinn Fein was preparing to join Northern Ireland's government.

Willie had lost an astonishing number of close relatives to the IRA. Most were killed because they'd joined the Ulster Defence Regiment to combat terrorism. 'They stood up for right against wrong because they believed in the system, believed in government and believed that they might have to pay the price but ultimately there would be justice,' he told me. Now they had been betrayed. Their families felt their suffering had all been for nothing. Sinn Fein and the IRA weren't really interested in peace – 'I don't think they'll be satisfied until they've driven every Protestant out of Northern Ireland.'

In Northern Ireland I frequently felt that it was impossible for an outsider like myself to understand the hatreds and the passions of either side, but Willie took me on a 12-mile via dolorosa across South Armagh that went some way towards enlightening me.

Every mile we passed the scene of some atrocity. At the brow of a hill beyond Bessbrook a wreath and some faded poppies were tied to a gatepost; this marked the site of the 1976 Kingsmills massacre, where the IRA ambushed a minibus one January evening and slaughtered 10 Protestant workmen with machine guns after letting the Catholic driver go. 'They cut them down like dogs,' said Willie as we surveyed the green and tranquil countryside. 'It's lovely terrain, but so deadly.'

We passed the Kingsmills Presbyterian Church where in 1980 the 'provies' shot Willie's uncle, Clifford Lundy, a former UDR member, as he was returning home from his work as a lorry driver.

We drove through the village of Whitecross where Willie was raised until local republicans drove out his family with stones and petrol bombs when he was 12.

Just north of the village a black marble monument lists the three UDR soldiers who died in 1991 when the IRA rolled a 2,000-lb lorry bomb down a hill into the Glenanne UDR barracks that used to stand there.

Just west is the farm where the IRA ambushed Willie's father one August afternoon in 1975. A small brick memorial marks the spot where he was 'murdered by the enemies of Ulster'. Willie, 14 at the time, knows exactly who did it. Someone saw the killers but did not dare tell the police. 'There were ten involved, from the scout car to the man who pulled the trigger,' he said. Most were local, most he knew, and a few days later he faxed me all their names.

Another mile along the lane Johnny Bell, another of Willie's uncles, was gunned down ten weeks after his father's murder. Three IRA gunmen ambushed him as he arrived home.

Beyond that is the tranquil country churchyard where Willie's father and uncle are buried. 'My father knew he was going to die. He told me so,' said Willie as he showed me their graves. 'But he wouldn't move. These UDR men were all the same. They believed they had to stand their ground to give the government time to get its act together. They thought if they moved out the IRA were winning, and that they were the only protection the Protestant people had.'

A hundred yards beyond the church was another roadside memorial – this one to a 12-year-old Catholic girl named Majella O'Hare who was caught in the crossfire of a gunfight between soldiers and the IRA as she was on her way to confession.

In Newtonhamilton the once-pretty town square was still being rebuilt following a car-bomb attack on the security base a year earlier. The base itself was virtually unscratched.

Beyond Newtonhamilton we came to a low grey building with steel mesh windows at a quiet country cross-roads where the air reeked of slurry. This was the Tullyvallan Orange Hall. In 1975 two gunmen burst in and opened fire, killing four men including one aged 80. 'It was ethnic cleansing that went on here in the 1970s,' said Willie.

We had traversed the northern part of South Armagh, where there was still a significant Protestant population, but as we headed south towards the border the towns and villages became almost entirely Catholic and republican.

Here the Irish tricolour, not the Union Jack, flies from every flagpole. Here signs are written in Irish as well as English, and the roadside memorials are to 'volunteers' killed by the security forces. Here the Queen's writ seems scarcely to apply, and you stand about as much chance of seeing a bobby on the street as you would of seeing Gerry Adams at Buckingham Palace. The few remaining Protestants are tolerated provided they don't inform, and the security forces really do seem like an army of occupation.

What was also striking was the number of palatial new homes tucked away down the back roads. Republicans may consider themselves oppressed, but there is no shortage of money in South Armagh and little doubt where much of it comes from.

One traditional source was the Army. In 1994–5, to pick a year at random, farmers lodged 38,634 complaints of livestock being killed or injured as a result of helicopters flying overhead or other military activity, and £6.2 million was paid out in compensation. The compensation process has since been greatly tightened up after it was discovered that three or four claims were being made for the same cow, that 'dead' sheep were turning up at auctions in the south, and that the hapless civil servants dispatched to investigate claims were being intimidated into reporting that whole flocks of chickens had died of heart attacks.

The even bigger source of money is smuggling. The border here is criss-crossed by tiny lanes and as porous as a sieve. You hear endless variations on stories of farmers with barns that straddle the border who put the cattle one end and the feed the other so that the animals smuggle themselves across. This is the United Kingdom's only land frontier. Drugs, alcohol and tobacco all come across in large quantities. Any number of commodities are smuggled north or south depending on the prevailing duties and exchange rates.

Diesel and petrol were the hot commodities while I was in Northern Ireland. The duty was at least 20 pence per litre less in the Republic, and a veritable tidal wave of the fuel flowed northwards. Customs officers in Belfast showed me a yard full of confiscated vehicles ranging from 18,000-litre tankers to elderly grocery vans with tanks inside, to a battered old trailer with a layer of turf covering one small metal fuel container. As many as half the petrol stations in Northern Ireland were believed to be selling at least some smuggled fuel. 'Huckster' stations consisting of a single pump in the back of a cargo container sprang up in back streets. By the most conservative estimates, the scam was costing the taxman £100 million a year in lost duty.

Willie grew noticeably tenser as we drove into the border town of Crossmaglen where, as an old song goes, there are 'more rogues than honest men'. Crossmaglen is a town that belongs in the north in no sense except the geographical. The place is such an uncompromising republican stronghold that even mail and newspapers have to be delivered to the Army base by helicopter, and rubbish leaves the same way. In fact a helicopter clattered in as we arrived, a machine gunner clearly visible by its open door.

Willie had more or less completed his tour by now, which was just as well as Crossmaglen made him distinctly nervous. In fact he wouldn't leave the car. South Armagh is a small place and someone could well recognise him. He wasn't afraid, he insisted. 'It's the fact that no one would come to your aid.'

This angry young Protestant dropped me in Crossmaglen with a parting shot. 'As far as I'm concerned this is our home,' he said. 'Ulster belongs to us. No IRA man or anyone else will push me out of it. They may carry me out, but they'll never push me out.'

Crossmaglen's huge town square would have been quite attractive were it not dominated by a grotesque, paint-splattered military watch-tower which the IRA twice tried to burn down after spraying it with petrol from a slurry tanker. The Army called it the Borucki sangar after James Borucki, a 19-year-old soldier blown up by a bomb left in a bicycle basket. There were always two soldiers on duty in the sangar, looking for any slight change in Crossmaglen's routine that could signal trouble, until it was finally dismantled in August 2000 as part of the peace process.

Borucki was one of at least eight soldiers killed in this town square, which must also be the only such square in the United Kingdom with a memorial not to the dead of the two World Wars but to fallen republicans. The memorial depicts a young man straddling an eagle with outstretched wings. 'Glory to you all, praised and humble heroes, who have willingly suffered for your unselfish and passionate love of Irish freedom,' reads the inscription. Again, it was hard to equate the bravery of the IRA bombers and gunmen with that of Captain Crozier or Charles Lucas.

I had an appointment in Crossmaglen. It was with a young lady named Michelle Boyle who has, on the face of it, one of the most impossible jobs imaginable. She is South Armagh's tourism officer, and spends her days battling the sort of advice offered by Harvard University's 1998 *Let's Go: Britain and Ireland* guide: 'Stay out of South Armagh altogether'.

We went for lunch in Murtagh's pub. Neither she nor I mentioned the fact that a sniper killed a 23-year-old soldier named Daniel Blinco right outside it in 1993. The men at the bar fell momentarily silent when we walked in, sized us up, and then resumed their conversations.

I suggested to Michelle that South Armagh had a bit of an image problem. 'Oh yes!' she replied cheerily. 'In any place there have been things that have happened. Nobody's denying that. But curiosity is going to bring people into South Armagh, and once they're in I've no doubt they're going to come back.'

It certainly had name recognition, I conceded, but wasn't it a bit like promoting a war zone as a holiday destination? 'Definitely not,' she retorted. 'The media have a lot to answer for. Life here's great. The people, the landscape, the culture are great. It's ideal for activities like angling, walking and cycling . . .' I cut her off. 'Show me,' I said.

And so began my second tour of South Armagh, though it might have been a different country. On a brilliantly clear and sunny afternoon she drove me around the Ring of Gullion, the beautiful circle of unspoiled hills surrounding the mystical mountain of Slieve Gullion which has a supposedly bottomless lake on top.

Michelle showed me megalithic tombs, ancient cairns and ring forts. She showed me the Ballykeel dolmen or portal tomb which consists of three standing stones supporting a huge cap-stone, and the carved Kilnasaggart stone that dates from AD 700 and is Ireland's oldest Christian monument.

As we drove along tiny lanes she pointed out lone thorn trees or 'fairy thorns' in the middle of little green fields that the farm-ers dare not cut down. Superstitions retain a powerful grip on the people of South Armagh. On 1 February each year they still hang out St Brigid's crosses woven from rushes to keep them and their animals safe. Michelle was a graduate, had lived in England and travelled extensively in America and Australia, but still believed in 'cures'. Someone had cured one of her own two chil-dren of chronic whooping-cough by passing him three times under a donkey, she told me.

South Armagh's fearsome reputation may deter visitors, but it acts as a magnet for international donors anxious to do their bit for peace. My tireless guide took me to two brand-new golf courses, a spanking new equestrian centre, the Cardinal O'Fiaich heritage centre and the Ti Chulain cultural centre which teaches Irish song, dance and folklore – all built within the last few years and each costing hundreds of thousands of pounds pro-vided primarily by the European Union and America.

My particular favourite was Creggan Church near Crossmaglen, a little haven of Anglican tranquillity in the very engine room of militant republicanism. It is a lovely old stone building with an historic graveyard fringed by woods and a small river. Those buried there include at least seventy members of the O'Neill clan, whose skulls and bones fill an underground vault, and three eighteenth-century Gaelic poets. One, Art MacCooey, was allegedly banished from Creggan for writing a wicked lam-poon about the priest's sister called 'Squint-eyed Mary', and only allowed to return when he wrote an obsequious sequel.

In the course of the Troubles the church's congregation

shrank to just nine die hard Protestants and their children; but thanks to its enterprising rector, Reverend Mervyn Kingston, it is now one of the most lavishly funded churches in the entire British Isles. Indeed, international donors consider an Anglican church struggling to survive in the heart of 'bandit country' so utterly irresistible that the cheery rector jokes about being a 'proxy millionaire'.

Amongst other things Mr Kingston has opened a visitors' centre, converted 13 acres of the church's grounds into a park, and put weirs into the river to improve the angling. He is restoring the old rectory's Victorian walled garden, commissioning statues of the three Gaelic poets, and planning to build eight self-catering holiday cottages and a caravan park.

Mr Kingston has yet to have an application for money refused. He had already secured £600,000 for his various projects, and was working on applications for another £500,000. 'I take the view that if the money's there you should use it,' he told me with refreshing candour. He has no trouble with the local republican chieftains. Not only do their people benefit from the improvements, but they actually now seek his advice on procuring public funds. Mr Kingston readily gives it, but on condition that the tricolour is not flown outside his church.

Michelle's enthusiasm was infectious. The people really were warm and welcoming, the country was beautiful and unspoiled. I soon stopped noticing the letters I-R-A nailed to telegraph poles, or the 'Sniper at Work' signs showing silhouettes of gunmen with rifles, or the Army helicopters clattering overhead. I stopped wondering which farms concealed arms dumps, or in what yards the Omagh or Canary Wharf bombs were built. At a quiet cross-roads we passed a pub called the Three Steps Inn, and it was with a jolt that I realised why I knew the name. It was in the pub's car park that the IRA seized Robert Nairac, an undercover SAS man, in 1977. His body was never found.

That evening we ended up at the opening night of the 18th

Lislea drama festival. Lislea is no metropolis or mecca for the arts; it is a cluster of 20 houses and a chapel in the middle of nowhere. Three hundred men, women and children had nonetheless crowded into the village hall to watch a group of amateur thespians from Newtownstewart in County Tyrone perform *All Soul's Night* by an Ulster playwright named Joe Tomelty. It was a tragic play about a fisherman's wife in a County Down fishing village whose two sons drown because of her greed. There was no Shakespeare at the festival, explained Liam Hannaway, whose family is the driving force behind it. The plays were about people and situations with which the audience could immediately identify. This was 'rural drama', not 'furcoat drama'.

It was also very, very good drama. The audience was transfixed, and moved. There were no missed cues, no lines fluffed, none of the wooden delivery often associated with amateur dramatics. These were serious actors hoping to win the coveted award for best performance when the festival concluded two weeks and six plays later. It was past 11 p.m. when we poured out into the clear, cold night air. There was a full moon, a sky full of stars, and lights twinkling on the black silhouettes of the surrounding hills. Once again this blood-soaked land seemed really magical.

Michelle deposited me that night at a luxurious bed-and-breakfast somewhere near Forkhill, but I had completely lost my sense of direction as we weaved through the dark lanes leading from Lislea.

I woke the next morning to thick snow, breathtaking views of lake and gorse-covered mountains fore and aft, and a large plate of bacon, eggs and tomatoes. My hosts were a retired publican and his wife who had returned from America in the early 1970s thinking that the Troubles would soon blow over. Six years later the IRA blew up their pub while they were in it, alleging that they had been serving soldiers. That hadn't put them off. Where else could they live amid such beauty, they asked? Guests exclaimed at all the helicopters flying overhead, and at the armed troops on the ground, but they themselves no longer paid them any attention. 'It's like living next to a railway. After a bit you just don't notice it,' said my hostess.

Michelle was the same. She rightly complained that the media's preoccupation with the IRA gave a distorted picture of South Armagh, but then she and many others whom I met had almost entirely tuned out the men of violence. Provided they minded their own business, did not speak out of turn and were not Protestants, they could lead perfectly normal, happy lives in idyllic surroundings. The IRA was always there, however. The gunmen were always lurking in the background. They were a taboo subject, something people simply did not speak about, said Michelle. How much support did the IRA really have in South Armagh? She simply could not, or would not, say.

People had been so friendly that I decided to make one more visit before I left. I decided to go and see Thomas 'Slab' Murphy. This strongly built, balding, middle-aged man is an IRA commander of fearsome reputation. He is the republican to whom the security forces have probably devoted more time and resources over the past thirty years than any other. According to Sean O'Callaghan, a prominent IRA defector, Murphy was once asked how the British could be persuaded to talk to the IRA. 'Bomb them to the conference table, then booby-trap the table,' he allegedly replied.

This charming bachelor and his elder brother, Patrick, live on a farm that very conveniently straddles the border between South Armagh and the Irish Republic. Why would I want to meet such a man? Perhaps because I'd been inspired by the bravery of Nicholson, Crozier and Lucas. Perhaps because – like Mount Everest – he's there. Perhaps because his infamous lair seemed as good a place as any to end this particular journey. To be honest the idea filled me with dread, but some journalists will do anything for a story.

Somebody had kindly divulged to me the location of his house. I drove back through the melting snow to Crossmaglen, and was stopped en route at a police checkpoint protected by half-a-dozen camouflaged soldiers crawling around the adjacent fields. I made a point of saying where I was going in case I did not come back. In Crossmaglen I took the little road that leads south-eastwards from the square. After a couple of miles I reached a T-junction, turned right and immediately left on to the really tiny lane that led to Slab's house and the border two miles further south.

By now I was in remote, featureless country except for the occasional farmhouse or abandoned cottage. I became conscious that there was no conceivable reason why a stranger would be driving along this lane, and that he or she would stand out a mile. I began to imagine the occupants of the farmhouses calling ahead to warn of my approach. My only comfort was the near certainty that two distant Army observation posts, one to the east of Slab's house and the other to the west, were also keeping a close eye on me.

I rounded a corner and there was the Murphy homestead. It was unmistakable. On the left of the lane were corrugated-iron screens erected to block the view of the eastern observation post. To the right was a gloomy old two-storey farmhouse, painted dark green and surrounded by trees, with three cartons of milk sitting on the brick gatepost. Beyond was a veritable fortress of a farmyard with high steel gates and even higher breeze-block walls designed less to keep animals in than snoopers and enemies out. Half-way along this little complex I crossed into the Irish Republic, according to my large-scale ordnance survey map, but there was nothing physically marking the border. At the far end there was a concreted yard open to the road, but a long, low cottage blocked any view of the interior. The place seemed deserted.

I drove straight past this little complex, and past three smart Dallas-style bungalows on the left, until I reached a crossroads where I stopped to take stock after my initial recce. It was now or never, I decided, so I turned round, drove back and parked by the gates of the old farmhouse. With pounding heart and a strong sense of being watched, I walked up the drive and rang the bell.

A rusty old car was parked to one side. There were net curtains in every window, and it was not clear whether the house was even occupied. I waited in the silence and then rang again, but nobody answered. As I walked back to the car, I noticed powerful floodlights hidden behind the bushes.

My courage had not yet quite deserted me; I drove back to the cottage at the southern end of the complex and parked in the yard alongside two other vehicles. I remembered reading how Slab had once escaped a raid by the Irish police by running across his property into Northern Ireland, abandoning his elderly mother in the process. There were dogs in the yard, but they did not bother me. There was a pair of muddy boots lying on their sides by the cottage door. I knocked. Again nobody answered.

I briefly considered whether to venture beyond the cottage and into the middle of the complex, but that really would have been an act of folly. Slab was definitely not the sort of person who would take kindly to strangers snooping around his property, and who knows what I might have stumbled on? Instead I returned to the car and drove back to the crossroads, half relieved and half disappointed, to consider my position.

As I sat there a large turquoise Mercedes swept up the road from the left. It braked just after it had passed me, reversed into the road opposite and then drove forward until it was right alongside me. The driver, a burly young man with crooked teeth, lowered the electric window. 'Looking for something?' he asked.

'I'm looking for a Mr Thomas Murphy – "Slab" Murphy,' I replied.

'Don't know anyone of that name living around here,' he said.

'I'm a journalist. I want to talk to him. I'm told he's quite well known around here,' I said with a half grin.

To my relief, the man grinned back. 'There's lots of Murphys in this area, but I don't know a Thomas Murphy. You're wasting your time.' It was obvious that he knew that I knew that he knew, and off he drove towards Slab's complex.

I was about to give up, but then I spotted an old man in the yard of a cottage opposite. I went over. 'Do you know where I'd find Thomas Murphy?' I asked. 'Try the third bungalow on the right,' he said, though it actually sounded like 'Troi tuh turd bungalow on tuh roight.' That was where Slab's brother Patrick lived, he said. He'd know how to find him.

Back I went, and parked outside the third bungalow. The blinds were drawn, but there were three cars outside. I walked up the driveway and found the front door enclosed by a porch of thick – probably bullet-proof – glass. I knocked on the sliding glass door, but that was transparently hopeless. Should I slide it back and venture in? I looked back at the road and saw the Mercedes cruising slowly past. Enough, I told myself. I was tempting fate. I walked smartly back to my car, half expecting to hear a gunshot behind me.

As I sped thankfully away, I noticed a small blue sign on the verge opposite the farmhouse. It was a community watch sign. Model citizens, these Murphys.

6

Westward Bound

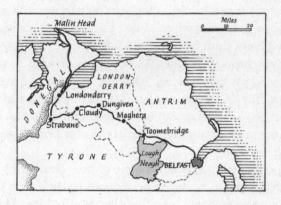

It is the Easter Monday bank holiday, but the streets around the City Hall are thronged. There are grey armoured police Land Rovers at every junction. The air reverberates with the beat of drums from more than fifty different bands. Tens of thousands of loyalists and their families are pouring into Belfast from across Northern Ireland for the opening day of the marching season. It is a prospect that delights the marchers, but fills almost everyone else in the province with dread.

Between now and the autumn the so-called 'loyal orders' – the Orange Order, the Royal Black Institution and the Apprentice Boys of Derry – will stage roughly 2,500 parades to celebrate William of Orange's victory over Catholic King James II at the Battle of the Boyne in 1690, the thwarting of James's siege of Londonderry the previous year, and other glorious moments in

Ulster's Protestant history that are remembered as if they happened not three centuries ago but yesterday.

The parades virtually guarantee long hot summers in Northern Ireland, however miserable the real weather. Nationalists consider these constant celebrations highly provocative, particularly if they happen to pass right through their communities. Even if they didn't mind, Sinn Fein activists would tell them that they did and make sure they mounted vigorous counter-demonstrations.

'Every year it gets worse,' complains Billy Irvine, a 43-year-old drum major, as he manoeuvres into position his 40-strong Millar Memorial Band from Finaghy in South Belfast. 'Every year the contentious areas get bigger. They're just growing in number and Sinn Fein is behind it all. It's going to come to a head, and there can only be one winner because there will certainly be no compromise.' There is no doubt in Billy's mind who that winner will be because 'no one fights harder than a loyalist when his back's to the wall'.

The parades are a classic example of how Northern Ireland's two traditions are incapable of understanding the other's point of view. Billy, a printer and keen fly-fisherman in normal life, sees today's annual Apprentice Boys march through Belfast not as an exercise in triumphalism, but simply as a 'celebratory day out' for himself and his family. He views it as a harmless expression of Protestant history and culture with no political or sectarian overtones whatsoever. His eight-year-old son is playing the triangle in the band, his wife and two daughters will be watching in the crowds, and he is dressed to the nines for the occasion. He has the same bright blue uniform as the rest of his band, but with a peaked cap, silver shoulder 'wings', sashes, a silver ceremonial sword brought back from the Battle of the Somme in 1916, and a mace with a silver crown on top.

'We're very keen on royalty,' he tells me somewhat superfluously, but our conversation is abruptly terminated as an almighty cacophony signals the start of the parade.

The bands stream into Donegall Place, lower their banners as they pass the war memorial and head off down Bedford Street – a long, colourful river of noise between banks of applauding, flag-waving spectators. On and on they come, their deafening marching tunes shaking your bones and causing your feet to tap in rhythm whether you like it or not.

Behind the 'Sons of Ulster' from Ballynahinch come the Armagh 'True Blues', the Portadown 'Defenders' and the Mourneview 'Young Loyalists'. Each is preceded by bearers of Union Jacks, the Ulster flag and beautifully painted banners depicting heroic historical scenes above embroidered mottos like 'No Surrender' and 'Fear God. Honour the Queen'. Each band sports its own brightly coloured uniforms. Most consist of ear-ringed, crew-cut young men playing flutes, while the biggest and beefiest of their number furiously bangs out the rhythm on a large bass drum.

It is the older men who march behind the bands that really interest me. They wear black suits and bowler hats, crimson collarettes and white gloves, and carry rolled-up black umbrellas. They are sturdy, dour Ulstermen of pedigree Protestant stock whose forefathers settled the province almost before America was discovered. They are men who see their life, like their fathers before them, as a constant battle against a perfidious Albion and southern papists.

They ignore the crowds; they do not smile as they march. There is none of the gaiety or levity of a St Patrick's Day parade. There are no jugglers, clowns or stilt-walkers to provide comic relief, and the bands' music is more martial than festive. The parade is not really a celebration at all. It is a statement – an awesome, high-decibel declaration that this is who these men are and this is their land and this is where they're staying. Like the Boers of South Africa, they are simultaneously noble and pathetic.

The procession kept coming, band after band, but after a

while their attractions palled and my eardrums begged for mercy. The Apprentice Boys of Derry had come to Belfast, but I was going to Derry via the annual Easter Monday horse fair in Toomebridge. I slipped away, but because the city-centre streets had been blocked off to traffic I had to walk to where I'd left my car outside St Anne's Cathedral.

The noise of the bands receded as I cut up a deserted Queen Street past the bland post-war building which houses the US Consulate and Belfast's entire diplomatic corps of three. The consulate, opened in 1796, is America's second oldest continually operated diplomatic mission and testimony to the extraordinarily strong historical links between Ulster and the New World.

The great myth is that today's Irish-Americans are all descendants of those impoverished Catholics who fled to America in nineteenth-century 'coffin boats' to escape famine and oppression. It is a myth so strong that most Irish-Americans identify with today's nationalists and republicans and regard Unionists as the bad guys. The first mass emigration to America actually took place in the eighteenth century, and was undertaken by Presbyterians of Scottish descent. They were mostly poor tenant farmers who were imported to settle Ulster, but were abused by avaricious landlords and the Anglican establishment and – unlike their present-day descendants – were not determined to stay in Ulster at all costs.

Tens of thousands of these 'Scotch-Irish' risked the perilous voyage to the American colonies in search of greater political, religious and economic freedom. By the end of 1775 at least 250,000 had settled there and formed more than a sixth of the total population. They took with them those qualities of industry, independence, religious fundamentalism and distrust of government that became such a quintessential part of the American character.

They provided the cutting edge of a pioneering nation.

Drawing on their experiences settling Ulster, these 'Scotch-Irish' led the march into the untamed American hinterlands and – as acolytes of King William – spawned the term 'hillbillies' in the process. 'They formed the kernel of that American stock who were the pioneers of our people in their march westward,' wrote President Theodore Roosevelt, and that is one reason why their story is less well known. The Catholic Irish who arrived in the nineteenth century tended to settle in what were, by then, well-established cities where they maintained a stronger sense of their cultural identity.

The 'Scotch-Irish' also played a central role in both the political agitation for American independence from Britain and the Revolutionary War itself. They provided many of the generals and half the rebel troops. 'If defeated everywhere else,' George Washington declared during that war against the British, 'I will take my last stand for liberty among the Scotch-Irish of my native Virginia.'

Frontiersmen like Davy Crockett, Kit Carson and Jim Bowie (inventor of the Bowie knife), soldiers like Sam Houston, Stonewall Jackson and Ulysses Grant, half-a-dozen signatories of the American Declaration of Independence and at least eleven American presidents were of direct Ulster Presbyterian stock. So too were the Mellons, the Gettys and Cyrus Hall McCormick, inventor of the mechanical reaper, who helped to transform infant America into a world power.

I'd parked my car on the corner of Donegall Street and Talbot Street, and not just because it was the most convenient spot. This site also has a surprising connection with America's early history.

Until the mid-1990s the Belfast *News Letter* occupied a lovely old sandstone office on this corner. The *News Letter* – Northern Ireland's pro-Unionist morning newspaper – is a mid-market tabloid, but one with an illustrious past. It is Britain's oldest daily newspaper, having been founded in 1737, and on 27

August 1776 enjoyed the biggest scoop of the eighteenth century. It was the first newspaper anywhere in Europe to publish the American Declaration of Independence, a mere 54 days after the document was signed in Philadelphia, because the ship carrying it to England stopped at the port of Londonderry on the way.

Within another two years a peripheral skirmish of the American War of Independence was actually fought in Belfast Lough when Paul Jones, an American privateer, sailed in on the *Ranger* and was confronted by a Royal Navy sloop called the *Drake*. The two vessels pumped shot and shell into each other for 43 minutes before the *Drake* surrendered.

I headed north up Donegall Street into Clifton Street where Belfast's elegant eighteenth-century poorhouse still stands, where the novelist Brian Moore was born in 1921, and where a two-ton statue of King Billy on horseback atop Belfast's heavily fortified Orange Hall miraculously survived the Troubles. The IRA had rather more luck in destroying the statue of 'Roaring Hugh' Hanna, a nineteenth-century Presbyterian evangelist and Orangeman, in the middle of shabby Carlisle Circus at the top of Clifton Street. Only the plinth still stands.

I took the Crumlin Road, which leads off Carlisle Circus, and almost immediately passed the famous old Crumlin Road jail on my right – its high walls still topped by coils of barbed wire – and the courthouse opposite. An underground tunnel links the two buildings, but neither is still used. The courthouse had just been sold to developers for £1, and the fine old Victorian jail – a listed building complete with a hanging cell and trapdoor in the floor – was still for sale. Buried in unmarked graves in its grounds are the remains of 17 men hanged in the 'Crum', the last in 1961.

Towards the top end of the Crumlin Road stand two huge defunct linen mills. Just beyond them, where the road divides the fiercely loyalist Upper Shankill to the south from the equally republican Ardoyne area to the north, there is the Ardoyne ambulance station; this is where Laurence Robertson works.

Laurence is a large, cheery fellow in his early forties who has probably attended more victims of paramilitary 'punishment' beatings and kneecappings than anyone else in Northern Ireland. In more than two decades on the front line of the Troubles, he has been called out hundreds of times to treat those attacked on waste ground or in back alleys by the paramilitary thugs who control their housing estates through naked terror. 'The stories you hear in the back of an ambulance are unbelievable,' he told me as we sat in the station's spartan television room one evening.

He said the paramilitaries often call the ambulances themselves and wait until they hear the sirens before kneecapping their victims. That way, the victims do not actually die if the bullets hit an artery. On one occasion Laurence's ambulance was called to a shooting off North Belfast's Antrim Road just as it was returning from another job. It arrived so quickly that 'as we came into the street a man approached with a mask and his hand in his breast pocket and said just drive around the block. We heard the bang. When we came back there was this guy lying in the road.'

He told how the victims are often summoned to be kneecapped and duly present themselves because the alternative is exile or worse. 'They're told, "We want you behind here 9 o'clock tomorrow night. We're only going to do one leg. If you don't show up we will get you tomorrow or next week or the week after that, but we will get you." They go because they live in the community, have lived there all their lives, and their families live there.'

He'd much rather be kneecapped than beaten. 'If someone came up to me today and said you can have five men with sticks or a gun, I would say shoot me. I would take my chance. Some of these beatings are absolutely horrific.' He has seen men with multiple major fractures to their legs and arms requiring plates, pins and screws. 'You could never go on a beach again anywhere in the world,' he said with typical Belfast black humour.

Local communities tolerate the hundreds of beatings and shootings each year because the victims are generally reckoned to have deserved them, but Laurence demurs. 'Nobody deserves to be shot or beaten to a pulp by a mob of masked men,' he said. 'The law is there to deal with persistent joyriders, or breaking into old people's houses and taking £10. Some are picked out on word of mouth and are totally innocent of anything. Some are 16-, 17- or 18-year-olds. Some are tragic, absolutely tragic.'

One consolation for men like Laurence, who deal daily with Belfast's horrors, is that it is an easy city to escape from; there are no sprawling suburbs. Barely half a mile beyond the ambulance station the rows of houses abruptly end and the Crumlin Road begins to zig-zag up the side of the Black Mountain. Within minutes I was up on the top of the windswept, sheep-cropped hills and looking back down over the city stretched out beneath me.

It was a stunning panorama – a great long, smoky swathe of docks, factories, high-rises and terraced housing bounded by hills and the glistening expanse of Belfast Lough to the north. Church spires, cranes, chimneys, the City Hall's green dome and Harland and Wolff's two great yellow arches provided tiny per-pendicular punctuation points. The setting was beautiful and the sight of this old industrial city – this former engine-room of empire and veritable cockpit of construction and destruction – quite compelling.

Since the Second World War no other city in Europe has suffered such continuous conflict. British troops first arrived on Belfast's streets in 1969, and only began to withdraw in the late 1990s. 'A city built on mud and wrath' with 'murdering miles of terrace houses' was how the poet Tom Paulin described the place. Louis MacNeice wrote:

See Belfast, devout and profane and hard,
Built on reclaimed mud, hammers playing in the shipyard,
Time punched with holes like a steel sheet, time
Hardening the faces, veneering with a gray and speckled
   rime
The faces under the shawls and caps . . .

There is another verse by Maurice James Craig that runs:

   Oh the bricks they will bleed and the rain it will weep
   And the damp Lagan fog lull the city to sleep
   It's to hell with the future and live on the past
   May the Lord in his Mercy be Kind to Belfast.

But let the people of Belfast speak for themselves. A 1997 survey asked them to describe their city as if it were a person. 'Belfast isn't a woman. A woman wouldn't be so harsh,' said one. 'Had a good job and lost it. He never recovered,' commented another. 'He has mood changes – he's a nasty annoying brute, ignorant, then he surprises you,' said a third. 'He has a vicious sense of humour – laughs at himself,' remarked a fourth.

I turned my back on the city and found myself looking across wide-open country with stunted trees and the odd white cottage and the first green fur of spring appearing on the hedgerows. Back in the car, I consulted my old friend Ernest Sandford to see if there was anything of interest between here and Toomebridge. In Crumlin, he informed me, there was a nineteenth-century folly called the Cockle House that faces towards Mecca because the landlord built it for his Moslem servant. That was a bit out of my way, but he did strongly recommend a visit to the graveyard of the Duneane Presbyterian Church which contained another in Northern Ireland's collection of bizarre tombs.

The hamlet of Duneane is about 25 miles north-west of Belfast, just before Toomebridge. Its graveyard sits in gentle,

rolling countryside, and in the midst of the tombstones stands
the most vainglorious monument I've ever seen. Erected by a
nineteenth-century eccentric called John Carey in honour of
himself, it consists of a tall, octagonal stone column topped by a
large stone urn with a white hand pointing heavenwards, and
the sides of this column are covered in plaques.

One is an 'obituary to John Carey, founder of this monument
and of the Temple Institution Careyvale and of the free public
fountain of water in Toome and of the Free Christian Church at
Balac, British India, for the converts from heathenism there and
of the foundation Carey lectureship at Derry and Belfast and
many other founded bequests religious, moral, literary and charitable Et Cetera'.

Another charts his 'lineage' which was from 'a very ancient
race . . . renowned for courage, equity and learning, honoured
with many prominent state offices, elevated to several peer-
ages . . . claiming kindred with the highest ranks in the empire
and a nuptial affinity with the Crown itself since the 16th century.'

A third, his 'biography', concludes: 'In life he was most ingenious, persevering and benevolent, in death an example to all for
those great moral virtues.' Yet another advises visitors to consult
Burke's Landed Gentry for more information on the deceased.

Arranged around the base of the monument were other great
slabs of stone inscribed with biblical quotations describing 'the
terrors of the broken law' and 'the consolations of the glorious
gospel', and the whole thing was surrounded by heavy railings
with iron hands for joints.

I didn't know who Mr Carey was, but a few days later I looked
him up in the library. He was a Presbyterian minister who was
drummed out of office on suspicion of fiddling the books and
attempted murder, and later became a money-lender who
charged impoverished farmers exorbitant rates of interest. I
somehow suspect there was no great sorrow when he died,

especially as his will demanded he be borne to his grave 'not by horses but by his kindly fellow creatures'.

I drove on into Toomebridge, commonly known as Toome, but I hadn't quite seen the last of Mr Carey. There by the side of the road as I entered the town was an old cow-tailed pump. Next to it was a circular stone structure from the top of which protruded another iron hand holding up a sign: 'This fountain free to all. The design and gift of John Cary (sic) 1860,' it said.

Toome is a small town located where the River Bann flows out of Lough Neagh. Its annual horse fair is the first of the season. Nobody organises it; it just happens, and has been happening for as long as anyone can remember. Anybody with a horse to sell just brings it along, ties it to a railing and waits for a buyer. In recent times bouncing castles, a funfair and dozens of stalls selling everything from cheap plastic toys to back-of-the-lorry clothes have sprouted on the margins, and for several hours the event brings traffic to a virtual standstill on the main Belfast–to–Londonderry road which runs through the centre of Toome.

The stalls were cheap and tacky, but the horse fair itself was traditional, timeless, cunning Ireland. Horseboxes lined the pavements down near the river. Men in grubby old clothes stood around in clusters. Horses, ponies and donkeys were tied to every post and pillar, and ranged in price from £150 to £1,500. Young men riding bareback skittered up and down the road, showing off their animals, or ran along pulling trotting foals with ropes. A silver-tongued salesman hawked cut-price saddles and harnesses from his van.

The crowds stuck to the stalls and the funfair. The horse fair was for insiders only. This was the black economy in action, and strangers were viewed with evident suspicion – especially if clutching a notebook. 'Didn't I see you at the "broo" last week?' one man asked me with a hint of menace. 'I think you're a policeman,' a young boy with a horse said accusingly. I was writing a book, I explained repeatedly, and slowly they opened up.

It's not often that you discover an entirely new profession, but I found one here. It is called 'guinea hunting', and it seems no horse fair is complete without half-a-dozen 'guinea hunters' loitering among the horseboxes. They are men like 'Wee Wheels' – the little wheeler-dealer – who learned the trade from his father, or Paddy Kelly, a pipe-smoking Derryman in his mid-sixties dressed in an old wool coat. Both his parents were guinea hunters and he's been at it for 50 years. 'It's all I know,' he told me.

These 'guinea hunters' go to all the two dozen horse fairs in Ireland each year, and it seems few deals are struck without their involvement. They don't advertise themselves, but they don't need to; they know all the dealers and most of the horses. They are the ones who step in to arbitrate between buyers and sellers, keep them haggling and finally decree a price. 'We're a cheaper version of a solicitor,' said Wee Wheels, who'll receive a cut of the profits for his services. And as he will almost certainly know what the same horse sold for at one of last year's fairs, and what the seller's profit is, he'll adjust his fee accordingly.

The deal is actually sealed when the buyer and seller spit on their palms and slap hands. Traditionally the seller then returns a few pounds to the buyer, and some particularly superstitious buyers will not proceed without such a 'luckpenny'. It is a little world of its own, one where a novice is likely to be ripped off horribly, but just as I was beginning to appreciate the finer points of the ancient art of horse-trading the heavens opened, the road turned to liquid horse dung and the fair was brought to a premature and very wet end.

I'd driven the main road to Londonderry countless times during the previous two years, but seldom turned off it. I did so the next morning as I had time to spare. A few miles beyond Toome I picked a little road off to the right at random and found myself driving up through an avenue of beech trees into the little village of Knockloughrim. 'Whomsoever shall call on the name of the Lord shall be saved,' proclaimed a large yellow sign nailed to one of the tree trunks. You find these all over Northern Ireland, just as you do in the American boondocks. 'Eternity – where?' is one of my favourites, or 'Booze – the Devil's Vomit'.

It was a fine spring day. I meandered along an empty back road bordered by fields of lambs and little woods and newly trimmed hedgerows. There were clumps of daffodils on the verges, hints of blossom on the trees, and to my left I had a breathtaking view across a broad green valley to the bald Sperrin hills beyond.

I drove into Maghera past the ruins of a thirteenth-century church. The gates were padlocked, but a man wandered over to say I could get the key from the leisure centre if I wanted. A sign on the Ulster Bank building in the main street announced: 'We are now open at lunchtime.' The town was not quite as unworldly as it seemed, however. On the far side lamp-posts were decorated with tricolours and the letters 'IRA' were spray-painted on road signs. I'd been here before – to interview a founder member of the Provisional IRA who was involved in the alleged diversion of Irish government money to procure arms at the beginning of the Troubles.

The man lives in a comfortable bungalow with a wonderful view of the Sperrins, and is a classic example of the problem that confronts so many British journalists covering Northern Ireland. It is very hard to portray him as the embodiment of evil; he and his wife were open, hospitable and eminently likeable. How to reconcile the charm of republicans with the evil deeds done in the name of republicanism was a question I never resolved.

Maghera has other figures of note. One Peter Henry was for a time Napoleon's personal physician, and in 1729 a certain Charles Thompson was born here. When Thompson was 10, soon after his mother died in childbirth, he sailed for America with his father and two brothers, but his father died within sight of the New World. He was reared by an elder brother who was already in America, became a teacher and befriended the Delaware Indian tribe who adopted him and gave him the title 'Man of Truth'.

Thompson rose to become secretary of the revolutionary Continental Congress and was one of those 'Scotch-Irish' Presbyterians who played a key role in securing America's independence. As secretary, he wrote out and publicly read the Declaration of Independence. In 1789 he rode 250 miles from New York to Mount Vernon, Virginia, to inform George Washington of his election as America's first president. He designed the Great Seal of the United States, and for nearly fifteen years he minuted the birth of a nation, but later earned every historian's wrath by destroying all his records lest they embarrassed any of the famous figures of the time.

Beyond Maghera I had to rejoin the main Londonderry road because that is the only way over the Sperrins. I enjoyed a spectacular 10-mile drive over the high Glenshane Pass where the only human habitations amid the moors, streams and geometrically shaped conifer plantations are the Ponderosa pub and the occasional white farmhouse in a hollow. On the far side I coasted happily down towards Dungiven where the ruins of a twelfth-century Augustinian priory stand in an ancient graveyard on the town's periphery.

A stunted tree also stands in the graveyard, its branches adorned with little strips of cloth. The tree conceals a smooth boulder with a water-filled hole in the middle. This is a 'wart well'; you dip a piece of cloth into the water, wipe any part of your body afflicted with warts, rheumatism or arthritis, then tie the cloth to the tree. Sadly I had no such afflictions to try it on, but made a mental note to return when I grew older.

Beyond Dungiven I continued my westwards ramble along the back lanes. My car was heavily outnumbered by tractors. Outside whitewashed cottages home-made signs offered Kerrs pink potatoes for sale. An occasional old man touched his cap by way of greeting as I passed. Except for Belfast, Northern Ireland is really just one huge farm.

I came to the little hillside village of Claudy with its credit union, post office and inevitable Spar grocery strung along the neat main street. Women were chatting on the pavements in the sun. The postman was doing his rounds. It was the very picture of tranquillity, and you would never guess that on 31 July 1972, three large car bombs tore the heart out of the place. There were no warnings given. Nine villagers – Protestant and Catholic – were killed. The youngest victim was an eight-year-old girl, and another was the mother of eight.

A local poet, James Simmons, captured the horror of the event in his poem 'Claudy':

> *The Sperrins surround it, the Faughan flows by,*
> *at each end of Main Street the hills and the sky,*
> *the small town of Claudy at ease in the sun*
> *last July in the morning, a new day begun.*
>
> *How peaceful and pretty if the moment could stop,*
> *McIlhenny is straightening things in his shop,*
> *and his wife is outside serving petrol, and then*
> *a girl takes a cloth to a big window pane.*
>
> *And McCloskey is taking the weight off his feet,*
> *and McClelland and Miller are sweeping the street,*
> *and, delivering milk at the Beaufort Hotel,*
> *young Temple's enjoying his first job as well.*

And Mrs McLaughlin is scrubbing her floor,
And Artie Hone's crossing the street to a door,
and Mrs Brown, looking around for her cat,
goes off up an entry – what's strange about that?

Not much – but before she comes back to the road
that strange car parked outside her house will explode,
and all of the people I've mentioned outside
will be waiting to die or already have died.

An explosion too loud for your eardrums to bear,
and young children squealing like pigs in the square,
and all faces chalk-white and streaked with bright red,
and the glass and the dust and the terrible dead.

For an old lady's legs are ripped off, and the head
of a man's hanging open, and still he's not dead.
He is screaming for mercy, and his son stands and stares
and stares, and then suddenly, quick, disappears.

And Christ, little Katherine Aiken is dead,
and Mrs McLaughlin is pierced through the head.
Meanwhile to Dungiven the killers have gone,
and they're finding it hard to get through on the phone.

The atrocity was widely blamed on the IRA, but in this instance the organisation was evidently too embarrassed to claim responsibility. It is said that the gang responsible failed to give any warning because the telephone box they intended to use had been vandalised.

Beyond Claudy I crossed the River Faughan, and was following the windy, undulating road towards Strabane when I spotted the shell of a great square stately home standing on a hill above the road.

Crows flapped out of the top of this three-storey, crenellated ruin as I approached. Two eroded sandstone coats-of-arms flanked the gaping orifice that was obviously once a grand front door. Tufts of grass and bushery had taken root in crevices. The whole building was surrounded by stinking slurry. There was nothing left inside, just mud floors, bare walls, the empty squares of former windows and an uninterrupted view of the sky above.

A few hundred yards down the road I spotted a middle-aged, ruddy-cheeked woman in the garden of a farmhouse. She was a friendly soul with an accent as broad as Lough Neagh. 'That old castle's called Ogilby's Castle,' she told me over her gate. 'The ones that built it came from Dublin. They were party people, but I suppose it didn't suit them up here and they went away again. It wasn't good enough and they headed back to Dublin.

'They left a son but he ran out of money. He sold it and went to live in Dunnamanagh. The Robertsons bought it, then the Eatons and they're away now. They had to take the roof off for the lead and things. Now there's nothing but muck.'

In her house she had a large, white marble fireplace that her grandfather had salvaged from the castle. Every time she had a fire, it got covered in wee black smuts. 'It's a hateful thing,' she said. 'It should have been left in the castle.'

A few miles on I found yet another ruined castle in the village of Dunnamanagh. This one – Earl's Gift Castle – was never even completed. A gentleman called Sir John Drummond abandoned it after his French fiancée was shipwrecked and drowned on her way to join him.

I reached Strabane late in the afternoon and almost wished I hadn't. It's a rather miserable town on the banks of the River Mourne afflicted by rampant unemployment and famous primarily for the people who managed to escape from it. These include yet more remarkable Presbyterians – Thomas Kean and Thomas Nelson who signed the American Declaration of

Independence, and John Dunlap, the man who actually printed it. Dunlap also fought in and helped finance the American War of Independence and started America's first successful daily newspaper, the *Pennsylvania Packet*, which enjoyed a scoop to rival that of the Belfast *News Letter*. It was the first to print the American Constitution.

Dunlap left Strabane for America in 1757 when he was 10, but the town likes to think he learned his trade in Gray's printing shop in Main Street and has turned the building into a little museum. From the audio-visual display, I learned how Dunlap sent a letter back to Strabane saying how there was 'no place in the world where a man meets so rich a reward for good conduct and industry as in America', and how that letter inspired another apprentice printer named James Wilson to emigrate in 1807. A century later James Wilson's grandson, Woodrow Wilson, became President of the United States.

I was the museum's only visitor and fell into conversation with Dorothy Smith, the genteel lady who runs the museum for the National Trust. She regaled me with the tale of how an IRA car bomb intended for a nearby hotel had destroyed her house in 1972 – once again demonstrating that hardly anyone in Northern Ireland was unaffected by the Troubles. She also told me that members of the Wilson family still lived on the farm from which James Wilson emigrated, so I decided to search out these presidential kinsmen.

I drove out of Strabane through the Drumrallagh estate, which is as grim as any in Northern Ireland. I'd been there once before, to interview a young man who was quietly watching television one night when an IRA gang burst in, beat him senseless with baseball bats, then realised they'd got the wrong house. They went next door and repeated the exercise on a neighbour who had slipped back to see his girlfriend in defiance of an exile order.

Half-a-mile beyond the estate I was climbing up into lovely

hills dotted with small farms and marvelling once again at yet another extraordinary juxtaposition of the ugly and the beautiful. The Wilson farm was about three miles out of town. The last few hundred yards lay up a narrow, grassy track between high banks. The ancestral homestead still stood – a thatched and whitewashed cottage with red wooden doors, but behind it was a bland, square box of a house rather unworthy, I thought, of a family with such grand connections.

There was nobody at home, and my quest for the presidential relatives would have ended there had I not met a man driving up the track as I drove down it. He told me that Andy Wilson was the fellow I wanted, but Andy was now living down at Magheramason on the road to Londonderry.

I drove back through Strabane and turned northwards up the broad, rich valley of the River Foyle with the hills of County Donegal on the far side. After about 10 miles I reached the village of Magheramason, and in the middle of a small loyalist housing estate I found the end-of-terrace, pebble-dash house with a neat little garden and gnomes on the doorstep where the president's kinsman lived.

Andy was a far cry from the austere, high-minded man who led America through the First World War and then formed the League of Nations. A short, humble fellow in his mid-sixties, with absolutely no pretensions to grandeur, he was dressed in blue overalls, wore thick glasses, smoked heavily and had a heart condition. He was a man of few words, but his favourite one was 'aye'.

He offered me tea. He had never established exactly what relation he was to the president, he told me; he had no letters or mementos of any sort from his distant cousin's time in the White House. He himself had spent most of his adult life working as a maintenance man at an oil refinery on Humberside in England, and had never even visited America. He would be the last Wilson to live on the farm as he was in the process of selling it.

He told me he had no regrets that his side of the family had not emigrated to the New World, and was quite happy where he was.

Our talk about matters presidential was quickly exhausted, so Andy took me out to see the splendid garage-cum-workshop he'd just built around the side of the house. He might lack his more illustrious namesake's political acumen and leadership skills, but I'd bet he was a damn sight better with his hands.

It was dusk by the time I drove into Londonderry along the south-eastern bank of the Foyle, but it was still a great sight. Across the broad sweep of water Northern Ireland's second city rose steeply above the old mill buildings, its ancient walls and cathedral spires framed by the Donegal hills beyond. It is little wonder that unlike Belfast, where people feel much more allegiance to their immediate neighbourhood than to the city, both Protestants and Catholics are immensely proud of Londonderry. They also like to point out that it was a city when Belfast was a mudflat.

Londonderry is a spirited place, its people are talented and wryly humorous, and its history is as striking as its appearance. St Columba founded a monastery here in the year 546. The settlement grew, became known as Derry after the Irish 'Doire' meaning 'place of oaks', and was ransacked by Scandinavian raiders at least half-a-dozen times before the year 1200. In the early 1600s the City of London's wealthy livery companies – the Grocers, Mercers, Fishmongers, Drapers, Skinners, Goldsmiths, Merchant Tailors, Tallow Chandlers, Haberdashers, Salters, Ironmongers, Vintners and Clothworkers – built a new fortified city on the site as part of Ireland's colonisation. It was the jewel in the crown of the Ulster 'Plantation', and the companies renamed it Londonderry.

Then came the siege of 1689, the events of which are still taught to all good loyalists at their mothers' knee. Catholic King James II was seeking to use Ireland as a springboard for recapturing the English throne. While their elders dithered, 13 young apprentice boys slammed shut the city gates to keep his forces out. Against all odds the 30,000 settlers huddled inside the walls held out for 105 days until ships sent by the newly installed Protestant King William relieved the siege by breaking through a wooden boom the Jacobites had thrown across the Foyle.

By that stage the settlers had been reduced to eating rats, which were selling for a shilling each, and dogs which were selling for half-a-crown. One particularly fat man had hidden himself away for fear of cannibalism. As many as 7,000 men, women and children died from starvation, disease or mortars. Londonderry became known as the Maiden City because she was never violated, and 'no surrender' remains the loyalist battle-cry to this day.

In the eighteenth and nineteenth centuries emigration to North America was the city's great industry. Towards the end of the nineteenth century Londonderry became the world's leading shirt manufacturer because linen was plentiful, so many men had emigrated and the women who remained were desperate for work. The city actually provided shirts to both sides in the American Civil War, and for a long time presented a gift of ten new shirts to each incoming US president.

At its peak in the 1920s the shirtmaking industry employed 18,000 women while most of the city's men were unemployed, and Londonderry still has a reputation as a place where the women wear the trousers. 'While men on the dole played the mother's role/Fed the children and walked the dog . . .' runs Phil Coulter's song about Londonderry, 'The Town I Love So Well'. A standard joke asks how many Derry men it takes to change a light bulb, to which the answer is: 'None, because their Mammy does it for them.'

In the Second World War the Allies waged their battle against the German U-boat fleet from Londonderry, Britain's most westerly port. In 1945 more than sixty U-boats sailed up the Foyle to surrender, and many of them were subsequently towed back out to sea for bombing practice or to be scuttled.

But Londonderry is best known, of course, as the place where the Troubles erupted at the end of the 1960s. The city's ruling Unionists engaged in blatant gerrymandering to retain political control of a predominantly Catholic population. There was discrimination against Catholics in housing and employment. Civil rights marches were brutally suppressed, most notably when British troops shot dead 13 unarmed demonstrators on Bloody Sunday in 1972, and the city quickly became synonymous with riots, bombs and appalling urban conflict.

Evidence of that conflict was still visible as I entered the gothic Guildhall, which houses the council chamber, the next morning. A 2½-ton marble statue of Queen Victoria stands in the entrance hall. In 1972 the IRA placed a bomb beside Her Majesty's pedestal and she landed several yards away, distinctly unamused. She has since been restored to her original position, but minus her hands and on a pedestal still badly chipped and pitted.

The bomb was one of two that rocked the Guildhall in the same week. Most of the building's splendid stained-glass windows were destroyed, though happily the blast spared the one that depicts King George V wearing his shoes on the wrong feet at his coronation.

I had come to meet John Kerr, a friend of a friend who was a nationalist SDLP councillor and former mayor. He ushered me into the Mayor's Parlour – an oak-panelled room with a blazing fire where he had laid on coffee and biscuits. I hadn't been there a minute before he was presenting me with a large wooden plaque and a tie, both bearing the city's coat of arms. I don't think he went as far as declaring me a freeman of Londonderry, but if he did he'll surely retract the honour if I persist in calling the city by that name.

People are fond of saying that history and current affairs are one and the same in Northern Ireland, and the issue of the name is a perfect illustration. Nationalists insist on calling the city by its original name of Derry. Unionists insist on Londonderry. The dispute places visitors like myself in the invidious position or having to choose between the two and give offence to one side or the other, or else trying to guess the allegiance of everyone you talk to and adapting accordingly.

One recent mayor achieved the remarkable feat of going an entire year without naming the city once – he used formulae like 'this lovely city on the banks of the Foyle'. The BBC ducked the issue by calling its local radio station 'Radio Foyle'. President Clinton, during his 1995 visit, referred to 'Derry in the county of Londonderry', and some people jokingly call the place 'Stroke City' as in London/Derry.

The issue may seem trivial, but Unionists boycotted the council for several years in the mid-1980s after the nationalist majority voted to change its name to 'Derry City Council'. 'It's a nightmare in marketing terms,' Mr Kerr admitted as we set off under grey skies for a tour of the finest walled city left in Europe.

The Germans bombed Derry just once in the Second World War, but the IRA subsequently detonated so many bombs that by 1975 three-quarters of the buildings inside the walls were damaged or destroyed, and one journalist memorably dubbed the place 'Tumbledown Derry'. You'd never believe it now. The historic area has been magnificently restored and is now an architectural delight full of little surprises.

Here, for example, is the lovely Georgian house occupied until recently by The Honourable The Irish Society, the body set up by the London livery companies in 1613 to manage their affairs in Ulster. Nearly four centuries later the society still exists, is still composed of 'six and twenty honest and discreet citizens of London', and still owns all the fishing rights on the River Bann, but it is now primarily a charitable organisation.

Opposite is an equally fine house, once the Bishop's Palace, where Mrs Cecil Frances Alexander wrote, 'There is a Green Hill Far Away', 'Once in Royal David's City' and 'All Things Bright and Beautiful'.

In ancient St Columb's Cathedral there is a huge iron mortar ball that was fired into the city during the siege, only this one contained surrender terms not explosives. Local wags like to call it the first ever air-mail letter. In the cathedral grounds is the Heroes' Mound created from the remains of those who died in the siege.

The only vandalism I saw was in the Diamond, the central square, where one of the four old trees around the war memorial had been cut down. This was allegedly at the insistence of Mr Clinton's secret servicemen who feared it would provide cover for a sniper during the president's 1995 visit.

The walls themselves are the city's crowning glory. They are about 20 feet wide and form an unbroken circle of roughly a mile with bridges over the seven old gates. The problem is that when you walk on them you are tempted to look outwards as well as inwards. It is then that you realise that Londonderry's ancient heart is ringed by ugly post-war housing estates whose architects deserve early, painful and singularly unpleasant ends.

The most notorious of these estates is the fiercely republican Bogside which you look right down on from the north-west side. You cannot mistake the place. For a start this stretch of the wall is ringed by high steel bars. It is unclear whether this was to prevent incoming or outgoing missiles, but it was doubtless connected to the fact that the Apprentice Boys memorial hall is just inside the walls at this point. Several times a year the descendants of the original apprentice boys insist on parading around the walls to celebrate the events of 1689, much to the disgust of the Bogsiders.

Then there are all the murals and graffiti directed at the casual visitor above. Some commemorate Bloody Sunday and those early battles with the security forces. Others proclaim Sinn Fein's latest gripe – 'No Sectarian Marches' or 'Disband the RUC'. One shows a woman being beaten by police beneath the legend: '1968 to 1996 Nothing Has Changed'. There is even a lone gable wall – the rest of the house having been long since demolished – which is painted white and bears the words: 'You are now entering Free Derry'. This marks the spot where, in the early 1970s, the Bogsiders briefly established a police no-go area.

Unionists like to accuse republicans of suffering from the MOPE syndrome, of constantly presenting themselves as the Most Oppressed People on Earth. Looking down on the Bogside, with all its reminders of old battles, I could see their point. Exploiting grievances – past or present, real or imaginary – is Sinn Fein's forte. If its constituents felt content, its *raison d'être* would vanish. But the truth is that in Derry, at least, it is now the Protestants who feel threatened and beleaguered.

Only a few hundred Protestants still live on the city side of the River Foyle. They inhabit a small, fenced-in estate abutting the south-western walls called the Fountain that is awash with the usual loyalist insignia of Union Jacks, painted kerbstones and 'GSTQ' (God Save the Queen) graffiti. I even spotted a washing line with red, white and blue clothes pegs.

An unemployed man named William Jackson took me into the hallway of his home where, to demonstrate his absolute Britishness, he had hung all the medals and military regalia of relatives who fought in the two World Wars. 'We're under siege twenty-four hours a day,' he told me. 'But I couldn't leave. Jacksons have lived here since the 1800s. I was born and raised here. If I did move out and thought a nationalist was coming to live in this house, I would vandalise it so it wouldn't be fit to live in.'

Mr Jackson is an exception. The vast majority of Derry's Protestants have long since moved across the river to an area known as Waterside. It was an exodus greatly accelerated by the actions of the IRA, and because the city is now so segregated there is little of the naked sectarianism you find in Belfast with its patchwork quilt of orange and green communities. Indeed, people here regard Belfast with something akin to horror.

The truth is that the Catholics have finally captured a city that King James's army failed to take by force three centuries earlier. About 70 per cent of Derry's 100,000 population is Catholic, nationalists now enjoy a comfortable majority on the council, and while the city is *in* Northern Ireland it is not quite *of* it.

Derry is tucked away in the north-west corner of the province, right on the border with the republic, with poor transport links. Its hinterlands include County Donegal, which is in the Republic, and it looks more to Europe and America for aid and investment than it does to Belfast or London. Its football team plays in the Republic of Ireland's league, not Northern Ireland's. There is even a joke that the skeleton on the city's coat of arms used to represent a Catholic looking for work in the city, but now represents a Protestant.

The real story of late twentieth-century Derry is one of Catholic empowerment, not Catholic suppression. It is the tale of a city that produced two Catholic Nobel prize-winners in the 1990s, Seamus Heaney and John Hume, though I will not repeat the mistake of saying that St Columb's College is the only school in the world to have produced two Nobel laureates. When I wrote that in *The Times*, I inevitably received letters from readers who gleefully informed me that St Mary's College in St Lucia and Todmorden Grammar School in West Yorkshire had done the same.

It is, above all, the story of a friend of mine – let's call her Mary McCullough – who has risen from the humblest of beginnings in a back street of the city to become a senior public servant with a large house in an affluent area of Belfast, a weekend cottage in Donegal and a BMW. It is a Derry version of *Angela's Ashes* with a happy ending.

Later that morning I went to meet Mary in a tiny two-up-two-down red-brick terraced house in the Pennyburn area of the city down by the river. Her grandparents first rented this house soon after they were married at the turn of the century. Her grandfather was lucky; he was the foreman of one of the council's paving teams and the only man in the street with a regular job.

Mary's grandmother gave birth to 14 children in the tiny back bedroom. She raised them in a house with an outside toilet and no hot water; she cooked on a range in the back room, and went out only to shop or attend Mass. The children slept head-to-toe in three double beds squeezed into the front bedroom.

Four of the children died young; the rest left school at 14 with minimal prospects of advancement. Two of the boys emigrated to America to find work. One moved to the Bogside and became a paver like his father. Another moved to the next street and worked for an engineering company. The other two boys were twins, found a variety of odd jobs here or in England, but eventually returned to live at home and died in the early 1990s.

The four girls all remained in Derry too. One worked in a canteen, and two in a shirt factory. The youngest escaped that fate because she objected to the factory's smell. 'It's a poor house that can't keep one lady,' her father declared. She married a delivery boy.

Mary's mother was one of the two daughters who went to the shirt factory; she worked there most of her life, sewing or pressing for £8 a week. She married a man from the Bogside and gave birth to Mary in the same bed in the same back room in which she herself was born, but her husband went off to England to get work and never returned.

Mary was raised in her grandmother's house. Her mother and grandmother slept in one of the two bedrooms, her twin uncles in the other, and she alternated. She played in the streets while her mother worked, but her grandmother set great store on education and made her do her homework. In 1961 she passed the new 11-plus exam and became the first member of her family ever to go on to secondary education – but only after a desperate search for money for the uniform.

That was the turning point, when Mary suddenly discovered a world beyond the narrow streets of Pennyburn. She discovered that not everyone was deprived; that Protestants, unlike Catholics, aspired to and usually got good jobs and houses. She learned to her amazement that people actually bought books and had things called bookshelves in their homes. She went to university in Belfast, fell in love with a Protestant boy and married him despite his mother's initial strong objections. Mary now has two children, takes holidays abroad and enjoys an affluent upper middle-class life in Belfast, though her heart remains in Derry. 'Once a Derry girl, always a Derry girl,' she told me.

What made the difference, she said, was Northern Ireland's 1947 Education Act – which made secondary education available to all – and subsequent fair employment legislation.

Mary showed me round Pennyburn. The neighbourhood has changed enormously. The shirt factory is now a supermarket; the local fish-and-chip shop is now a decent pasta restaurant where we had lunch. The little corner shops have gone, and the terraced houses have been taken over by students and other young single people. But Mary's mother, a diminutive lady in her late seventies, still lives in the same tiny house and told me she would never leave. 'I just love this house. It's not great, but it's just home to me,' she said.

After lunch we sat and chatted in front of the coal fire in the back room for a while, and then Mary showed me the minute upper bedroom where she and her 14 uncles and aunts were all born, and the kitchen and bathroom extension with which the family replaced the outside toilet only 30 years ago. The extension all but fills the back yard, but there is still an opening in the stone wall that is covered by fine wire mesh and served as the fridge.

As we left, Mary pointed to the brickwork surrounding the front door. Scratched, carved or etched into the soft red surfaces were the names or initials of a century's-worth of McCulloughs – sons, daughters, uncles, aunts, parents, grandparents and, of course, those big strapping cousins with gleaming white teeth and money in their pockets who came back from America to find their roots.

Once I looked at the map I realised I couldn't really end this journey in Derry. The city sits at the eastern foot of the Inishowen peninsula, which juts up into the Atlantic. The most northerly point on the peninsula, and of the entire island of Ireland, is Malin Head. Like Fair Isle, Ronaldsway and Rockall, Malin Head is one of those tremendously evocative names that I have known all my life thanks to BBC Radio's twice-daily shipping forecasts. I simply had to go and see what it was really like.

I set off early the next morning, driving northwards out of Derry past the field where Amelia Earhart landed in 1932 after becoming the first woman to fly solo across the Atlantic. She was aiming for Paris but knew she had veered off course, and her first words to an astonished labourer were: 'Where am I?' Fifty-five years later, incidentally, Richard Branson touched down just a few miles further east after completing the first crossing of the Atlantic by balloon.

The Foyle River on my right soon broadened into Lough Foyle, glistening in the early sun and fringed by distant misty mountains. There was no border post. I knew I had crossed into the republic only when the post office vans turned green and the signposts began giving directions in kilometres not miles.

I left the lough shore at the little town of Moville and continued north through gorgeous empty country ringed by hills, riven by streams, and dotted with sheep or cattle. The occasional shower created brilliant rainbows over the road ahead. I met only a couple of ancient buses coming the other way.

I passed through the tiny villages of Gleneely and Culdaff where piles of turf were stacked outside the cottages. Beyond Malin with its village green, ancient store and lovely old stone bridge, I followed an estuary bordered by grassy bluffs and sandy coves until finally I drove up on to one last headland and there it was – the great heaving blue Atlantic smashing on to the last few fractured rocks of Europe.

In the lee of the hill behind me were a few white cottages with smoking chimneys. On the headland itself there was nothing except an abandoned concrete tower from which the Lloyds shipping agency used to signal to vessels out at sea, a little car park with a map, and lots and lots of very cold wind.

It was a wonderful, wild, breathtaking view, but no place to linger. I retreated back the way I'd come, and sought out the meteorological office – a low, square building with a tall mast, a key in the door and another wonderful view of the sea. I went in and there was Jim – a short, cheery, red-headed fellow with smiling blue eyes who for the past 20 years has been the source of all those shipping reports.

Every hour of every day of every year, he or one of his four colleagues measure the wind speed, temperature and other vital statistics and dispatch them by teletext to Dublin. Malin Head had never failed to report, he said with pride. 'That's not done. You just don't miss reports. You don't fall asleep. It takes a special breed.'

Jim was unmarried. He lived alone, and would never live in a city. He laughed when I suggested the wind that day was strong. It was a mere 25 m.p.h., he said. 'Strong here is 60 to 70 m.p.h. The highest wind we've had here in my time was 103 m.p.h.' In the summer it was lovely at Malin Head, but 'there are days when you see that sea out there and you think it's boiling and you get hailstones cutting your nose.'

Jim giggled when I asked what else happened in Malin Head. There was a school, five pubs, a few fishermen and farmers who eked out a living, he said. After a moment's pause he added: 'We've definitely got a lot of weather.' With that he pulled on a very thick jacket and hurried out to take the readings for the benefit of some equally lonely skipper far out in that vast expanse of ocean.

7

The Sporting Life

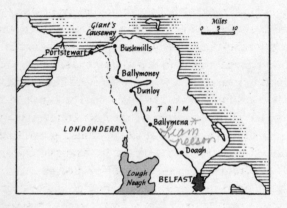

Just north of Belfast's city centre there is an underpass beneath a ring road called the Westlink. High on one of its walls is a faded floral wreath and a plaque. 'To the memory of 15 innocent civilians murdered by a pro-British loyalist gang in a no-warning bomb attack on McGurk's Bar December 4th 1971,' it reads. Below are the names of the 15 victims including those of Paddy McGurk's wife and 14-year-old daughter. The plaque is all that remains of the bar.

The Ulster Volunteer Force attack on McGurk's Bar was 'perhaps the most horrific single incident of the Troubles', wrote the historian Jonathan Bardon in 1982, though sadly his words proved premature. 'By the light of arc-lamps surgeons treated the injured in the open; gas escaping from fractured pipes flamed in the rubble as all through the night the dead and mutilated were uncovered brick by brick; and rescue operations were hampered as nearby the Army came under fire and rival crowds fought in the darkness.'

A week later the IRA bombed a furniture shop on the Shankill Road. It too gave no warning, and the four victims included a seven-month-old boy. A terrible cycle of tit-for-tat bombings had begun.

Nowhere suffered worse over the next quarter of a century than the square mile of Belfast immediately north of where McGurk's Bar once stood – a patchwork quilt of Protestant and Catholic working-class enclaves where the strength of the paramilitaries matched the depth of sectarian hatred.

The postal areas of BT14 and BT15 were the killing fields. These labyrinthine streets witnessed nearly a fifth of all the killings of the Troubles. They are riven by no fewer than 14 of Belfast's 17 'peace lines' – great steel, military-green walls that slice whole streets in half to separate, for example, the loyalists of Tiger's Bay from the republicans of New Lodge.

McGurk's Bar was on the southern edge of New Lodge, a ghetto whose representative in Northern Ireland's assembly is Gerry Kelly – the man who helped to mount the IRA's first bomb attack on London in 1973.

New Lodge is the sort of place where mothers do not sleep until their sons come home at night and boys all too easily grow into criminals or paramilitary thugs. It is a place where the walls are daubed with IRA graffiti and vivid murals commemorate the 1981 hunger-strikers; where the once-neat rows of terraced homes have mostly been abandoned, bulldozed into wasteland, or replaced by a clutch of far grimmer high-rise blocks.

On the seventh floor of one of these high-rises a 79-year-old man named John Browne was woken by an IRA gang one night in 1998, tied up and made to sit on the lavatory with a cushion cover over his head. The gang then shot him in both knees and both ankles. It later transpired that they were after a child molester who lived on the same floor, but had broken into the wrong flat.

I remember knocking on the doors of that high-rise after Mr Browne's shooting. Most of the residents were far too frightened to talk to a journalist, but one woman did usher me inside and chatted for a while about the paramilitaries' iron grip on the area. As I left, I noticed a wooden club studded with nails hanging behind her front door beside a picture of Jesus. She kept it there to protect herself, she told me.

But even in New Lodge it is possible to find inspiration, so let us begin this journey in an old red-brick building – a former barracks – that sits in the shadow of these high-rises. It is early one May evening, and in a cramped gym on the first floor two dozen men, teenagers and mere boys are pummelling punchbags and making skipping ropes whistle. Welcome to the Holy Family Golden Gloves boxing club, one of Belfast's more remarkable institutions.

Boxing is big in Northern Ireland. A common joke, which also happens to be true, is that the only medals the province consistently wins at the Commonwealth Games are for fighting and shooting. Belfast's huge working-class estates support at least two dozen clubs, but what makes Holy Family unique is that for over half a century it has been easily the most successful and, despite its location, the only one that has consistently attracted both Catholics and Protestants even during the darkest days of conflict.

In this noisy, sweaty room with its bare floorboards and harsh strip lighting Gerry Storey, the club's veteran coach, trained the former world featherweight champion Barry McGuigan, four Olympians, 15 Commonwealth Games medallists and countless internationals. Their photographs, and posters advertising their fights, adorn the walls like some boxing Hall of Fame, interspersed with admonitions like 'Winners Don't Quit' and 'Quitters Don't Win'.

Here the Marquess of Queensberry's rules apply, not the gunman's. Here youths are offered discipline, purpose and an outlet for aggression. Here swearing, smoking, alcohol, drugs and – above all – sectarianism are forbidden, and offenders are ejected.

The club brings young Catholics and Protestants together in a manner normally impossible in rigidly segregated Belfast. It takes them to tournaments in Britain, Ireland and America. It keeps them out of trouble, as they themselves admit. Without boxing, 'I'd probably have wrecked the joint like everyone else,' confesses Tommy Waite, a 26-year-old Protestant from the Shankill who is the Irish bantamweight champion.

'All I wanted to do was keep kids off the street,' explains Gerry, a former dock worker who became the club's coach when an eye problem forced him to abandon his own promising career at the age of 21. He is now in his mid-sixties and has run the club on a shoestring for most of his adult life.

Holy Family was one of the inspirations for a club of the same name that featured in Jim Sheridan's 1998 film *The Boxer* starring Daniel Day-Lewis. The club falls foul of the IRA in the film, but not in real life. Those self-styled enforcers evidently recognise the role Holy Family plays in combating drugs, joyriding and other anti-social activities. 'They never interfere with us,' Gerry shouts above the din. 'They appreciate what I've done.'

He recalls the IRA once suspending a gun battle with the Army in the New Lodge Road in order to let him through. He remembers loyalist paramilitary godfathers summoning him to the Shankill one Sunday night in the mid-1970s and telling him to keep bringing teams into their communities – they even offered escorts. In the 1980s loyalist and republican prisoners invited him to coach them in the Maze, and several are now coaches themselves.

Gerry believes the IRA would long ago have turned the gym

into one of its drinking clubs had anyone but the club been
using it. He also believes that the IRA has been giving safe passage to Protestant boxers like Waite who venture nightly into the
heart of republican New Lodge. Because of that 'unwritten rule'
not one boy was so much as scratched in 30 years of sectarian
conflict.

My ultimate destination on this particular journey was the
coastal resort of Portstewart and the North West 200 motorcycle
race, the biggest event in Northern Ireland's sporting calendar –
bigger even than Glasgow Rangers versus Celtic football
matches. But that was a few days off, so I had plenty of time to
dawdle on the way.

The next morning I headed north up the Antrim Road, whose
lower stretches earned the sobriquet 'murder mile' during the
Troubles. Here the bars are still fortresses and the shops have
steel grilles across their windows. Here the police barred Belfast's
predominantly Catholic Cliftonville football club from playing
home games against Linfield, which has a big working-class
Protestant following, after riots in 1970.

In 1998 I'd gone to Solitude, Cliftonville's dilapidated stadium, to watch Linfield return for the first time in 28 years. It
was hardly a conventional game. The crowd was limited to
1,500, the Linfield fans were bussed in with a police escort from
the other side of the city, and they were heavily outnumbered by
police officers and journalists. For Belfast, however, the game
represented a major step back to normality.

Further up the Antrim Road the houses become bigger and
finer, and the side streets wider and leafier. There was a time
when this was the fashionable place to live, but then came the
Troubles. It was too close to the flashpoints and the affluent
middle classes fled, leaving behind some excellent schools and
Northern Ireland's only synagogue.

The latter is a circular brick building standing in its own peaceful gardens on the corner of Somerton Road. I went into the reception area, but there was a service in progress and I couldn't interrupt. Someone was chanting the Torah. I stood and listened for a minute, rather enjoying this novel sound in a land of diehard Protestants and Catholics, but it was all a little poignant.

There used to be a thriving Jewish community of at least 1,200 in this area, many of them driven from Eastern Europe by the pogroms of the 1880s. One of its number was Sir Otto Jaffe, Belfast's Lord Mayor in 1899 and 1904, though he himself was actually a prosperous linen merchant of German descent. Another was Gustav Wolff from Hamburg, who founded the Harland and Wolff shipyard. A third was Rabbi Herzog, who lived in No. 135 Cliftonpark Avenue where most of the houses have now been either demolished or abandoned. In 1918 his wife gave birth to a son, Chaim, who later fought in the Second World War, emigrated to Palestine, became an army general and ended up as President of Israel from 1983 to 1993. I'd like to report that Belfast made Chaim Herzog what he was, but unfortunately his father became the chief rabbi of Ireland and the family moved to Dublin when he was just nine months old.

Yet another member of this community at the beginning of the twentieth century was a woman of Polish origin called Rifka Levinson. She also lived in Cliftonpark Avenue, at No. 15. In 1908 her brother arrived on her doorstep with a suitcase full of stolen Russian roubles. A Bolshevik on the run who lived with her for the next two years, Maxim Maximovich Litvinov was a colourful character who wore a white suit and Panama hat, and carried a pistol and Ghurka knife because he believed the Russian secret police were after him. After the Russian revolution, he made his way to Moscow and became Stalin's foreign minister.

The synagogue was built in 1964 to replace an older one, but Belfast's Jewish community was already declining and the onset of the Troubles five years later hastened its demise. Members dispersed to England, Israel and America. The cultural centre was sold off to become a nursing home. The 600-seat auditorium was cut in half, and the barely 200 men, women and children who remain can't fill even that. There is no longer a rabbi, just a lay minister. Belfast's last kosher butcher closed in the late 1970s, and kosher meat now has to be imported from Manchester every six weeks. 'We have another ten or 12 years, and the last one left will put the lights out,' one member told me.

It will be a shame if that happens. Northern Ireland desperately needs more, not less, religious and cultural diversity. There is an old joke about a Jewish boy walking up the Shankill Road when some thugs accost him. 'Are you Protestant or Catholic?' they demand. 'Jewish,' he says. The thugs pause. 'A Protestant Jew or a Catholic Jew?' they ask finally. 'A Protestant Jew, of course,' he replies, and is allowed to go on his way.

At the top of the Antrim Road I found myself right beneath Cave Hill, its lower slopes adorned by the city's zoo and a Scottish baronial pile called Belfast Castle. To my right I enjoyed a stunning view back across the city and the lough. I hurried through Glengormley, a place of distinctly limited attractions, and was soon in open country where Ernest Sandford once again dictated my route.

He took me north-west to the village of Doagh, pronounced 'Doke', a few miles beyond Glengormley. Here a large stone obelisk in a little walled enclosure on the main street commemorates a linen spinner named John Rowan who lived from 1787 to 1858 and was, according to the inscription, 'the founder of one of the best engineering establishments in Ireland, the dispenser of employment on an extensive scale and the untiring advocate of improvement in art and science'.

Curiously the inscription fails to spell out Mr Rowan's particular claims to fame. He was another of those extraordinarily innovative Ulstermen. He invented not only an early form of piston ring still used in nuclear power plants, but Ireland's first steam-powered vehicle which he drove through Belfast on 5 January 1836 accompanied by a military band and a large, excited crowd.

'We rejoice that it has been accomplished by an almost unassisted native genius,' the *Belfast Commercial Chronicle* wrote of Mr Rowan's achievement in building the 'Perseverance'. 'We therefore trust that the singularly persevering inventor may reap the benefit of his ingenious discovery.'

As it happened Mr Rowan built no more vehicles, but he did start a long tradition of vehicle-building in Northern Ireland. John Dunlop developed the first successful pneumatic tyre. Jack Chambers designed the first Vauxhall car. In the early twentieth century Chambers and Fergus cars were built in Belfast, and in the 1930s Harry Ferguson developed the tractor. Rex McCandless was responsible for the 'featherbed' Norton motorbike which dominated world motorcycle racing in the early 1950s. Shorts, the aircraft manufacturers, briefly built three-wheeler Nobel bubble-cars in Northern Ireland before the advent of the Mini in 1959 destroyed the market.

Small companies that built cars like the Sullivan Special and the Devin came and went. George Dennison built lorries in Glengormley until Crane Freuhauf of Michigan bought him out in the 1960s. Racing cars are still produced in County Down by Crossle. Then of course there was John De Lorean, the tall, silver-haired American who coaxed vast grants from the government for a project that would bring jobs and hope to this troubled province. Just 8,583 of his revolutionary gull-winged sports cars had rolled off the production line at Dunmurry in south Belfast by the time the whole caboodle collapsed in February 1982 at an estimated cost to the taxpayer of nearly £80 million.

In my own rather clapped-out and distinctly unrevolutionary
Vauxhall Cavalier I drove on through Doagh and up a hill to a
Presbyterian church with a fabulous panorama across hundreds
of square miles of lush green farmland. The sun had come out,
and in the freshly mown graveyard was another little treasure I
would never have found without Mr Sandford's guidance.

The Stephenson family mausoleum was erected in 1837. The
vegetation sprouting from its cracks has hastened its crumbling,
but you can still recognise it for what it was – a miniature Taj
Mahal complete with a splendid pointed dome. It was apparently
the brainchild of a Stephenson who served in the Dragoon
Guards in India.

It was while admiring the Taj that I spotted the grave of a certain William Gault, who died in 1812 at the age of 61. 'He was
the first to establish a Sunday school in Ireland,' read the rather
unorthodox inscription, 'and he had to bear with much opposition and reproach from the prejudiced. But a better age has
arrived and all men now unite to approve his philanthropy and
bless his memory.'

People think of Northern Ireland as being divided between
Catholics and Protestants, but the divide between Presbyterians
like Mr Gault and the established church, the Anglican Church
of Ireland, was also great – and to some extent still is.

Another few miles of country lanes and rich farmland brought
me to the town of Ballymena. I had prepared for this moment by
reading not Mr Sandford but a publication called the *Ulster Joke
Book* that made Ballymena a particular butt of ridicule. The
theme was always the same. 'Why are 50p coins shaped the way
they are? So you can use a spanner to get them off a Ballymena
man,' ran one. Another had a Ballymena man counting his
change six times. 'What's the matter?' asked the shop assistant.
'Didn't I give you enough?' 'Yes, but only just,' the man replied.

As you will have deduced, Ballymena has a certain reputation.
It is said to be stuffed with parsimonious Scots Presbyterians and

frugal farmers, and to have more millionaires than any other town in the United Kingdom. I have no idea whether or not that's true, and I was certainly not about to quiz its citizens about their pecuniary status, but it did colour my outlook as I drove in past a large open-air market offering six bars of soap for £1 or nine toilet rolls for £1.50.

In the bustling town centre I parked outside Poundstretcher, and every window I looked in seemed to be advertising some bargain to lure the canny shopper. The Going Places travel agency was offering four nights in self-catering cottages in Holland for £44 including a 'free grocery starter pack worth £25'. Devlin's greengrocery was offering 1 lb of carrots, 1 lb of onions, a cabbage and a turnip for 99p. It is surely no accident that apart from the actor Liam Neeson and the Olympic pentathlete Mary Peters, the town's most illustrious son is Timothy Eaton who founded the Canadian chain-store Eatons.

I wandered past shops called Budget Shoes, Bargain King and Wyse Byse and spotted the tourist office, so in I went. The place doubled as a small museum whose central exhibit was an antique till. 'Is Ballymena really full of skinflints?' I asked the lady behind the desk, though I phrased the question a little more delicately than that.

I'd expected a flat denial, but to my astonishment she said yes. 'People here like to hold tightly on to their money,' she chuckled. 'They're quite thrifty. They do like a bargain.' She herself took her husband to McKillens Fashions every New Year's Day to 'rig him out because everything's half price'.

The business of Ballymena is business, to coin a phrase, but that is not the only manifestation of the town's Scottish Presbyterian roots. It boasts no fewer than eight Presbyterian churches; it elects that extreme Calvinist, Ian Paisley, as its MP. The people have an accent that sounds more Scottish than Irish, and Ballymena Academy's emblem is, appropriately, an industrious ant.

The town is the very buckle of Northern Ireland's bible belt where a strict Calvinistic moral code still prevails, but it is being slowly eroded by outside influences. Newcomers to the town's housing estates have brought a big drugs problem with them – the worst in Northern Ireland – and Ballymena's rigid observance of the Sabbath is under threat.

British chain stores like Tescos and Sainsburys have introduced Sunday opening, for example. The town's leisure centre only began opening on Sundays in the mid-1990s and was picketed for its pains. Not until 1999 did Ballymena rugby club play its first Sunday game – and that was away. The town's cricket club still refuses to play on Sundays. It did play one Sabbath game in 1997, because it had such a backlog of fixtures after a particularly sodden summer, but in Ballymena's version of *Chariots of Fire* half-a-dozen of its best players refused to turn out on religious grounds.

I could hardly leave Ballymena without buying something. As it happened, I needed some jeans. I found a pair for £12.99. The shopkeeper refused to sell them for £10, but I left a few minutes later having bought two pairs for £20, and drove happily on.

In the countryside a few miles beyond Ballymena I came to Cullybackey, a village whose name allegedly means 'the lame dog's leap'. It is a singularly undistinguished little place except for the fact that the father of Chester Arthur, America's twenty-first President, was born there. By the same token, Mr Arthur was a singularly undistinguished president. Even after eight years covering politics in America, I used to discover presidents I'd never even heard of – men like Millard Filmore or Franklin Pierce or William Harrison, who died of a cold within weeks of taking office. Mr Arthur didn't even win an election. He inherited the Oval Office in 1881 after another complete unknown, President James Garfield, was assassinated, and he failed to win his party's nomination to run in the next election.

I found 'Arthur Cottage' up a farm track behind the village. Unfortunately it was closed, but I picked up a leaflet which told me how it had been 'carefully restored to let you see how the Arthur family lived there two centuries ago'. I had rather naïvely imagined that the Arthurs had lived in a hovel, but not a bit of it. They lived in a beautifully thatched and whitewashed cottage with freshly painted doors and window-frames, neat flower-beds, picnic tables, litter-bins, floodlights and their very own car park. Heaven knows why they wanted to leave this rural idyll and emigrate to America.

I couldn't linger. I had an appointment in Dunloy, a staunchly nationalist village about 10 miles north of Cullybackey, but I didn't know quite who I was meant to be meeting.

I'd spent months trying to track down one of Northern Ireland's few remaining poteen-makers. Everyone says they can get you some of that fiery liquid, and I'd actually drunk some in a police officer's home. But finding a maker was a different matter. I had asked around, put out feelers, and discreetly made my interest known until one night I received a telephone call from a man I'd never met who said he understood I was interested in meeting a 'character'.

It was all delightfully cloak-and-dagger. He told me to meet him at 7 p.m. on this particular evening outside a baker's shop in Dunloy's main street. The morning's sun had long since vanished, it had turned into a wet, dank evening, and I felt somewhat apprehensive as I waited at the rendezvous. By 7.30 I had virtually decided the man wasn't coming when a car drew up alongside mine and a cheery fellow with a baseball cap and two days' stubble invited me to hop in.

Sean – not his real name – drove me eastwards towards the Glens of Antrim for about 15 minutes along windy little lanes that I would never recognise again. We finally pulled up outside a small bungalow in the middle of nowhere. 'Yer man will be sizing you up before he talks,' warned Sean. 'He'll want to be sure of you.' And in we walked to the most basic of front rooms.

There was a coal fire burning in the grate, a battered old sofa, an ancient rug on a lino floor, a couple of holy pictures on the walls. Assorted grandchildren and great-grandchildren were watching television. Sitting in an upright chair was 'yer man' himself, now well into his seventies with white hair, bushy white eyebrows, a red nose and substantial girth.

Let us call him Patrick. He sat down, and dispatched a grandson to fetch us both a glass of his 'holy water'. His short, wonderfully spherical wife came in with tea and plates of buttered drop scones, radiating good cheer and mercilessly teasing her husband of 50 years. Patrick was equally genial and seemed only too happy to talk about his art. The only trouble was that his brogue was so thick, and his teeth so few, that he might have been speaking in ancient Urdu. Sean had to act as interpreter.

It was emigrants from Ulster who carried the art of poteen or moonshine-making to America, where it still thrives in the Appalachian mountains. About the only places where the art is still practised in Northern Ireland, however, are the Sperrin Mountains and here near the equally wild Antrim glens. Patrick told me he had learned his skill more than forty years ago from Mickey McIlhatton, the 'King of the Glens'. 'I asked if I could watch him and he said "Aye". I watched and I thought I could do that myself.'

In those days Sean knew of at least two dozen poteen-makers, but people were poor, the demand was high and he sold around 1,000 bottles a year to supplement his farm labourer's income. He got caught twice. The first time he was fined £5 and the second – 30 years ago – £100, but he carried on regardless. 'If they caught me now it'd be jail,' he reckoned, but there is little chance he will be.

The local police turn a blind eye. Customs officers are far more concerned about the huge quantities of alcohol, tobacco and diesel being smuggled into Northern Ireland from the south. Patrick was nearly caught a few years ago when security forces searching for arms stumbled across some of his brew in a neighbour's hen-house, but with the Troubles dwindling even that danger has receded.

He took us into a shed behind his house where two 20-gallon barrels of fermenting 'wash' – sugar, treacle, grapes, raisins, yeast and water – were emitting a strong, sweet smell from beneath their canvas covers. His neighbours all knew when he was brewing, he chuckled.

After three weeks he strains the 'wash' into a milk churn and carries it into a tiny outhouse lit by a single naked light bulb. There he transfers it into a large steel boiler beneath which he places a propane gas ring. It takes an hour for the 'wash' to start boiling, by which time the room is sweltering. The steam is funnelled into a coiled copper pipe – the 'worm' – that spirals down into the blue barrel filled with cold water. The steam condenses and trickles out through a spout at the bottom as pure poteen.

'Don't drink it yet,' he warns. 'Wait till it gets weaker.' The first litre or two is 'poison' – so strong it would kill you. The entire 'run' takes about three hours, and produces enough to fill a dozen gin or vodka bottles with a fluid twice as strong.

Nowadays Patrick makes only about 100 bottles a year, which he sells by word of mouth for £6 each. He no longer drinks the stuff himself, having given it up a few years ago after a fearful binge. 'I was that sick I didna care if I died or no,' he said. His wife now does his tasting.

Patrick goes to Mass three or four times a week. He has six 'wains', 14 'grandwains' and five 'great-grandwains' to whom he is evidently devoted. He certainly doesn't consider himself a criminal – merely a provider of a service and a practitioner of a dying skill. He knows of nobody else in the area still making poteen, and none of his sons has shown any interest, but he has taught one of his teenage grandsons who plans to keep the art alive.

The evening became distinctly jolly, and ended with us performing various tests of Patrick's poteen. We lit pieces of newspaper covered in the stuff and watched it burn off with a bright blue flame while leaving the paper unsinged. We then did the same using our fingers instead of newspaper. Happily the poteen passed both tests, and Sean and I walked out into the night each clutching a couple of bottles as trophies.

I managed to get stopped for speeding on my way home. The officer fined me £40. Fortunately he ignored the two bottles of 'vodka' lying in full view on the seat beside me.

The following morning was clear and sunny as I resumed my journey at Dunloy. This time I actually went into the baker's shop to seek directions to my next port of call. Drive three or four miles up the back road towards Ballymoney, I was told, and look for a bungalow with a children's playhouse in the garden.

I found it all right. There was nothing remarkable about the bungalow, but its owner is a legend. If Mickey McIlhatton was 'King of the Glens', this man is 'King of the Roads'. His name is Joey Dunlop, MBE OBE. He has won more motorbike races than almost anyone else in history, and even in his late forties he continues to risk life and limb at 170 m.p.h. Nor does he do circuit races; he prefers road-racing, which is far more dangerous.

Motor-racing, in cars or on bikes, is another of Northern Ireland's particular passions. The province has produced no end of champions, the most recent being Eddie Irvine, and we have friends in and around genteel Helen's Bay who spend most of their holidays travelling to Grand Prix races around the world.

There are historical reasons for this. In the earliest days of motoring there was a strict 4 m.p.h. speed limit in Britain, and cars had to be preceded by men with red flags, but that law was widely disregarded in Ireland. When a British driver won the prestigious Gordon Bennett race in France in 1902, entitling Britain to stage the race the following year, Parliament passed a special act permitting it to take place on public roads in Ireland because it didn't want it in England.

That helped to spark Irish interest in motor sport, and soon after Ireland's partition in 1920 Northern Ireland's new Stormont government passed a bill to allow racing on the province's public roads. It remains the only part of the United Kingdom where road racing is permitted, though the Isle of Man allows it too. During the summer there are a couple of motorbike races every month in Northern Ireland, the biggest of which is the North West 200.

You can hardly write a travel book about Northern Ireland without writing about motor sport, and you can hardly do that without writing about Joey Dunlop, but he is an elusive man. He owns a bar in Ballymoney, and I'd written to him there asking if I could talk to him but he never replied. I telephoned several times and left messages, but he never called back. In desperation I found out where he lived and decided simply to arrive. Knowing nothing of motor-racing, I had this vision of Joey as some aggressive, leather-clad Hell's Angel, so it was with some trepidation that I knocked on his front door.

There was a Mini parked in the drive, but it seemed nobody was at home. I wandered round the back and heard a radio playing in a shed. I looked in, and there was a slight, silver-haired man in a dirty blue-checked shirt and jeans working on a stripped-down bike. He looked like neither a sportsman nor a legend. 'I'm looking for Joey Dunlop,' I said. 'That's me,' he finally replied in a murmur.

There was nothing faintly aggressive about Joey – perhaps he reserved that for the racetrack. He was a diffident, soft-spoken man who was at first reluctant to say anything. 'I'm very busy,' he explained apologetically. 'I've got to get ready for the North West

200.' I pleaded, he finally relented and we chatted while he worked, but Joey was clearly a man who expressed himself more through his racing than his mouth.

He'd been competing since his late teens, he told me in an accent almost as broad as Patrick's. He'd won five world titles, 23 Isle of Man TT titles, 13 North West titles and heaven knows what besides, but he'd also had dozens of spills. He'd broken his collar bone 14 times, his back, his leg, his ribs, his shoulder-blades. He held up a hand to show where he'd lost the end of a finger. He used to do circuit racing, he said, but he'd given it up because a broken wrist prevented him changing gears fast enough. Anyway, road-racing was 'the way we're brought up in Ireland'.

He did it for the thrill, for the excitement, for that indescribable feeling you got when you crossed the line first, he said. Did he ever think of retiring? 'I think about it now and again. I think about it until the next race comes along,' he replied with a smile. 'It's a bit like smoking. Once you start it's hard to stop.' Didn't it put him off seeing colleagues killed? 'It does at the time.'

The bike Joey was preparing was a 125cc Honda. Next to it was a 750cc Superbike. In the other half of the shed were three more bikes of intermediate sizes. The place was stuffed with machinery, tools and spare parts. Joey still goes to two dozen meetings a year, and rides four or five races at each, but nowadays he'll only go flat out if he gets a good start, he said. Nowadays 'I enjoy working on bikes more than I do riding them.'

Joey relaxed a bit; he laughed when I referred to his reputation for drinking the night before a race. 'If I did things like that I wouldn't be here now,' he said. His wife, Linda, watched some of his races, but no longer worried: 'She's been used to it that long.' Fortunately his two eldest children were daughters, but his two sons were growing up and he was concerned they'd want to follow in his footsteps. 'I'd rather they didn't.'

He described the North West as 'a family outing', though it seemed to me that watching your father dice with death was a curious form of pleasure. It was not his favourite course, however. About twenty years earlier both his brother-in-law, Mervyn Robinson, and a close friend, Frank Kennedy, had been killed on it. 'I've never really liked the course ever since,' he said. 'It's still on my mind whenever I go back.'

I left Joey tinkering with his bikes and drove on up the road into Ballymoney, which is less than 20 miles from Ballymena but, in the usual way of things in Northern Ireland, has a subtly different ethos, accent and vocabulary. A local could instantly tell which of the two you were from.

Ballymoney is a small market town that produced the winner of the marathon in the 1912 Olympics, but it is another of those places that I'm afraid I'll remember for all the wrong reasons.

On the town's southern edge is the loyalist Carnany estate. At the height of the province-wide riots that erupted after the Orange Order's Drumcree parade was blocked in July 1998, Richard, Mark and Jason Quinn – three young brothers aged from seven to eleven – were burned alive here when their house was petrol-bombed by members of the Ulster Volunteer Force in the small hours of a Sunday morning. It was an atrocity so dreadful that the riots stopped almost instantly.

There were three things that really struck me at the time. One was the complete lack of privacy on these estates. Everyone knows exactly who is who. The Quinn brothers' mother was a Catholic, and the previous week almost every other Catholic living on the estate had received through the post a bullet and a UVF greetings card bearing the words 'Get Out Now'. Within ten days of the three boys' deaths, an eighth of the approximately 200 families on the estate had applied to be moved.

Another thing was that the police soon knew precisely who the arsonists were, but were able to charge and convict only one man, the driver. Two-thirds of all the 3,600 killings of the

Troubles remain unresolved. The problem is lack of cooperation from terrified local communities, witness intimidation, and a judicial system tilted heavily in favour of defendants.

The third thing was the fundamental decency of the vast majority of people in Ballymoney in particular, and Northern Ireland in general. Thousands of Catholics and Protestants demonstrated their grief and outrage in the only way they knew how – by attending the boys' funeral. 'I couldn't do anything else,' one elderly Protestant gentleman told me as he stood, close to tears, in the huge overflow crowd outside the Church of Our Lady and St Patrick. 'It's terrible. It's a crime against our community.'

Out of a sort of morbid curiosity, I now found myself turning into the Carnany estate instead of driving straight on into Ballymoney. It was nearly a year after the fire, and workmen were demolishing the row of houses that included the burned-out shell of the Quinns' old home. These were to be replaced by a small play park commemorating the three dead brothers.

Not much else had changed. The kerbstones and lamp-posts were still painted red, white and blue. Ulster flags – red crosses on a white background – still hung outside several homes. Paramilitary slogans were still daubed on the walls of an estate now almost entirely purged of Catholics. On one side of a shed at the entrance to the estate someone had scrawled, in very large letters, the highly questionable proposition: 'UFF – Simply the Best'.

North of Ballymoney the country grows ever more gorgeous – smooth green hills, little white cottages and bright yellow gorse. The air is brilliantly clear, and in front of you the land gently rises until it ends abruptly in a jagged line beyond which lies the vivid blue Atlantic.

Before I reached the rugged cliffs of the North Antrim coast, however, I came to Bushmills, another place where the ancient art of distilling is still practised. Unlike Patrick's operation, however, this one is legal. In fact the Bushmills Distillery is the oldest licensed whiskey distillery in the world, having been authorised by James I in 1608, though whether it has been in continuous production since that date is somewhat less clear.

Irish monks allegedly brought the art – or at least an earthenware vessel called an 'alembic' used for distilling purposes – back to Ireland from the Middle East in the sixth century. 'Uisce beatha' or 'water of life' was the early Irish name for the product. That was shortened to 'fuiske', which was then anglicised into 'whiskey'. Manufacture of the Scottish version began much later, and is spelt without the 'e'.

The recipe hasn't changed much over the centuries, only the quantities in which it's made. In fact, you could get drunk on the smell inside the distillery. A guide called Paddy showed me how 'malted' Irish barley, now imported from the south, is turned into 'grist', 'mash', 'wort', 'wash', 'feints' and finally 'spirit' or – to put it in layman's language – crushed, stewed in water from a local stream called St Columb's Rill, left to ferment, then distilled three times in great copper stills. Scotch is only distilled twice, and American bourbon once.

The spirit is then diluted to lower its strength, put into oak barrels previously used for bourbon, port or sherry, and stored in large bonded warehouses. Only when it has spent three years maturing can it legally be called whiskey. The cheapest Bushmills is blended with coarser grain whiskey and bottled after about five years, while the most expensive 'single malt' is left for 16 years. In 1975 some bright spark had the idea of selling 350 barrels for $5,000 each which were allowed to mature until late 1999. Each purchaser then received about 250 bottles of 25-year-old whiskey in time for their millennium celebrations.

Bushmills and the distillery are brilliantly marketed, with dreamy pictures of idyllic Irish landscapes and constant references to tradition and much talk of how Bushmills Malt is becoming 'a legend among whiskeys'. But personally I found Patrick's poteen-making more romantic. Unlike Bushmills, he has not been owned in quick succession by Great Universal Stores, Bass Charrington, Seagram's, the Irish Distillers Group and now Pernod Ricard of France, which also owns almost every other whiskey distillery in Ireland. As I said, he produces just 100 bottles a year which he sells by word of mouth, compared with Bushmills' 2½ million litres which is shipped to 50 countries. His poteen is also a fraction of the price – and twice the strength.

Bushmills is, of course, of infinitely higher quality, but I have to confess to being a total dunce when it comes to whiskeys – or for that matter whiskies. At the end of my tour Paddy took me to the distillery's bar where I proved an immense disappointment to my hosts. The barmaid poured shots of the cheaper blended whiskey, the costly 12-year-old single malt, and one in between. She then mixed them up. I managed to identify the best as the worst and vice versa.

As I was leaving, I noticed a framed letter on the wall written by George Bush when he was America's vice-president. 'I just wanted to thank you for the photograph of the outdoor sign that you sent me. I found it very clever indeed,' he said. Next to the letter was a copy of the photograph. Taken in Ballyporeen, County Tipperary, just before President Reagan visited his ancestral home there in 1984, it showed a CIA man standing on a ladder with a paintbrush and amending an advertisement to which the White House had evidently taken exception: 'Bush – The President's Choice' it read. The agent was painting out the 'P'.

Bushmills is a pleasant little village with a nice old hotel and, in the middle of its main junction, the inevitable memorial to those who died in the First World War. Just as every little town in the American Deep South has a memorial to Confederate soldiers who died in the Civil War, so practically every town or village in Northern Ireland has one commemorating the count-less Ulstermen who died fighting for Britain. They are more than mere memorials, of course. In America they are statements of defiance. In Northern Ireland they serve as constant reminders of the sacrifices the province has made for Britain – and the support it expects in return.

Northern Ireland's memorials differ from those elsewhere in Britain in two respects. They are usually very warlike – this one, for example, is topped by a statue of a soldier wielding a rifle with a fixed bayonet. They also tend to focus much more on the First than the Second World War. There's a very good reason for that. Nobody here advertises the fact, but the government felt unable to impose conscription on this unsettled province in the Second World War and relatively few signed up.

I could hardly write a travel book about Northern Ireland and not go to the Giant's Causeway, just three miles beyond Bushmills on the North Antrim coast. Nor did I have any wish to avoid the place. I'd been there many times before with visitors, and it was always a pleasure. The Causeway may have been des-ignated a World Heritage site like the Grand Canyon, the Great Wall of China and the Great Barrier Reef, but it is rarely crowded and eminently accessible.

From the visitors' centre – largely financed by the European Union, like the one at the Bushmills distillery – there is a road down to where the causeway juts out into the sea, and even a small bus if you're feeling really lazy. But my favourite way of approaching it is to walk along the cliff top from which you can not only see miles out to sea, but look right down on what appears from that height to be a rather insignificant little promontory. After another half-mile there is a steep path down the cliff face past a cluster of 40-foot-high basalt columns called the Giant's Organ. At the bottom you double back along a grassy track and you can't really see the Causeway until you're actually standing on it.

It is at that moment that its uniqueness really hits you. You suddenly find yourself standing on a rocky spit formed from roughly 40,000 upright hexagonal columns, each of a different height but slotted together as neatly as a perfect honeycomb. The tops of some of the columns are concave and filled with water. Others are convex and warmed by the sun. The higher columns form a great hump and central spine that runs away from the shore until it vanishes beneath the foam and spray of the Atlantic rollers.

The prosaic explanation for the Causeway is that it was formed by volcanic disturbances 50 or 60 million years ago. I prefer the legend that the giant Finn McCool built it so that he could lure his rival, Benandonner, across from Scotland. Benandonner came, but he was much bigger than Finn had expected so Finn's wife quickly disguised her husband as a baby, complete with bonnet. Benandonner was so impressed by the baby's size that he feared to meet the father and fled back to Scotland, tearing up the Causeway as he went.

The other funny thing about the Causeway is that some people come away enraptured, while others remain quite indifferent. It was always thus. 'One of the most wonderful sights that, perhaps, is to be seen in the world,' wrote Mrs Delaney in 1758. 'Worth seeing? Yes, but not worth going to see,' was Samuel Johnson's verdict in 1776. 'Mon dieu! And have I travelled a hundred and fifty miles to see that?' exclaimed William Thackeray when he first set eyes on it in 1842.

I find all this coastline impressive, not just the Causeway. Its rugged cliffs are broken by perfect white sandy beaches that could be in Antigua, not Antrim, were the weather 20 degrees warmer. It is also dotted with the romantic remains of ruined castles, the most dramatic of which teeters precariously atop a sheer rocky outcrop just a few miles west of the Causeway.

Dunluce Castle is linked to the mainland by a single narrow bridge. Below its jagged walls a long, deep cave runs down through the rock to the sea, affording a safe way in and out when the castle was besieged. Even Thackeray was impressed by Dunluce, writing of its grey towers 'standing upon a leaden rock and looking as if some old, old princess of old, old fairy times were dragon-guarded within'.

Exactly how old Dunluce is nobody really knows, though it certainly dates back to the fourteenth century.

In 1584 the English captured it from Sorley Boy MacDonnell, but almost immediately lost it again when one of Sorley Boy's men, employed in the castle, hauled various MacDonnells up the cliff in a basket.

In 1588 the MacDonnells strengthened the place with cannon and treasure salvaged from the *Girona*, a Spanish vessel that sank offshore as she limped homewards with 1,300 men aboard after the rout of the Spanish Armada. Just nine survived, and 260 of the dead are allegedly buried in the ruined church nearby.

In 1636 the 2nd Earl of Antrim built an elegant manor house inside the walls for his new bride, Lady Catherine Manners, but she loathed the sound of the sea and abandoned the place when part of the kitchen fell into the waves on a stormy night in 1639, carrying several servants with it.

Dunluce has been battered by wind and sea for centuries, and has witnessed plenty of bloody battles in its time, but I arrived to find it tranquil and deserted except for a couple of men mowing the grass in the late afternoon sun. From the vertiginous walls I looked down on the gulls and the heaving water below. To the north the sea washed around the odd rocky islet as it stretched away to the horizon, while to the west I could just make out the misty hills of Donegal's Inishowen peninsula. To this part of Northern Ireland, at least, peace had finally returned.

I stopped briefly at the ruined church, but was unable to find any memorial to the *Girona*'s dead so drove on another few miles to Northern Ireland's 'Riviera' – the adjacent resort towns of Portrush and Portstewart.

Portrush has a celebrated golf course, one of the world's 'top 20' along with the Royal County Down in Newcastle, but it is the Blackpool of the pair. Portstewart is normally a little more genteel, more Bournemouth than Blackpool, except when preparing (as now) for the North West 200. My immediate preoccupation, however, was another sporting event – Portstewart Football Club's last home game of the season against Coleraine University in one of Northern Ireland's obscure junior leagues.

I had some trouble finding the pitch as it was hidden away in the middle of a housing estate and supporters were not exactly flocking to the game. I finally arrived half-way through the first half, but that didn't matter as it was not the game I had come to see. I had come to find out what happened to once-great football players when their glory days were over.

It was a fine if rather chilly evening, and beyond the rooftops the sea glistened in the setting sun. There were a few dozen spectators on the touchline. I couldn't see my quarry, but I could hear him. Harry Gregg, the former Manchester United star who was once the world's most expensive goalkeeper and hero of the 1958 Munich air crash, was bellowing from the dug-out. 'Stay up,' he shouted at Portstewart's players. 'Get on to them.' It was a very, very far cry from the days when this man played before 50,000 adoring fans in the cauldron of Old Trafford.

Mr Gregg owns a hotel on Portstewart's promenade whose walls are covered with photographs, shirts and other memorabilia from his years with Manchester United. As you eat your cornflakes you can read the front-page story of the *Manchester Evening News* headlined 'United Cup XI Crash: 28 Die' and examine pictures of the wreckage.

I'd called him several times during the previous few days and left messages, but he hadn't phoned back. At half-time I approached him with the same sort of apprehension I'd felt when knocking on Joey Dunlop's door that morning, for he was notoriously prickly. He was wearing a track-suit and Atlanta Falcons baseball cap. He looked in remarkably good shape for a man in his late sixties, and still had the clean-cut look of comic-book sporting heroes. He stared at me with piercing blue eyes, then spoke: 'So you're the persistent bastard that keeps telephoning me?' Finally, as I'd come so far, he agreed to give me a few minutes after the game.

Portstewart romped home 5–1. The team and its followers adjourned to the bar. Harry took off his baseball cap to reveal silver hair, ordered a lemonade and lime and lit the first of many cigarettes. My few minutes came and went, but Harry didn't stop. In fact he was only warming up. For all his outward aggression he obviously loved an audience. The minutes turned to hours as he reminisced about his glory days with the likes of Bobby Charlton, Denis Law and George Best in the same way that an old soldier talks of bygone wars.

It was a story tinged with pathos. Harry was born and raised just four miles up the road in Windsor Avenue, Coleraine. He was signed by a Belfast club called Linfield at the age of 15 and progressed to Doncaster Rovers. In 1957 he helped Northern Ireland beat England 3–2 at Wembley for the first time ever, and within weeks had transferred to Matt Busby's incomparable Manchester United for what was then a world record fee for a goalkeeper of £23,750.

Three months later he was pulling his fellow 'Busby babes' from the wreckage of the plane bringing the team home from a European Cup match against Red Star Belgrade. After a refuelling stop in Munich, the aircraft had crashed on its third attempt to take off in dreadful conditions. Harry returned repeatedly to the burning fuselage, rescuing a baby girl and her mother, but 23 passengers died including eight of his teammates. Harry was saved, he reckoned, because he'd cleaned up in a poker game and gone to sit near the bulkheads. Most of the remaining poker school were killed.

He was playing football again within two weeks. He kept goal for United for another nine years, won championship and FA Cup winner's medals, and was named the world's best goal-keeper in 1958 when he helped tiny Northern Ireland reach the World Cup quarter-finals in Sweden. He was also awarded an MBE.

When United bought Alex Stepney in 1966, Harry left to become Stoke City's player-coach. Some stars quit when they're on top, while others slowly fade away. Harry was one of the latter. He played his last game for Stoke in 1968, and was succeeded between the posts by Gordon Banks. Apart from a brief return to Manchester United as goalkeeping coach, and stints in the Middle East and Hong Kong, he spent the rest of his coaching career drifting around the lower divisions of English football with less-than-glamorous clubs like Shrewsbury, Swansea, Crewe, Swindon and near-bankrupt Carlisle.

After he finally parted company with Carlisle in the late 1980s, his sister told him that a hotel overlooking Portstewart's little harbour was for sale. His wife persuaded him to buy it, and so his life came full circle – from Windsor Avenue in Coleraine to the Windsor Hotel just down the road.

Running the hotel was 'the hardest work', he said. He misses the camaraderie of football clubs. He misses the limelight, and recounted with evident pleasure how someone had recently come up to shake his hand while he was waiting at the Belfast ferry port: 'It's nice when people recognise you.' He hopes people will remember him as 'a decent old goalkeeper'. But although the glamour has gone and Portstewart is hardly Manchester United, he still gets pleasure from coaching the team and bringing on new players. 'It's still the same ball. It's still round,' he said.

Nor has the competitive urge yet left him. A few months earlier he had appeared at a charity event on Portstewart's beach. 'I stood in a goal and was supposed to let the kids beat me,' he recalled with a laugh. 'I just couldn't do it.'

On the eve of the big race, I drove back up to Portstewart from Belfast on a glorious evening when the sky was impossibly blue, the gorse impossibly yellow and the fields impossibly green. For once, however, the road was far from empty.

An estimated 100,000 spectators flock to the North West 200 each year, and I found myself in a slow-moving queue of cars with a stream of giant motorbikes weaving in and out of the oncoming traffic. At a junction just before Ballymoney I passed a fearful smash, with one car completely written off and firemen cutting someone from another.

Portstewart was jam-packed, or 'bunged' as they say in Northern Ireland. The pavements and car parks were thick with motorbikes. Harry's hotel was fully booked two years ago for this weekend, and every hotel and bed-and-breakfast within 30 miles was chock-a-block. However, a few days earlier I'd taken the precaution of telephoning Ross Wilson, the sculptor responsible for the statue of C.S. Lewis's magic wardrobe in East Belfast and the only person I even vaguely knew in Portstewart.

Ross's wife, Liz, runs a bed-and-breakfast on the seafront. That, too, was completely full, but no matter. Would I mind staying with Liz's mother in Coleraine, asked Ross? Of course not, I replied, and so it was that an elderly but hospitable widow named Doreen Caskey ended up having a complete stranger sleeping in the spare room of her bungalow that night.

What I didn't realise until Ross delivered me to Doreen's house was that she did not live alone. She looked after another daughter, Aileen, who had been grievously injured when a young man returning from a motor rally some ten years earlier had hit her car head-on.

Aileen, who was then engaged to be married, lay in a coma for many weeks and her doctors had wanted to turn off her life-support system. Miraculously she had survived, but the wedding never took place, her right side was entirely paralysed and she was confined to a wheelchair. She could barely read or watch television because her eyes were affected. She couldn't speak, but with her left hand she could tap out messages on a little machine that spoke what she wrote.

In this way we conversed until nearly midnight. Her mental faculties were entirely unaffected. As she told me what had happened to her, she appeared remarkably free of bitterness. Before going to bed I asked her what she thought about motorbike racers who knowingly take the risk of ending up like her. I'd expected her to say they were mad, but not a bit of it. 'I enjoy watching them,' she typed. 'It's a brave sport.'

The next morning dawned clear and sunny, and I drove over to Liz and Ross's house for breakfast. It was right on the seafront, with a fabulous view across strand and sea to the distant Inishowen peninsula. The house had been taken over by a bunch of high-spirited bikers from Scotland who had been coming to the North West 200 for the past 12 years or so. The meet was the inevitable topic of conversation as we ate our Ulster Fries, and in no time a scrap-metal merchant from Ayrshire was offering to take me round the course on his bike before the racing began. He was called John, bore an uncanny resemblance to the actor Simon Callow, and had already regaled us with the story of how he'd lost his licence for six months after being caught doing 103 m.p.h. But naturally I accepted.

I borrowed a jacket and helmet with darkened visor that made me look like Darth Vader. We went round the back of the house and there was John's bike – a huge 1100cc Honda Blackbird. We jumped on, I heard a deep rumble from somewhere beneath me, and we roared off with such violent acceleration that I nearly fell off the back.

The course is nine miles long – a triangle between Portstewart, Coleraine and Portrush. There were still a couple of hours before the racing began, but the roads were already stiff with cars and motorbikes. John was entirely unfazed. He roared down the country stretches at 80 m.p.h., weaving in and out while I clung on behind, more exhilarated than fearful.

I began to understand why road-racing fans consider circuit racing 'sterile' – and why most circuit riders will not road-race. Circuits are purpose-built and obstacle-free, with cambered corners. Road-racing is a throwback to an earlier, more daring age before the nanny state took over. For this occasion the local council had removed the traffic islands and groomed the road surfaces. The organisers had tied straw bales around the telegraph poles, erected some fencing and painted the kerbstones white – which made a welcome change from red, white and blue – but that was about the extent of it. We hurtled round roundabouts, over grates and manhole covers, down streets lined with brick walls, lamp-posts and metal road signs – and we were travelling at half the speed the racers would be doing. 'If you crash, you're in someone's front room,' John shouted back at me.

It was hard to establish exactly how many riders had been killed at the North West 200 since it first began in 1929, but ten had been killed since 1972 and this is one of the safest road-races. Just four days earlier a 45-year-old rider named Donny Robinson from Cullybackey had died after coming off at a roundabout while practising in the rain – the third member of his family to die on motorbikes. For today's races there would be 22 ambulances, 26 first-aid posts and 12 doctors scattered around the course, plus two doctors on motorbikes, two cars equipped with the latest heart equipment and an emergency helicopter. Back in the 1970s the organisers had begun asking the riders if they were Protestants or Catholics, lest they needed last rites, but the riders understandably suspected there were ulterior motives for the question and refused to answer.

Even John was forced to slow down as we turned left in Portrush and headed along the seafront to the starting line past burger stands, programme sellers and fields jam-packed with tents and caravans. By this point the traffic had come to a virtual standstill. The world and his wife, all dressed in brightly coloured biking gear, seemed to be making for the paddocks where in a veritable city of vans and pantechnicons the riders and their mechanics were making last-minute adjustments to their machines. In this sport at least the riders remain just regular guys, not prima donnas, and happily chat to their fans.

The excitement was building almost palpably. The biggest crowd of all had gathered around Joey Dunlop's predictably modest van, and the man himself was quietly readying his bikes with the same calm smile I'd seen a few days earlier. If he was tense, he didn't show it. Not until the riders were actually summoned for the first race did he slip into the back of the van to change into his leathers and trademark yellow helmet. As he did so, an assistant wheeled his silver 250cc Honda to the start line where the noise of revving engines was positively deafening. 'Keep 'er lit, Joey!' read a banner draped over a trackside fence. The Clerk of the Course stepped aside and 60 brightly coloured bikes sped off for a warm-up lap.

Five minutes later they were back on the grid. Mechanics were wrapping mini-electric blankets around the bikes' tyres to keep them warm and enhance their grip, but something was wrong. Joey's bike was missing. There was no time to find out what had happened before a klaxon sounded. Girlfriends, groupies and mechanics rapidly removed their equipment from the track, and the Clerk of the Course held up a wooden sign with the instruction 'Engage Gear'. The flag fell, and with a mighty roar a pack of nearly 60 jostling bikes took off down the straight with just inches between them.

I'd never watched a motorbike race before, and it struck me as a really peculiar pastime. In no other sport can spectators witness such a tiny fraction of the action. The bikes vanished in seconds, and we didn't see them for another four minutes or so when they flashed past again at an astonishing speed. In between we had to rely on commentary from the loudspeakers to follow what was happening.

Six laps later a Scotsman named Callum Ramsay took the chequered flag. Joey's bike had seized up, someone informed me, but I wasn't too perturbed as there were still five more races to go.

The next race was for superbikes – those up to 1000cc. You could have told that simply from the deep roar of the engines, compared with which the 250cc bikes had emitted high-pitched whines. This time the start was more like one of those scenes from a Vietnam war movie when the thunderous noise of incoming helicopters makes the entire cinema vibrate, except that it was also accompanied by a powerful smell of exhaust and burning rubber. It was a terrifying, awesome sight, rendered all the more riveting by the knowledge that one tiny miscalculation would spell disaster not just for the rider who made it, but for several others right behind him.

For this race I had repositioned myself next to a chicane – a deliberate twist in the course to slow the bikes down. The first riders sped through it, their knees grazing the ground as they leaned first one way and then the other on their half-ton steeds and did virtual wheelies as they accelerated away. Then suddenly one rider cut the corner too fine. What followed seemed to happen in slow motion. His front wheel reared skywards right in front of me; he was thrown off, landed heavily on the small of his back and was hurled across the road where he cracked his head against the opposite kerb and lay motionless. The bike careered towards the crowd, hit a steward and stopped just inches from a bank of terrified spectators.

The rider lay there, apparently lifeless, as other stewards frantically waved red flags to stop the rest of the bikes. Ambulances and the motorbike doctors raced to his assistance. He was carried away on a stretcher with serious head and chest injuries and a broken leg. Half of me was horrified, but the other half felt as if I'd won the lottery on my very first attempt.

I didn't know it then, but I'd backed a loser that day. After a brief interlude the race was rerun, but Joey came in seventh and a young Yorkshireman named David Jefferies won his first-ever North West title with an average lap speed of 120 m.p.h. 'I'm absolutely over the moon,' the winner exclaimed.

In the 600cc race Jefferies won again and Joey came in eleventh. 'I must admit, I'm over the moon,' Jefferies declared once more before calling his father on a mobile phone. That was followed by the race for 125cc bikes, which sounded like a swarm of angry hornets. Joey came in tenth – 'This is certainly not going to be the year of Joey Dunlop,' remarked the commentator.

This chapter was supposed to end with a string of victories for Joey, but he simply refused to follow my script. In the second superbike race he retired to the pits with mechanical problems after one lap, and Jefferies grabbed an astonishing third win. 'Sweet fucking hell! Yessss!' the young man cried as he tore his helmet from his sweating head. 'This is unbelievable,' he said.

In the final race Joey's bike seized up on the very first lap. 'What a very disappointing day for Joey Dunlop,' proclaimed the commentator, but it didn't really matter. The good-humoured crowd talked motorbikes, soaked up the atmosphere and basked in the sun, their common interest generating an easy camaraderie. They whooped and cheered as men and machines flashed past a backdrop of cliffs and dazzling sea. They had seen a new champion emerge, but Joey's place in their hearts – and in the history of road-racing – was assured long ago.

The following summer Joey Dunlop was killed, racing in Estonia. More than 50,000 people – Protestant and Catholic – attended his funeral in Ballymoney.

8

Bowls and Bullets

It is a fine day in late May, and I'm walking away from the City Hall down Howard Street where, in 1984, loyalists came within an ace of assassinating Gerry Adams as he was being driven from a court appearance. Being lunchtime, I turn left into Great Victoria Street and duck into another of Belfast's great pubs, the Crown Liquor Saloon.

Some people, especially travel writers, seem able to go into pubs and instantly strike up lively conversations with all around them. I'm afraid I'm not one of them. I met no great characters as I enjoyed my pint and a large plate of beef-and-ale pie. I did admire my surroundings, however, for the Crown is an almost pristine Victorian gin palace that miraculously survived the IRA's many attacks on the Europa – the world's most bombed hotel – directly across the street.

A young man called Michael Flanagan created the Crown in the 1890s after travelling extensively in Italy and Spain, and he evidently felt the staid and rather prissy Belfast of his time needed something a little exotic. He imported skilled craftsmen and the finest materials, and the result is an Aladdin's cave of mirrors, mosaics, marble and mahogany, of granite counters, oak casks, carved woodwork and painted windows. Even the loos are tiled masterpieces, though the Durex machine strikes a slightly jarring note. The place is so exuberantly, extravagantly ornate that Sir John Betjeman called it a 'many-coloured tavern', and in 1978 it was acquired by the National Trust which is more used to protecting its properties from dry rot and rising damp than terrorist bombs.

Little has changed over the past century. The place is still lit by gas-lamps. Customers still sit in little wooden 'snugs' – or cubicles – with closing doors, bells for summoning barmen, and carved lions and griffins. There are still gunmetal plates for striking matches. The engraved front windows were destroyed during the bombings of the Europa, but have been faithfully recreated.

Just outside the swing doors there is a mosaic crown in the floor. The story is that Flanagan's wife was an ardent Unionist and chose the pub's name; he – a nationalist – got his own back by placing a crown where customers could wipe their feet on it. Amply fed, I stepped over the crown, retrieved my car from a car park just behind the equally ornate Grand Opera House across the road, and sped off south on the M1 motorway out of Belfast. Within 20 minutes I was being admitted through the steel doors of the legendary – and far from ornate – Maze prison a little beyond Lisburn.

The Maze – which should perhaps be protected by the National Trust as well – has a history as colourful as that of Alcatraz. It began life in 1971 as a series of makeshift prison huts or 'cages' erected on an old airfield to house internees – terrorist suspects detained without trial. It was known in those days as Long Kesh, and its alumni still call it 'the Kesh'.

The inmates organised themselves along military lines, reinforced each other's political beliefs, and developed long-term strategy. They enjoyed 'special category status' to distinguish them from regular criminals, but when internment ended in 1975 the government removed that special status and in doing so triggered the subsequent 'blanket' and 'dirty' protests.

The inmates had burned down much of the Maze in 1974, and in 1976 they were moved into eight new H-blocks. The IRA prisoners refused to wear prison uniform and began wrapping themselves in blankets. In 1978, when 300 'blanket men' were harassed while slopping out, they stopped washing and began smearing their excrement across their cell walls.

The 'dirty protest' was succeeded by the 1981 hunger strike. Bobby Sands, aged 26, and nine other republicans demanding political status starved themselves to death. This helped change the course of the Troubles. Some 30,000 voters elected Sands to parliament in a by-election shortly before he died. Two other hunger strikers were also elected to the Irish parliament. The republican movement realised its political potential, and began to consider the advantages of unarmed struggle.

The strike also won the prisoners de facto political status. They were allowed their own clothes, and excused prison work. In 1983 – the year 38 IRA prisoners staged the biggest breakout in British prison history after hijacking a food lorry – loyalist and republican prisoners were segregated. Over the following decade the regime became increasingly liberal as the authorities reasoned that a prison housing 500 terrorists could only be run with their cooperation.

By the time of the 1998 Good Friday peace accord, the authorities secured the perimeter, the inmates ran their own wings and guards entered only with their permission. They had computers, mobile phones, generous arrangements for compassionate and Christmas leave. Then suddenly it was all over. The accord provided for the release of all paramilitary prisoners by the summer of 2000, and the Maze began emptying as fast as it had filled.

I had telephoned the prison service and asked to visit this unique testament to the Troubles while it was still in use. A German television crew had made the same request, so we were taken in together. A heavy steel door in the 2½-mile outer wall swung open to admit our vehicles. We were photographed, body-searched and taken into the prison's inner sanctum through a bewildering series of steel gates and grilles and airlocks. There were notices offering the 1,100 prison officers advice on redundancy and retraining, and advertisements for 'HMP Maze Tie Badges £1.50 each. Get One Before You Go.'

Inside the inner wall my immediate sense was of space and light. The sun was shining and the buildings were low, well-spaced and divided by broad roadways. But then I looked up and saw the watch-towers, the ubiquitous security cameras, the coiled barbed wire on top of every wall and the great long cables stretched over our heads to prevent prisoners escaping by helicopter.

An officer – let us call him Albert – showed us a little walled-off enclave containing a memorial to 29 of his colleagues who were killed during the Troubles, most assassinated while off-duty. We walked past the hospital where the hunger strikers died, past a prison chapel inside a giant cage, and past H-block Six where republican inmates shot dead Billy Wright in December 1997 as the infamous Loyalist Volunteer Force leader sat in a van taking him to the visitors' centre. For some reason loyalist paramilitaries always seem to have nicknames like 'Mad Dog' and 'Swinger'. Wright was always known as 'King Rat'.

Our destination was H-block Eight, and it was quite extraordinary. The wings had been vacated by IRA prisoners a few months earlier, and left exactly as they were when the men moved out.

The cells were still strewn with old shoes, clothes, tooth-brushes, air fresheners, ash-trays and unwashed coffee mugs with mould growing in the bottom. In one cell a withered car-nation sat in a jam-jar on the window ledge. On the walls were murals of gunmen, football posters, maps of County Donegal and the scribbled names of the inmates and the date of their release. In the kitchen there were still jars of Lea & Perrins sauce on the shelves, and the week's menu on the wall – 'Tuesday: Liver, carrots and potato. Apple tart and custard.' On the snooker table, next to a pile of Monopoly money, some hope-ful prisoner had left a copy of the *Belfast Telegraph* open at the jobs page.

An Irish lesson was chalked up on the blackboard in the edu-cation room. By the telephone box in the corridor was a box of expired green British Telecom phone cards stamped 'For Use in HM Prisons Only'. On the floor of the library were piles of books that said much about the inmates: *Papillon*, *The Kennedys*, *A Celtic Odyssey*, *The Beginner's Guide to Winning Chess*. In the loyalist block, said Albert, it would have been all porn and joke books.

I began chatting to Albert, who had been an officer at the Maze for more than 25 years. He told me he'd worked through the 'blanket' and 'dirty' protests, and actually guarded Bobby Sands as he starved himself to death.

Sands – the first to refuse food – was moved to the hospital about 30 days into his hunger strike, said Albert. There was already enormous international media interest in the hunger strikers, and Albert's job was to sit in their rooms and ensure that visitors could not photograph or record them. He caught one person smuggling in a camera. When visitors left, he had to lift the prisoners and search their beds, and once found a tape recorder hidden between the cheeks of a prisoner's bottom.

The prisoners completely ignored Albert and his fellow guards, just as they ignored the meals that were delivered to their beds three times a day. 'The thing that took me to the cleaners, and I'm a guy that likes my grub, is that they would bring fish and chips and mushy peas, all the things that make your nostrils flare, and they wouldn't lift a finger at it,' said Albert.

The evening meals were left by the prisoners' beds all night. The trays were weighed before and after to see if anything had been eaten. 'The best grub went in,' said Albert. 'We were out to break them, but you've got to hand it to them. There was not any of them ever tried to break off and eat, not once.

'When you look back on the history of the dirty protests, we detested them because we couldn't understand how anyone could live in their own shit and piss. They were the lowest form of life as far as we were concerned. But during the hunger strike we began looking at them in a different light. We began thinking there must be something more to these guys. Anyone who can stand 30, 40, 50 days without food must have something. They never wavered once.'

It was not just the prisoners. Even as they grew progressively weaker and Margaret Thatcher's government showed no sign of backing down, Albert never heard their families try to dissuade them from continuing. They ignored appeals by the prison chaplain. 'They would come in, pat them on the back, tell them they were doing a great job, how everyone was asking about them outside, giving them encouragement, telling them they looked great. This was to a boy whose stomach had shrunk down till you could see the spinal cord. It was like looking at Belsen photos.'

Only when Albert escorted the families out of the prison did they break down. 'Whenever they got out they were emotional. You could see the anguish. You could see the mothers' tears all right, but not in front of the prisoners.'

Sands, by then an MP, increasingly drifted in and out of consciousness. 'When you're sitting with someone dying there's a smell of him,' said Albert. He was in Sands' room, along with Sands' parents and siblings, when he finally died just past midnight on 5 May 1981, after 66 days without food.

The moment the doctor pronounced Sands dead, 'the balloon went up', Albert recalled. The family were 'terribly upset. They wept then.' The prison governor immediately informed the Northern Ireland Office, who delayed the formal announcement while troops and soldiers were rushed on to the streets to contain the inevitable rioting. A great throng of demonstrators had gathered outside the main gate of the Maze and, as Albert recalled it, a decoy hearse containing an empty coffin was subsequently driven out of the gate lest republicans tried to seize their martyr's body. Sands' body was actually smuggled out of a back gate to be taken to the mortuary at the Forster Green hospital.

But inside the Maze itself 'you could have cut the atmosphere with a knife', said Albert. 'You could have heard a pin drop. Even from the loyalists there was no shouting or cheering or banging.' The other hunger strikers in the corridor were told immediately. 'I tried to imagine myself lying there, number three or four or five. One goes, and you know your turn is coming,' Albert told me. In the event nine more died over the next three-and-a-half months, their names scarcely now remembered.

The loyalist silence did not last for long, of course. Belfast's notorious and perhaps indispensable black humour quickly reasserted itself. Soon graffiti appeared on the walls of loyalist estates proclaiming Sands 'Slimmer of the Month'. That may be tasteless, but it is par for the course. After Billy Wright's murder in the Maze the republican joke was, 'What's the difference between a black taxi and Billy Wright? Answer: A black taxi can take five in the back, no problem.'

Before we left H-Block Eight, Albert started thrusting things into my hands as souvenirs – a wooden shield bearing pictures of the hunger strikers, a crudely framed copy of the 1916 'Easter Proclamation' of Irish independence, a book on the loyalist paramilitaries. They were only going to be thrown away, he explained.

By chance I glanced inside the book's cover and saw the name 'E. Gilmartin' scribbled inside. I did a bit of a double-take because I had come across Eugene Gilmartin a few months earlier. The morning after he was released I went to interview Beryl Quigley, the widow of an assistant governor at the Maze whom Gilmartin had murdered in the driveway of his East Belfast home as he left for work one March morning in 1984.

Mrs Quigley was another of those astonishingly strong women you find in Northern Ireland. She and her three-year-old daughter had witnessed the murder, and Gilmartin had actually fired at her as well. Her husband died in a pool of blood 'while the moisture of our last kiss was still on my lips', she told me.

But she was a devout Christian who had long ago forgiven Gilmartin. She had spent the previous night praying that he would now be able to put his past behind him and use the rest of his life constructively. 'He's lost a lot of time, and some of that time he'll never be able to make up because you can't reclaim your youth,' she said.

From Mrs Quigley's comfortable middle-class home in East Belfast I had driven across to the bleak republican Twinbrook estate in West Belfast where Gilmartin came from. His terraced home was festooned with balloons, yellow ribbons and 'Welcome Home, Eugene' signs. I knocked on the door and Gilmartin's wife answered. She was still in her nightdress; they'd had quite a party the previous night, she explained a little sheepishly.

She was not hostile and was interested to know what had become of Mrs Quigley. Her husband had done his time and would not talk, she said. He regretted the hardship he had caused his own family, but not the killing. 'It was a war,' she insisted. 'He was a soldier. A lot of bad things happen in war.'

Ahead of me, the next morning, lay the grimmest area of Northern Ireland, a pit of sectarian hatred that incorporates Lurgan and Portadown and justifiably became known during the Troubles as the 'murder triangle'.

Sectarianism is nothing new to this patch of mid-Ulster. Some of the worst massacres of Protestants during the Irish rebellion of 1641 took place here. In the eighteenth century Catholics and Protestants were attracted in equal numbers by the booming linen industry, and became economic as well as ethnic rivals as they battled to rent patches of land close to the mills. Sectarian warfare inevitably erupted.

Protestant 'Peep O'Day Boys' terrorised Catholic families with tactics uncannily similar to those employed by today's loyalist paramilitaries – warnings to leave, arson attacks and kneecapping or 'peppering' as the practice was then known. Like the IRA, gangs of Catholic 'Defenders' responded in kind. The whole thing came to a head in 1795 when the 'Peep O'Day Boys' thrashed the 'Defenders' at the so-called Battle of the Diamond and formed the Orange Order at the village of Loughall just outside Portadown.

As I drove through the pretty village of Moira I wondered what I could possibly write about this area that was positive. In the 1800s Moira produced a remarkable lady named Anne Lutton who spoke passable French, German, Spanish, Italian, Portuguese, Latin, Greek, Hebrew, Irish, Arabic, Russian, Syriac, Persian, Samarian, Ethiopic and Chaldee, according to my guide and mentor Ernest Sandford, but the most striking thing about the village today was the wreckage of the RUC station half-way up the main street that was bombed by a republican splinter group in 1998.

I was still pondering the question as I drove into the former linen town of Lurgan with its wide and bustling high street. Here the IRA murdered two policemen in cold blood in 1997. Here I witnessed a baying mob of loyalists drive away David Trimble as the MP sought his own constituency's support for the Good Friday accord during the 1998 referendum. The last time I'd been in the town was for the funeral of Rosemary Nelson, a local solicitor who represented several prominent republicans and was killed by a loyalist bomb planted beneath her BMW in 1999.

Not even Mr Sandford could help me in Lurgan. The best he could come up with was a stained-glass window in the parish church commemorating Master McGrath, a champion greyhound, and an eighteenth-century grave whose inscription consists of the single word 'Tacet', meaning 'She is silent'. This was reputedly a bereaved husband's epitaph to an argumentative wife.

Of Portadown, a few miles further west, William Thackeray wrote rather verbosely in 1842: 'The little brisk town, with its comfortable unpretending houses, its squares and market-place, its pretty quay, with craft along the river, – a steamer building on the dock, close to the mills and warehouses that look in a full state of prosperity, – was a pleasant conclusion to this ten miles' drive.'

Nobody would write such things about Portadown today. Variously dubbed 'the Orange Citadel', 'the Town called Malice' and 'Northern Ireland's Alabama', it is a place where tolerance and compromise have long been dirty words. Rosemary Nelson used to describe it as more a malignant sensation than a location: 'You don't just go to Portadown – you feel Portadown.' After her death, loyalist graffiti on Portadown's walls proclaimed 'Bye Bye Rosemary' and 'Job Vacancy – Sinn Fein Solicitor'.

It is a town that witnessed almighty confrontations over the Orange Order's annual Drumcree church parade almost every year since 1995 – confrontations that have sparked riots and mayhem across the province and made July a month when the law-abiding citizens of Northern Ireland fled en masse.

The issue is simple to describe, but seemingly impossible to resolve. Every July since 1807 the local Orangemen have paraded to Drumcree's grey-stone parish church on the edge of Portadown for a Sunday service, then returned to the town centre along the Garvaghy Road.

That was fine while the Garvaghy Road was still a country lane, but in the 1960s council houses were built on either side of it. During the population shifts of the Troubles the area became almost exclusively nationalist and the approximately 5,000 residents grew increasingly resentful of the Orangemen's annual parade past their homes.

Both sides drew proverbial lines in the sand. The nationalists decided to take a stand against what they saw as displays of Protestant 'triumphalism' designed to underscore their second-class citizenship, and the Orangemen a stand against what they perceived as the steady erosion of their civil and religious liberties by governments bent on appeasing terrorists.

When the nationalists sought to block the march, thousands of irate loyalists massed at Drumcree and the RUC and Army found themselves caught in the middle. For the first three years the Orangemen got down the Garvaghy Road, although twice the police were forced almost literally to barricade the residents in their homes. Each year since 1998 the loyalists have found their route blocked by a massive police and army operation, and have engaged in pitched battles night after night with forces of the Crown to which they profess such loyalty.

There were never any real winners. Northern Ireland was racked by violence and wanton destruction, community relations across the province were poisoned, and it would have been far cheaper to fly every Garvaghy Road resident to the Caribbean for the week of the march.

Portadown itself was transformed into the United Kingdom's most polarised town, with its working-class estates almost completely segregated and the fifth of its population that is Catholic living almost exclusively in the town-within-a-town that is today's Garvaghy Road.

There are some good people in Portadown, there really are. I telephoned a young councillor named Mark Neale who is a moderate Unionist, which makes him an endangered species in these parts. Show me the pleasant side of Portadown, I begged, and after lunch with his charming wife Hazel and their high-spirited young children he duly obliged.

He took me down to the banks of the River Bann, to an area called Moneypenny's Lock, and very pretty it was too. The only snag was its history. During the Irish uprising of 1641 the Catholic rebels drowned about eighty Protestants just near here. It was said that you could walk across the river on the corpses. The town's Orange Lodge has pointedly erected a plaque in memory of those who died 'as a permanent tribute and a reminder to future generations of their faith, devotion and sacrifice'.

After that we rather gave up the pretence. Mark is an honest fellow. He loved Portadown, he said; it had a strong industrial base, good schools and a great future if only it could surmount its present problems, but he didn't even try to deny those problems existed. How could he when every other street is decked out in loyalist or nationalist colours to warn off the other side? How could he when his constituency included the Garvaghy Road but he could not walk around it? We changed tack and embarked on a Billy Wright tour.

Portadown is one of Northern Ireland's industrial hubs. Its factories produce carpets, textiles, furniture, foodstuffs and much else besides. However, its best-known human product apart from Sir Robert Hart, who founded the Chinese Post Office, is undoubtedly Wright, a lapsed born-again Christian who became one of the most brutal killers of the Troubles.

Wright formed the Loyalist Volunteer Force after the Ulster Volunteer Force expelled his infamous Mid-Ulster brigade in 1996 for breaching the loyalist ceasefire by murdering a Catholic taxi driver. He made Portadown the LVF's stronghold, and from here he conducted a blatantly sectarian murder campaign designed to strike such terror into the Catholic community that it turned on the IRA. His ruthlessness and efficiency won him plenty of admirers in Portadown. Thousands turned out for his funeral and the town's shops all closed, albeit under pressure from men in black leather jackets. Since then the Billy Wright cult has if anything grown, though it is a measure of the place that signs of a UVF revival in the town in 1999 were generally regarded as good news.

Mark showed me two huge murals glorifying Wright in the loyalist housing estates of Killycomain and Brownstown, where he lived. In the Seagoe cemetery we found his grave adorned with several red, white and blue floral wreaths and a Union flag. 'In loving memory of Brigadier William Stephen Wright, the beloved father of Sara, Ashleen and Stephen, murdered by the enemies of Ulster,' read the inscription. Against the headstone someone had propped a framed 'poem' that showed how, to some twisted minds, this man had become a hero:

Billy we never got to meet you. How I wish we had
The closest that we got to you was on that day so sad
We stood here by your graveside, tears trickling from our
  eyes
As your coffin was gently lowered we whispered our goodbyes
We admired you from a distance as you took your faithful
  stand
For your comrades, faith and truth and for Ulster our dear
  homeland.

It went on, but I'll spare you the rest. A respectable-looking lady was tending her mother's adjacent grave. I expected her to be appalled at having Wright buried so close, but not a bit of it. 'He has to be buried somewhere,' she told me. She didn't support violence, she said, but it was quite wrong that Wright could be killed in prison and she suspected official connivance.

We went on to the Pride of the Hill shop at the far end of the town's handsome old high street. This is owned by a short, bearded, heavy-set man named Stephen Millar. He opened it in late 1998, he told me, because his support for Drumcree's Orangemen had cost his cleaning company several lucrative contracts. It sold loyalist regalia of every description, and was doing so well that it was now open six days a week instead of weekends only.

There were several young men browsing, but I have to confess I found nothing that made me want to reach for my wallet. There were Billy Wright portraits selling for £60 each, videos of the annual Drumcree confrontations, counterfeit banknotes bearing pictures of gunmen, bars of chocolate inscribed 'We Demand the Right to March' and 'Proud to be a Prod' fridge magnets. There were orange 'no surrender' scarves, paramilitary insignia and T-shirts with pictures of loyalists battling with police. What did faintly amuse me were the 'walking Orangemen' windmills of the sort people stick in their front gardens. These consisted of dumpy wooden bowler-hatted Orangemen with legs that revolved in the wind.

The shop was giving one thing away: a booklet entitled *Is There Room in Heaven for Billy Wright?* The answer, needless to say, was 'yes' because Wright's was a 'just war'. It argued that the government had failed to take on the IRA and was conspiring to shunt a million Protestants into a united Ireland. Wright felt so strongly about this that he committed himself to the counter-terrorist struggle: 'Dear Loyalist, as you read these words, rest assured that Billy Wright, a true son of Ulster, died as a martyr for our faith and fatherland. His testimony is sealed in blood and one glorious day he will rule and reign with the Lord Jesus in the countless ages of eternity, shining in the image of the first begotten Son'.

The next day was a Saturday, but not just any old Saturday. It was the day of the all-Ulster Lambeg Drumming Championships, and shortly after midday I arrived at an old farmhouse tucked away in the hills near the village of Tandragee, a few miles south of Portadown. This is the home of Frank Orr, a genial plasterer in his early fifties who is in his own modest and diffident way a rather unique man.

Nobody knows for certain where the Lambeg drum came from. The oldest surviving Lambeg dates from 1849, the year of the bloody Battle of Dolly's Brae between Orangemen and Catholic 'Ribbonmen' near Castlewellan in County Down. Folklore suggests that it arrived from Holland with the troops of Protestant King William in 1690, or that it was made for the Battle of the Diamond in 1795, and it certainly featured in Orange parades from that time on. More likely, it evolved from an instrument called the 'Long Drum'.

Whatever its origin, the Lambeg must be one of the few musical instruments in the world associated exclusively with one small grouping – in this case the Protestant Orange Order. There are barely a hundred people alive who can play it, and fewer than twenty who can do so really well – and Frank is one of them. Not only that, he is also one of the half-dozen people who can actually make the things – and they are truly works of art.

Frank learned the skill from his father, who was taught it by his father. In a breeze-block workshop alongside his house, he constructs the shells of the drum from two thin strips of oak 12 feet long and 13 inches wide. These he bends into a complete circle over the course of a couple of months, and holds in place with three light rings of ash.

The 'heads' he makes from she-goat skins, those of billy-goats being far too thick. He removes the fat and the hair, then scrapes the skins until they are parchment-thin. Then he wets them and stretches them to remove the give. He treats them with a potion or 'dope' that he inherited from his father, the ingredients of which are more secret than the recipe for Coca-Cola.

After several months, when the skins are well and truly seasoned, Frank glues and tacks them to a pair of 'flesh hoops'. These are placed over the two sides of the shell with the line of the goat's backbone running top to bottom, and held in place by two large 'brace hoops' with 15 holes in each. A linen rope nearly 40 feet long is threaded through these holes in zig-zag fashion. The tighter the rope is pulled, the closer the hoops are drawn and the tauter the skins are stretched over the rims of the shell. A complete drum is more than three feet in diameter, weighs 30–40 lb, and costs up to £1,000.

For these championships, as for every other match, Frank started preparing his drum four days ago, tightening the skins a little more each evening. By now a pair of skins that began life soft and furry had been transformed into drumheads taut as steel, and Frank was a little bit tense himself. He has been drumming since he was ten, and won about 25 cups last year alone, but this is one of the really big Lambeg drumming matches.

Fortunately the weather was good, because rain wrecks the skins and the event would immediately be cancelled. We arrived in the car park behind the Orange Hall in Banbridge shortly before 2 p.m. As I opened the car door I was hit by the noise of what I took to be a passing train. It took a few seconds for me to realise that it was actually the din of Lambeg drummers warming up beyond the row of terrace houses dividing the car park from Victoria Street in front of the hall.

We walked in past lines of cars and trailers from across the province; experts claim they can tell where a drummer comes from by his beat. The hall itself was already packed, with a large temporary bar and food counter at one end. There were more than fifty giant drums standing around, and each drummer had two or three assistants helping him to prepare. One was leaning on the drum to hold it in place, while the other two wore protective gloves and were pulling the rope as tight as they could possibly get it. 'Taking the rope', the process is called, but someone across the far side of the hall took too much rope and a skin snapped with a crack so loud that the entire room jumped. For that drummer, the day was over before it began.

Frank didn't involve himself in this part. He sat quietly to one side while Victor Wilson and two brothers, Fred and Nigel Prentice, prepared his drum. All three work for the same building firm as Frank; Victor has been helping him for thirty years or more and comes to every match. 'I love the sport of drumming but I'd not be good enough to play,' he told me. 'We see more of each other than we do of our wives,' quipped Fred.

I wandered round the hall. Some drums were plain, others decorated. On one there was a painting of Princess Diana beneath the legend 'England's Rose'. Another bore a painting of the drummer's mother. There were portraits of 'The Late Bro. Hugh Chambers' and 'The Late Sir H. Wilson' – a former Chief of Imperial General Staff who was murdered in London by Irish republicans in 1922. Then there were the pictures of 'King Billy – The Orange Hero of Ulster', of 'Cromwell the Terror' and of Lord Kitchener that nationalists would denounce as triumphalist and provocative.

To Frank these portraits were purely and simply 'folk art'. To him and most of the other competitors I spoke to, the drum was something to be celebrated and enjoyed as it would be in any other culture. They said the Lambeg drum used to be played in processions of the Ancient Order of Hibernians, a Catholic organisation, and expressed deep regret that in Northern Ireland it had become – like so much else – a sectarian symbol. Some nationalists even call it the 'Drum of Hate'. 'It's sad that people see it as that. I see it as a musical instrument,' said Frank.

In fact few Orange parades still feature the Lambeg drum; it is considered too slow and cumbersome. Frank's playing is confined mostly to weekly drumming matches, and he plays 'just for the love of it'. Drumming, he says, 'is in the blood. It's a disease. If you don't do it you miss it, surely.'

As we waited, he explained how a whole combination of factors had to come together on the day: the thinness and quality of the skins; the secret recipes that the various tanners use to cure them; the weather conditions, which affect the skins and require the drummer to adjust their tautness and his beat. There were also a host of lesser factors like the thickness of rim over which the skins are stretched, the suppleness of the rope, and the quality of the shell's wood. Some drummers even smeared poteen on the inside of their shells before a match to try to give them extra life.

Frank repeatedly referred to his drum as 'she'. He talked of it as a sensitive female whose moods varied with the temperature and humidity and according to how she was treated. To be really successful, the drummer must be able to read those moods and adapt his rhythm or 'time' accordingly. He must search out the most sensitive spots on the skins with the flexible Malacca canes that he uses for sticks. When everything's perfect, said Frank, 'she's playing back to you as you are playing her'.

Finally the match begins. The first half-dozen drummers move outside, loop the leather drum-straps over their heads and lean back to take the weight. Then they start playing and the noise is quite fantastic – a relentless, deafening rat-a-tat-tat that hurts your ears, shakes your body and makes you feel as if you're standing in the *Titanic*'s engine room or the middle of a thundercloud.

The drummers are almost all male, many of them members of well-known drumming dynasties like the Careys, the Beatties and the Boyces. They are young and old, big and small, some too short to see over the tops of their drums. They have powerful shoulders and bulging forearms, many heavily tattooed. There is just one female drummer, a spirited 19-year-old slip of a girl called Caroline Stewart from Armagh who only took up the sport four years ago.

As they join the queue working slowly down the road towards the judging pen, their backs arched and knees bent, flailing the giant instruments resting on their stomachs, they make a bizarre spectacle. From the side they looked like grotesquely pregnant women, and from head on like weird headless creatures with short little legs and frantically waving antennae.

This is a real team effort. The helpers engage in urgent last-minute fine-tuning; they hop from side to side to make sure the two skins are 'levelled', or sounding the same; they tap the hoops with mallets to make the necessary micro-adjustments. When they are finally satisfied they nod to the drummer and he enters the pen, which is formed from two lengths of orange tape and some traffic bollards.

In the old days drumming matches were trials of strength, with large bets laid on the outcome. Two rivals would take each other on, beating out their rhythms hour after hour, wrists bleeding from contact with the shell, until one stopped from sheer exhaustion. Not any more. Nowadays the judges, clutching clipboards, listen intently as the drummer plays his heart out, his face a study in concentration. They too walk from one side to the other to check for balance. After about a minute they dismiss the drummer, who parades slowly back to the Orange Hall still drumming for all he's worth.

To the uninitiated like myself each drum sounded painfully the same, rather like machine guns. But to the knots of aficionados following each drummer on his stately progress, heads bowed and intently focused, there was evidently a world of difference between the good, the bad and the merely mediocre.

In snatches of conversation above the almighty racket, they explain that they're judging not the drummer but the tone he elicits from his instrument. They're seeking a certain quality they cannot readily explain. They talk of certain drums having a 'good upstairs', or 'plenty of bell in her', but it's like trying to describe a taste or a colour. They're listening for a resonance, a ringing, a music that lurks behind the beat and which you either recognise or don't. When these people hear it, they smile and nod in quiet approbation like connoisseurs savouring a vintage wine.

There is nothing short and sharp about the whole event, however. On this occasion there are 54 contestants, and three separate rounds before 25 are selected for the final. There are no breaks between rounds, no half-time, no tea-breaks or drinks intervals. The deafening noise goes on and on, hour after hour. No residents of the surrounding streets could possibly enjoy their Saturday afternoon sport on television.

For most of that time I found it quite impossible to tell one drum from another. I frequently had to turn away to protect my ears. Every hour or so I sought sanctuary inside the hall and found I'd been half-deafened. I struggled to think of a more painful way of spending a pleasant summer's afternoon.

But as the event wore on, a funny thing happened. I found myself unconsciously beginning to distinguish between the good and the bad drums, becoming quite judgmental. Then I listened to Frank processing down the road and suddenly I got it.

I heard not the beat itself, but the drum answering with a vibrant, ringing music of its own. I heard her responding to Frank's overtures like the chimes of a church bell that's been struck. It was like staring at one of those 'magic eye' pictures until the formless pattern on the page suddenly resolves itself into a crisp 3-D image and makes you gasp. It was a moment of epiphany.

Not until early evening did the last contestant strut before the judges, but still the music was not over. As the judges went off to reach their verdict, half-a-dozen of the leading drummers lined up outside the hall for a glorious grand finale. Each picked up the beat and off they went in deafening unison, sinews straining, teeth gritted, sweat pouring from their faces as the frenzy built, the crowd roaring them on in the mellowing sun and the very ground vibrating beneath the sustained onslaught. If King Billy did use Lambeg drums at the Battle of the Boyne, it's little wonder that he won. To hear that rolling thunder advancing towards them must have scared the life out of King James's men.

Then abruptly it was over. For the first time in six hours peace returned to Victoria Street, and everyone packed inside the hall for the results.

These took a long time coming. Over in Scotland that afternoon Glasgow Rangers had beaten Glasgow Celtic in the Cup Final and many of those present had been celebrating at the bar. They would not shut up. The speeches took an age, the raffle even longer. Then came the inevitable singing of the national anthem, and finally the verdict.

I thought I'd backed a certain winner in Frank Orr, but like Joey Dunlop at the North West 200 he failed to follow my script. He had made the final 25, but was not amongst the five cup-winners. He didn't care a jot. 'We never think anything of it,' he said as he loosened the ropes on his drum. 'So long as you've had a good day's drumming that's all that matters.'

Lambeg drumming is considered a Protestant sport, so being a good and impartial journalist I returned to County Armagh the next day for what is widely regarded as a nationalist sport.

I drove past orchards of blossoming apple trees to Armagh city, which is all that Portadown is not. A small but elegant old city which was chosen by St Patrick as the site of his principal church in AD 445, it has remained Ireland's spiritual and ecclesiastical capital ever since.

The Anglican Cathedral of St Patrick sits on a hilltop within an ancient ring fort, the latest of roughly eighteen churches which have occupied that site over the last 1,500 years. It looks across to the newer Roman Catholic Cathedral of St Patrick on another hilltop. The Catholic Cathedral was built over 70 years in the nineteenth century with money collected mostly from fund-raising events, and its sacristy contains a grandfather clock that was a prize in an 1865 raffle. The winner has yet to collect it.

Armagh is full of fine old buildings and institutions like the Royal School, founded by James I in 1608, the Robinson Library, founded in 1771, and the Observatory. The library boasts a first edition of *Gulliver's Travels* with annotations in Jonathan Swift's own hand – or at least it did so until the 273-year-old book was stolen in December 1999. The Observatory I had visited with my family one freezing night the previous December. We saw Saturn with all its rings as clearly as if a picture of the planet had been stuck on the end of the giant telescope, but what was really amazing was that Northern Ireland's sky was clear enough for us to do so. Of all the places to build an observatory, why here in this cloud-shrouded province?

The heart of Armagh also boasts a lovely Mall, a large expanse of grass ringed by trees and pleasant Georgian town houses, where preparations were being made for a cricket match that afternoon. Cricket is not something you see very often in Northern Ireland. It is an English import that has never really taken root here, perhaps because rain constantly stops play. Being an Englishman, I'd like to have lingered and watched, but I was on my way to see a much more indigenous Irish pastime almost unheard-of outside the Emerald Isle.

On the verge of a tranquil country road leading away from the city towards Dungannon, almost hidden by the thick green grass of early summer, stands a stone whose inscription might be in hieroglyphics for all the sense it would make to the uninitiated: 'July 1955 Joe McVeigh Played from Knappagh to Here in 22 Shots,' it says.

To understand these cryptic words you need to be standing with me on this unusually sunny Sunday morning amid the crowd of several dozen men – old-timers in cloth caps, beefy middle-aged fellows and mere teenagers – who are strung out along the road.

They are crouched, heads turned down the road, all intently watching a young man called Fergal about 100 yards back. Fergal shuffles forward, breaks into a run and as he reaches top speed leaps into the air with his right arm high behind him. As he lands his arm shoots forward, brushing his leg, and hurls an iron ball towards the crowd with immense velocity.

The ball hits the tarmac with a puff of grit, hurtles noisily along the road and scatters the crowd. 'She's battling well,' observes one gnarled veteran as the ball rattles by. It hits the verge but bounces back and finally comes to rest a couple of hundred yards from where it was thrown. 'Yes, Fergy boy!' cries one man in the crowd. 'That'll do, boy,' shouts another. The punters begin to adjust their odds as the crowd moves on up the lane. 'I'll lay two-to-one the score,' offers one, and he finds a taker.

Welcome to the centuries-old sport of road-bowling, or 'bullets' as it is known in Armagh. There was a time when the game was played across Ireland, and even in parts of northern England, but today it is found only in Counties Armagh and Cork, and in Dagenham, Essex where it was introduced by Ford's Irish workers.

The rules have not changed in generations, and could hardly be simpler. Two players compete to hurl 28-oz iron balls along two or three miles of winding, undulating country lane in as few shots as possible. If the ball hits a grate, or a signpost, or someone's leg, that's tough.

In Armagh the players throw underarm and spin the ball round corners. In Cork, where road surfaces tend to be more pitted, they throw overarm and lob the ball over the top of sharp bends. In both the game takes precedence over cars, which are waved through between throws.

This is sport in its purest form – a genuine community event undefiled by professionalism, commercialism or pay-per-view television, although thousands of pounds do sometimes change hands in bets. It is played not in a stadium, but on the public by-ways. It is played not for money, but for love and glory by men – and women – whose fathers, grandfathers and great-grandfathers would have passed their Sundays in exactly the same way.

The game has its own language. A match is a 'score', the first throw is the 'break off', and tufts of grass used to mark where the balls end up are 'butts' or 'sops'. The balls are 'bullets', and there is just one factory in Cork that makes them.

It has its own legends – men like Joe McVeigh, 'Hammerman' Donnelly or Danny McParland who once threw a ball a phenomenal 512 yards and has been commemorated in verse by the 'Armagh Bard', Harry McGrail:

> *Before they reached the finish*
> *Sure everyone had seen*
> *McParland was the master*
> *And his backers not so green*
> *His last bowl like a rocket sped*
> *Along the winning way*
> *Three cheers for young McParland*
> *He's the hero of the day*

The sport even has legendary courses – the Knappagh Road, the old Moy Road, the Dublin Hill, the Marshes – but where it originated nobody knows. Some say it was imported by northern

English linen workers in the 1700s, others that it was introduced by the Dutch soldiers who arrived in Ireland with William of Orange in 1689 and used cannon balls.

Two uncles of the Brontë sisters played it in County Down. Jonathan Swift mentioned it in a poem he wrote in Armagh in 1728. The earliest known reference is in the Londonderry council records of 1714 which state: 'No person shall play long bullets on the ramparts of the walls . . . on paine of paying five shillings for each offence.' That was a colossal fine for those days, suggesting the authorities didn't think much of the sport, and it remained illegal until at least the 1950s. Nobody could tell me why it was considered so heinous. Perhaps it was thought to be a danger to other road-users. Maybe it offended the churches because it involved betting on a Sunday.

In one respect only has the game changed: it has become more organised. In 1963 the men of Cork met the men of Armagh in the first All-Ireland championship – an event that now attracts thousands of spectators who fill the road and part like the Red Sea before Moses as the ball hurtles towards them. In 1985 Cork hosted the first World Road Bowling Championships, with teams from Holland and Germany where there are similar games called 'Klootschieten' and 'Klootschlessen', whose players throw from springboards.

On this particular Sunday two 'scores' are advertised in the *Armagh Observer*'s road-bowling page – Paul Grimley v. Malachy Lappin followed by Johnny Kelly v. Fergal Carr. All are competing for the right to represent Armagh in the All-Irelands.

Grimley is a genial, muscular, 6'4" tyre company representative in his mid-thirties. He was the 'Junior A' all-Ireland champion in 1991 – 'Junior A' being the third level of skill – and has been bowling for 20 years. Lappin, an electrician, is smaller, slighter and a mere 22 years of age. It seemed a lopsided contest, but then 'bullets' is a trial of skill as much as strength and both players have a couple of handlers who know every bump and pothole of the road ahead.

The players meet by the Armagh road sign on the boundary of Ireland's ancient ecclesiastical capital. They strip off their sweaters. Grimley wins the toss, which enables him to choose the best ball as well as deciding who goes first. He lets Lappin start, falls behind from the very first throw and never regains the lead.

By the time this pair reach Brannighan's Gate the punters are no longer taking bets on the result, only on individual throws. By the Big Tree Lappin has 'raised the bowl of odds', meaning he is a full throw ahead. Lappin's fourteenth throw takes his ball past the telegraph pole beyond Conlon's Lane that marks the finish line – a comfortable victory for a future champion over a past champion.

After a few minutes' break the crowd turns round and Johnny Kelly and Fergal Carr begin the second 'score' back towards Armagh's distant cathedral spires. The early money is on Kelly, an easy-going 28-year-old electrician who was the All-Ireland Under-18 champion in 1989. 'Take Kelly on score, take Kelly on the contest,' the punters cry. However, Carr, who has just turned 19, is the present under-18 champion and looks altogether leaner, meaner and keener – so I put £10 on him at 15–10.

This is serious stuff, with a lot of prestige and money riding on the outcome. The players each have a couple of older, more experienced advisers with whom they confer before each shot. They are advised to throw the ball high if the surface is rough, or to 'track it' along lines worn smooth by traffic, or to 'screw' or 'pitch' it – which means spin it right or left round corners. One of the advisers – the 'shower' – then scurries up the road and stands with his legs apart to show the exact line to be taken.

Carr takes an early lead. By the Coalsheds Kelly has more or less caught up, and large sums of money are now changing hands. At Donnelly's Cottage, egged on by his determined father, Carr produces a tremendous throw of about 300 yards and things begin to go wrong for Kelly.

Carr's ball seems charmed – it bounces off banks and kerb-stones and just keeps rolling along the road. Kelly's ends up in ruts or ditches, known hereabouts as 'sheughs'. He fails to make Campbell's Corner, meaning he needs another throw to get round it. By McVeigh's Stone he is one full throw behind. 'It's never over till it's over,' he insists, but by Gus's Corner he is two throws down and the 'score' is as good as over.

In the end it was a bit anti-climactic, but that didn't matter. The countryside was lush and green and beautiful, and a pleasure to be in. As this curious gathering made its way back towards the city, remarkably thick wads of notes appeared from trouser pockets and debts were settled. I collected my £25 and went on my way, happy at last to have backed a winner and happier by far than the man who'd bet £300 on Kelly and lost the lot.

I'd intended ending my journey at this point, but once again I made the mistake of examining my map too closely. Just a few more miles down the road, right on the border, was the village of Caledon. As that was the place which provided the spark that ignited the Troubles way back in 1969, it seemed almost churlish not to finish the chapter there.

One thing leads to another. I returned to Armagh, had a coffee in Our Ma's Café, and as I headed out on another country road towards Caledon I passed the entrance to Navan Fort, or Emain Macha, a place I'd excluded from my itinerary since it was on the tourist trail. Because it was a warm Sunday afternoon, and because I had time to spare, I relented – and I was pleased I did.

There was actually nobody about at all, and I climbed alone to the top of the 'fort' – a great round, man-made mound ringed with the remains of ancient earthworks and carpeted with daisies, dandelions and grass as thick as fur. I sat on the top, sur-veyed a breathtaking panorama of brilliant green countryside in every direction, and tried to get my mind around how very, very old this place was.

It was old long before St Patrick arrived in Armagh in the middle of the fifth century. It was mentioned by Ptolemy, the Greek geographer, in his second-century map of the world when it was still an important centre of whatever it was they did in those days. It was the principal stronghold of the Celtic kings of Ulster from about 700 BC, Ulster's Camelot, and in around 94 BC the people built a huge round, wooden temple on top of the hill and immediately set fire to it, perhaps as an offering to the gods. Earlier still it was the haunt of a Bronze Age aristocracy, Neolithic farmers and – we're back to about 7,000 BC by now – Mesolithic hunters. For good measure, archaeologists have discovered the skull of a Barbary ape from North Africa that Navan's inhabitants apparently kept as an exotic pet during the second century BC.

My imagination rather failed me at that point. Coming to grips with any time-scale beyond my own lifetime is something I find difficult. The effort also reminded me of one of the low points of my journalistic career in Northern Ireland.

Down in Newgrange, County Meath, there is a burial mound built around 3,200 BC that makes even Stonehenge and the Pyramids look modern. It was constructed with 200,000 tonnes of stone and earth by New Stone Age farmers, and with astonishing mathematical precision. At 8.58 a.m. each Winter Solstice, the beams of the rising sun penetrate a narrow slit above the door and work their way up a narrow 62-foot passage until a rod of intense golden light illuminates the central burial chamber. Minutes later it is plunged back into darkness.

For such an amazing spectacle, the audience figures were for a long time disappointing. This is because the mound was forgotten within 1,000 years of its construction, and not rediscovered until 1699. It was not until 1963 that an archaeology professor named Michael Kelly guessed the significance of the slit. Even then, it was another four years before the sun shone on the Winter Solstice and Dr Kelly became the first man in more than 4,000 years to see the inner chamber illuminated.

Since then the demand for tickets has been phenomenal. The authorities allow about twenty people a year into the chamber to witness this solar – as opposed to stellar – performance. The lucky few who get in nowadays applied a decade or more ago, but even they are likely to be disappointed as their chances of a clear sunrise are only about one in four.

Ever the optimist, I telephoned about two days before the 1998 Winter Solstice and asked whether they could possibly squeeze in a gentleman from *The Times*. To my absolute astonishment, they agreed. I got up at 6 a.m., thinking that would allow me plenty of time, sped through a deserted Belfast and headed south. A few lorries slowed me down, but I wasn't really worried. As the traffic on the pitifully inadequate Belfast–Dublin road grew heavier, I began to feel a few pangs of anxiety. By Dundalk I was feeling distinctly uneasy. In Drogheda, as the darkness began to lift, I hit almost stationary lines of rush-hour cars and panicked.

It was past 8.30 before I was through the town and hurtling along an icy country road in search of non-existent signs for Newgrange. Swearing at the top of my voice, cursing myself and Ireland's Roads Department, I chose a random turn to the left and careered around tiny, winding lanes getting ever more lost until suddenly, miraculously, I spotted the mound no more than half a mile away.

I reached the car park at 8.55. I screeched to a halt, leapt out and sprinted past a crowd of astonished onlookers to the entrance booth, waving my letter of authorisation. Some old fellow inside began reading it, very slowly. 'No, no,' I cried. 'You've got to get me in there – now!' He began hobbling up towards the entrance to the mound where another large crowd had gathered, and it was all I could do to refrain from bodily lifting him up and running.

On either side of the ancient doorway stood two guards. 'Please,' I begged. 'You've got to let me in!'

As they looked at me with a cross between pity and amusement, I turned round. Above the low hills on the far side of the frosty Boyne River valley, the first slither of sun was just beginning to illuminate a perfect, cloudless sky. I had missed the only chance I'd ever have of witnessing the oldest and most magical man-made show on earth – all for the sake of an extra 15 minutes in bed.

Navan, fortunately, you can enjoy at any time of day or night, and I lay in the sun for a while before completing the drive to Caledon.

I'd never been to the village before, but it was a name I knew well. It was here, in June 1968, that two homeless Catholic families were evicted from the newly built council houses in which they were squatting. One of the houses was then allocated to a 19-year-old single Protestant girl, Emily Beattie, a Unionist politician's secretary. Austin Currie, a nationalist MP in Northern Ireland's Stormont government, decided to take a stand. He broke into one of the houses and staged a sit-in that ended in his being evicted and fined. In the process he triggered the civil rights protests in Londonderry and elsewhere whose brutal suppression ignited the Troubles.

Caledon was not at all what I'd expected. I drove in across the beautiful River Blackwater that divides Counties Armagh and Tyrone. To my left, beyond an elegant gatehouse, were the parklands surrounding Caledon Castle, a great Georgian house where Field-Marshal Earl Alexander of Tunis was born. To my right, cows grazed on the football pitch down by the river. The main street, bordered by two long rows of fine old stone houses, looked as if it had been transported straight from the Cotswolds and was serenely empty on this somnolent Sunday afternoon.

I had no idea where the infamous houses were, so I went into a pub and asked. It was a little embarrassing to be honest – a bit

like asking a stranger why he left his wife. The lady behind the
bar didn't seem to mind too much. 'Kinnard Park,' she told me.
'Back up the road and to the left. Go and see Joan in Number
13 – she'll help you.'

Kinnard Park was a little cul-de-sac of about 14 houses set
back into fields. Behind the houses on one side was a green hill
crowned by an old stone church; on the other side the land fell
away towards the river. That this tranquil little backwater could
be the fount of such a long and bloody conflict was almost as
hard to grasp as the age of Navan Fort.

I knocked on Joan's door. There was a long pause before a
handsome, middle-aged lady in nightdress and dressing-gown
opened the door. She'd been having a nap, she explained as she
invited me in.

Joan was obviously quite used to 'Troubles tourists' like
myself. Indeed, I got the impression that she was the street's
spokeswoman. She told me that numbers 9 and 11 were the
houses that were occupied. She believed the whole thing was a
nationalist 'set-up'. Today the street was mixed, most of the
houses were owner-occupied, and 'you couldn't get anywhere
nicer. Everybody gets on with everybody. It's so quiet and peaceful.'

Joan advised me against knocking on the doors of numbers 9
and 11. 'People down here don't like it being thought of as the
place where the Troubles started. We don't look at it in that way.
It was an excuse. It didn't really start here at all.'

Whether or not the Troubles began in Caledon, this charming
little village did not escape the maelstrom that engulfed the
province for the next 30 years. This is border country. Opposite
the RUC station is a plaque commemorating three local policemen and a nun killed in an IRA ambush on the Armagh road.
On the edge of the Caledon Castle estate, at the top of an avenue
of trees, stands a plinth surrounded by the rubble of a monument destroyed by the IRA.

At least the castle itself survived. Just up the road the IRA torched the lovely eighteenth-century Tynan Abbey one January night in 1981, having first murdered its 84-year-old owner, Sir Norman Stronge – a former Speaker in the Stormont parliament – and his son James. The burned-out shell stood untouched behind padlocked gates for another 18 years before it was finally razed to the ground.

9
Thugs and Charmers

Across the road from Belfast's City Hall, in the north-west corner of Donegall Square, there is a fine old doorway hemmed in by shopfronts. This is the entrance to a former linen warehouse that houses the Belfast Library and Society for Promoting Knowledge. It is more commonly known as the Linen Hall Library, a charitable institution founded in 1788 that is now the United Kingdom's second largest independent library and a unique political archive.

The library's celebrated Political Collection was begun in 1968, just as the Troubles were brewing, by a librarian named Jimmy Vitty who was handed a civil rights leaflet in a Belfast bar. Mr Vitty was no cloistered academic; he had a shrewd idea of what lay ahead, and he began dispatching his assistants to the barricades to collect all the material they could. Three decades later the collection has grown to more than 135,000 items, a priceless and comprehensive record of the Troubles that is the envy of the Palestinians, the South Africans and numerous other former combatants who lacked anyone with Mr Vitty's foresight. Indeed, it is the only archive collection in the world gleaned from all sides of a localised conflict.

The library is one of the very few institutions in Northern Ireland that spans the sectarian divide. Unionists, nationalists, loyalists and republicans, even the most extreme paramilitary groups, voluntarily send it their material. Wildly diverse customers ranging from government commissions to terrorist prisoners in the Maze use its resources, and no serious book about the Troubles has been written without its help. 'We collect comprehensively. We don't select,' boasts Yvonne Murphy, the enthusiastic and endlessly helpful young woman in charge of the Political Collection.

The Collection itself has actually just expanded into a brand-new reading room, thanks to a £3 million grant from the National Lottery's Heritage Fund, but during my time in Northern Ireland it was housed in a wonderful Dickensian garret reached by creaky wooden stairs. There the shelves were stuffed with every book and document ever written on the Troubles, with 30 years of press cuttings and boxes full of posters, manifestos, leaflets, handbills and 50,000 photographic negatives. Yvonne has watched people pluck up the courage to come in, perhaps 20 years after a son's or husband's murder, to read the cuttings and find out for the first time what really happened. Many weep.

But the Political Collection is more than just an archive; it is half museum. On the walls hang *Belfast Telegraph* front pages proclaiming 'It's Over', 'Truce Lies in Tatters', 'IRA Calls Ceasefire' and 'It's Yes' – five years of tumultuous history summed up in 11 words. For my benefit Yvonne rummaged through drawers and produced gems like a hand-drawn map of the Maze showing the route IRA prisoners used in 1983 for the biggest break-out in British prison history, and four sheets of cigarette paper covered in tiny, dense writing – this was the 'com', or secret message, smuggled out of the Maze to announce the end of the 1981 hunger strike.

And then there was the display cabinet containing such delights as a 'Baby Prod' bib, a republican children's alphabet book – 'A is for Armalite that sends them all running' – and a 1993 calendar showing four armed and hooded men that the Ulster Freedom Fighters had sent out as a reminder to those it had maimed but failed to kill the previous year.

On New Year's Eve that same year, two young IRA thugs planted incendiary devices on bookshelves on the library's second floor. Had the fire brigade not been attending a nearby alert in the small hours of that morning, the whole priceless collection would have gone up in flames. The library is held in such esteem that this wanton act elicited a private apology from Sinn Fein's Gerry Adams, and this unprecedented notice in the republican newspaper *An Phoblacht*: 'The IRA wishes to reiterate its public apology for the unintended damage caused by us to the Linen Hall Library.'

It was into Mr Adams' personal fiefdom of West Belfast that I was heading. I walked up through pedestrianised shopping streets to the point where the infamous Falls Road – known as Divis Street in its lower reaches – ends in a large car park on the edge of the city centre.

Here you find ranks of old black London taxis that do nothing but drive up and down the Falls Road to republican strongholds like Andersonstown, Twinbrook and Poleglass. The service began in the early 1970s when municipal buses refused to travel through volatile West Belfast. It proved so popular that it has never stopped, and has been emulated on the Protestant Shankill Road.

The fare is 70 pence, you'll share the cab with four or five others, and there is a good chance your driver will be a former IRA prisoner. 'They can't find any other work. It's also relatively safe because you're only going up and down the Falls,' explained Adrian McCreesh, a cheery fellow in a thick jacket and black woollen hat whose job as a 'loader' involves filling each cab with passengers.

Adrian himself served seven years in the Maze for attempted murder. He was caught sniping at two police officers from behind a low wall in the Short Strand area of Belfast in 1977. I'd never met him before, but he told me this without a trace of shame because he felt none. 'It was all part of the war,' he said. 'We have a different attitude to people being in jail. As long as it's political you're all right. You've done your bit for the community and you get a lot of respect from people. It's as if you've been away in England or America working.' Welcome to the looking-glass world of republican West Belfast.

To outsiders, including much of the population of Northern Ireland, it is a no-go area full of IRA terrorists and fanatical supporters who would lynch you as soon as look at you. To those who live there it is a vibrant, resourceful community that has bravely defended itself against state oppression and loyalist attacks. One man's terrorist is another man's freedom fighter, as the saying goes, but I have to say that I never felt remotely threatened in West Belfast.

Tom Hartley, a Sinn Fein strategist and enthusiastic local historian, agreed to give me a republican's-eye view of his community, and together we set off up Divis Street.

He pointed to the last of half-a-dozen 1960s tower blocks called Divis Flats at the foot of Divis Street. Look at the top, he said. There was what I would call an Army observation post, and Tom called a 'British military spy post', with its cameras trained on the Falls and capable of reading the registration numbers of every car entering or leaving.

We passed what seemed to me high-standard public

housing built where the demolished Divis Flats once stood. Tom saw it as textbook 'defensive architecture', dictated not by the needs of the residents but by the demands of the security forces. The houses were set well back from the main road, and faced inward not outward to lessen the scope for sniping. The old terraced housing of West Belfast had a thousand ways in and out, but these were built in small, easily controlled units.

Imagine Belfast as a clock face and the Falls Road would point to 8 o'clock, the Protestant Shankill Road to 10 o'clock. This close to the city centre they run almost side by side, and we stopped at St Comgall's primary school where Tom pointed out the bullet holes pitting the façade of the old red-brick building. They dated, he said, from 1969 and the invasion of the lower Falls by loyalists from the Shankill at the beginning of the Troubles.

Beyond the school we turned right into a warren of back streets by the Clonard Monastery named with supremely inappropriate imperial names like Lucknow Street, Cawnpore Street and Kashmir Street. Bombay Street was the one we wanted. There on a wall was a plaque to 15-year-old Gerard McAuley 'who died defending the people of Bombay Street on August 15th 1969'. He was helping Catholics to escape loyalist mobs when he was shot by a sniper – the first IRA 'volunteer' to die in the Troubles.

Today Bombay Street backs on to one of the huge steel 'peace lines' that divide the Shankill from the Falls so absolutely that there are only two or three easily sealed crossing points. Tom hasn't been into the Shankill in 30 years, though it is less than a mile from his home. Nor has Gerry Adams, who can travel the world but not visit a part of the West Belfast constituency for which he is MP. Belfast is actually far more segregated than most American cities with their black–white divides, but while the 'peace line' keeps the two communities apart, it cannot stop missiles. The back gardens of the Bombay Street houses are covered by grotesque steel cages – a sight hard to credit in a supposedly civilised nation.

Our progress up the Falls Road was halting, to say the least. We had not yet travelled half a mile but, as Tom observed, almost every building has a story. One on our right was painted deep blue except for a giant mural of Bobby Sands, the IRA hunger striker. This was a bookshop, but quite unlike any other I have visited.

Officially called the Green Cross Book Shop, it gives its profits to the families of republican prisoners. It is more commonly known as the Sinn Fein Book Shop and was attacked several times during the Troubles. Next door, in the Sinn Fein advice centre, an RUC officer went berserk and killed three people. There were still huge boulders on the pavement outside to prevent car bombs. Admittance was through two heavy steel doors, and the lady behind the counter proudly pointed out a bullet-hole in the ceiling above the till.

Despite its unappetising exterior the place had become something of a tourist attraction, and had changed its wares accordingly. Beside the dry doctrinal tomes and standard biographies of republican heroes you could now buy a whole range of delightful gifts to take home. How about a Gerry Adams coffee mug, or an IRA T-shirt, or a sweat shirt emblazoned: 'Long Kesh – University of Freedom'? If you simply wanted a postcard, there was a very nice range depicting the best of West Belfast's paramilitary murals.

All those attacks had evidently taken an unseen toll on the bookshop. A few weeks after my visit, it moved to new premises around the corner because the building was deemed structurally unsafe.

On we went. Eamon de Valera spoke here. James Connolly lived there. Three men were killed by the security forces in that bookie's over there. Look how they bricked up the Falls Road entrance to the Royal Victoria Hospital's extension at the height of the Troubles. See that old Presbyterian church? It is now the Irish language cultural centre. And how about this? An entire terraced street built with American dollars to house Catholics ousted from their homes by Protestants during an earlier pogrom in the 1920s. It is called Amcomri Street after the American Committee for the Relief of Ireland.

At the junction of the Falls Road and Whiterock Road Tom interrupted his political tour of West Belfast to duck into one of his favourite haunts – the City Cemetery.

The City Cemetery is in its own way much more interesting than the better-known Milltown Cemetery, not least because it is divided by an underground wall so that even in death Catholics and Protestants would be separated. It was opened in 1869 because the other graveyards had been filled by the victims of the famine. In those days it was on the edge of the city, not in the heart of republican West Belfast. It is the resting place of the Unionist establishment of the late nineteenth and early twentieth centuries – MPs, prison governors, imperial grand masters of the Orange Order. They are buried beneath magnificent monuments and obelisks that are slowly vanishing behind trees or under the rampant undergrowth, in part because so few of their descendants have dared to visit.

Tom is an ardent republican, but for these Unionists at least he did express a certain respect – and not just because they were dead. For a start, many of the tombstones featured Celtic crosses and inscriptions in Irish. 'That generation saw no contradiction between being Unionist and Irish,' he noted approvingly.

But as we pulled back the ivy and the brambles to read the inscriptions, something else became obvious. One man was killed in the Boer War. Another was 'killed on the first day of the Battle of the Somme'. A third 'lies in an unknown grave in France'. The three Newell brothers were killed in action in 1915, 1916 and 1917, all in their twenties. Herbert Gifford was 'an

engineer on the RMS *Titanic* who went down in that steamer in
mid-ocean doing his duty'. Another memorial to a First World
War casualty quoted Tennyson: 'Not once or twice in our rough
island story/The path of duty was the way to glory.'

'You see the price Unionists have paid?' said Tom. 'What
becomes very, very clear is their sense of public duty.'

The cemetery sits in the shade of the Black Mountain and
offers a wonderful view across Belfast. We rooted around for an
hour or so. Tom has a wry sense of humour. He showed me the
grave of one Brendan Gamble whose inscription reads: 'Beam me
up, Lord.' He also showed me the garish plot of a traveller family
named Doherty which was adorned with flowers, a couple of
Guinness bottles, two plaster horses' heads and stone tablets
commemorating various Dohertys. 'B. Doherty. Contractor. He
was the best,' read one.

At the Milltown Cemetery, on the opposite side of the Falls
Road and a few hundred yards further up, Tom's republicanism
reasserted itself. Compared with the City Cemetery, Milltown is
a vast, bleak and cheerless place that slopes down to a motorway
and has none of the lush vegetation of its municipal counterpart.
For republicans, however, it has enormous cachet for this is
where the IRA lays its dead to rest.

Tom started to point out the graves. Over there was 'Volunteer
Joseph Malone. No. 1 Battalion Irish Expeditionary Force.
Captured in London and died in Parkhurst Prison 21 January
1942'. Beyond was Marie Drumm, a Sinn Fein vice-president
'murdered by pro-British elements' as she lay in a hospital bed in
1976. And here was 'Volunteer Patricia Black' who 'died on
active service'. 'She represents for me the pain of our society,'
said Tom. 'She died when she was 18. What do you know about
life when you're 18?'

Ms Black, I discovered later, blew herself up while trying to
plant a bomb at a concert given by an Army band in St Albans,
Hertfordshire, in 1991.

There was not a soul about – at least metaphorically speaking. We walked on in one of those damp, cold, penetrating Belfast winds past the grave of Guiseppe Conlon, who died in an English prison and was the subject of the movie *In the Name of the Father*. We passed a plot for members of the Official IRA, from whom the 'Provisionals' split in 1970; they seemed a bit short of martyrs, with only four names inscribed on a great expanse of wall. We passed another monument – this one engraved with a hand clutching an AK47 assault rifle – for the dead of another republican splinter group, the Irish National Liberation Army.

Finally we reached the republican holy of holies tucked discreetly away in a corner of the cemetery. Here, surrounded by a low green fence and small fir trees, were the black marble graves of particular IRA heroes like Bobby Sands and the three members of the active service unit shot dead by the SAS in Gibraltar in 1988. As that trio were being buried at this very spot a lone loyalist named Michael Stone hurled grenades and opened fire on the thousands of mourners, killing three before running down towards the motorway. There he was caught and beaten by the crowd before the police arrived just in time to save his life.

It is this plot that draws the tourists, but close by is the big, square County Antrim memorial inscribed with the names of all the IRA volunteers from Belfast who died for the cause over the past two centuries. Beside each name appear short inscriptions – 'Murdered at home', 'Killed in Action', 'Killed on Duty' – that mask a multitude of violent stories. So, too, does the inscription on a stone at the foot of the memorial which reads: 'This grave reserved for Lt Tom Williams IRA. Hanged in Belfast Jail 2 September 1942 and still interred there.'

Williams was the only IRA man ever executed in Northern Ireland. In 1942, when he was 19, he shot Constable Patrick Murphy of the Royal Ulster Constabulary in a Falls Road ambush. He and five colleagues were all sentenced to death, but a huge campaign on both sides of the border won reprieves for all but Williams. 'Don't worry about me . . . I'm fully prepared to die,' he told his fellow-prisoners in Belfast's Crumlin Road jail. Early on the morning of his execution, while the police separated throngs of baying loyalists and praying Catholics on the streets outside, he refused breakfast and twice celebrated Mass before walking calmly to the gallows.

One of Williams' fellow-prisoners was Joe Cahill, now the 'Grand Old Man' of the republican movement. He claimed that Williams' dying wish was to be buried with full 'military' honours next to his IRA comrades-in-arms in the Milltown Cemetery. The republican movement's grandly named National Graves Association fought a seven-year legal battle to retrieve its 'longest-serving prisoner', and in 1995 secured the Queen's approval to have his remains dug up from his unmarked grave inside the walls of the now-defunct prison.

They were duly disinterred in the summer of 1999, but unfortunately for the NGA Williams' relatives had other plans. Having established their legal title to his remains, they reburied him in early 2000 in his mother's overgrown grave in a far corner of the cemetery. Thousands turned out for the funeral, and Mr Cahill led the mourners.

Outside the Milltown Cemetery, the Falls Road turns into Andersonstown Road. The junction is marked by the Andersonstown police station – another huge, ugly fortress bristling with observation cameras atop high masts and deeply resented by the locals. For the best part of 30 years no uniformed policeman left here except in a convoy of slate-grey armoured Land Rovers, or guarded by a quartet of heavily armed soldiers if on foot.

The dangers were amply illustrated one March morning in 1988 just a few hundred yards further up the Andersonstown Road. It was three days after Michael Stone's Milltown attack and the tension was great. Two Army corporals in civilian clothes inexplicably drove into the funeral cortège of one of Stone's victims outside Casement Park, West Belfast's Gaelic Football ground.

A mob, apparently believing the two men were loyalist gunmen, dragged them from their car. They were stripped, beaten and taken on to waste ground opposite Casement Park where they were shot. What made the whole episode still more horrific was that an Army helicopter hovering overhead filmed the shootings but was powerless to intervene. Tom pointed out the waste ground up an alley between two buildings. There was no plaque or memorial marking these two deaths.

It was lunchtime. Fortuitously we had arrived at the large green, windowless box of a building that houses the republican Felons Club – a sort of drinking club and community centre wrapped into one. You have to have spent time in jail to qualify for membership, and there is no shortage of eligible people. One survey showed that just in the Springfield Road area of West Belfast one in every 10 adults had been imprisoned for paramilitary activities. Nelson Mandela is an honorary member. Happily Tom had served two brief spells in the Crumlin Road jail, so in we went through the security gate just as Gerry Adams came out.

It was a slightly awkward moment for the tall, bearded Sinn Fein president. He was off to watch his son play a Gaelic Football match in Casement Park. I had written to him a few weeks earlier asking if I could accompany him to a game so that he could explain the intricacies of that exclusively nationalist sport, but he had never replied. He had to retain some privacy, he now explained. The 'Shinners' are like that. They are always friendly, always helpful, but always keep their distance. You would never, ever be invited to their homes.

Inside, the ground-floor bar and the lounge, hung with portraits of republican heroes, were almost empty. But upstairs the large functions room, decorated with artefacts made by prisoners in the Maze, was packed for a party commemorating a famous republican singer who had died 20 years earlier.

A *Who's Who* of republicanism was sitting eating soup and sandwiches: Joe Cahill, the veteran IRA leader still going strong more than half a century after being sentenced to death; Martin Meehan, the legendary IRA hard man from North Belfast who commanded one of the IRA's most active battalions during the Troubles; Martin Ferris, caught smuggling seven tonnes of weaponry into Ireland in 1984; Danny Morrison, the former Sinn Fein publicity director who first coined the phrase 'the armalite and the ballot box', and so on. It all seemed utterly commonplace. But for the accents, we could have been in a popular Home Counties pub.

Beyond the Felons lay Ballymurphy, Turf Lodge, Twinbrook, Poleglass and other republican estates stretching south-westwards out of Belfast in a corridor between the motorway and the slopes of the Black Mountain. Their labyrinthine streets were plastered with murals, some paramilitary but others recalling the famine or Celtic myths. There were countless memorials and plaques on gable ends honouring 'volunteers' who 'died at the hands of the British army' or 'defending their community'. One commemorated 'Julie Livingstone, aged 14 years, killed by a plastic bullet 13th May 1981'. Tricolours fluttered from lamp-posts. Irish street signs had been erected in place of English ones. Tom even showed me a primary school built by local people so that their children could be educated in Irish.

In the midst of this sea of 'green' there is one small red, white and blue enclave. The Protestant Suffolk estate, built in the early 1950s, is almost entirely ringed by a steel 'peace wall' for protection. On the 'front line' of Stewartstown Road nearly every building has been abandoned and boarded up. The estate is periodically attacked by nationalists bearing petrol bombs, its population has declined from several thousand to just 800, and 145 of its original 583 properties have been demolished, but it survives.

I mention Suffolk because it illustrates the extraordinary complexities of housing in Northern Ireland. I once interviewed a grandmother there named Jean Brown who had bought her four-bedroom council house and kept it immaculately. It was worth about £16,000 and falling. Barely a stone's throw away, an almost identical three-bedroom home belonging to another grandmother named Briege Clarke was worth about £27,500 and rising.

The reason for this discrepancy was very simple. Mrs Brown lives in Suffolk, where the demand for housing is non-existent because Protestants have been abandoning Belfast. Mrs Clarke lives in Andersonstown, where the demand is sky-high because Catholics want to live in areas where they feel safe. Indeed, Gerry Adams' constituency has probably the highest rate of council-house sales in the United Kingdom.

The obvious solution is for Northern Ireland's Housing Executive to move Catholics into Suffolk, but this is Belfast where not an inch of territory is ever surrendered. In the mid-1980s the executive did try building homes for Catholics in Protestant Roe Street in North Belfast, but loyalists burned out the new residents and £500,000 almost literally went up in smoke.

For the executive to repeat that experiment in Suffolk 'would just be completely unacceptable,' Mrs Brown told me. 'People here feel so insecure. Their feeling is that all it takes is one or two Catholic families to move into the empty houses and the process begins of moving Protestants out. It would be only a matter of time before the Protestant community disappears.'

Mrs Brown and her husband were driven out of the nearby Lenadoon estate in 1972 when displaced Catholics moved in and broke her windows, burned her car and pelted the house with eggs. She admitted buying her house more as a statement of defiance than an investment. 'It's my home and my community,' she said, and insisted she would never leave. A couple of Catholic families had tried moving in, but Suffolk has its fair share of loyalist paramilitaries and 'quite honestly they were intimidated out'.

Suffolk is not a one-off. The same unwritten rules apply across Northern Ireland. The Housing Executive is thus left in the absurd position of having to demolish thousands of houses in run-down Protestant areas while struggling to build enough new homes for a young and growing Catholic population.

Tom had been at pains to demonstrate West Belfast's suffering, resourcefulness and cultural richness. He could have shown me much more in the same vein – the music, the dancing, the vibrant drama. It was not an inaccurate picture, but it was not complete. What it failed to highlight was the IRA's deliberate use of violence and coercion to keep the community in line.

Ask the local school principals who face pickets if they invite the police for something as innocuous as road safety lessons. Ask the players of the Donegal Celtic football club who were 'visited' at their homes and warned that their 'safety could not be guaranteed' if they played a cup semi-final against the Royal Ulster Constabulary.

Ask the family of Maureen Kearney, a woman with impeccable republican credentials whose 33-year-old son Andrew crossed an IRA commander in a pub in 1998. A few days later eight men burst into his eighth-floor flat as he was cradling his two-week-old daughter just after midnight, dragged him into the stairwell and shot him in both legs, severing an artery. He bled to death because the gang ripped out the telephone and jammed the lift doors as they left. The IRA were 'mere thugs who terrorise their own community in pursuit of money and power', Mrs Kearney told me shortly before she herself died, broken-hearted, in August 1999.

Ask Margaret McKinney, the mother of one of the so-called 'Disappeared' who were abducted, executed and buried in secret graves by the IRA in the 1970s. Margaret, a former school cleaner now in her late sixties, is yet another of those extraordinary Northern Ireland women who have somehow endured and survived the most unimaginable suffering. She told me her story as we sat in the same spotless little house in Andersonstown where she and her husband, a retired roofer, raised four children including a son named Brian.

One night in May 1978, when Brian was 22, he did not come home. Her husband went out, asked around, and was told the IRA had him. Brian finally returned 48 hours later, beaten and distraught; he admitted he had helped to rob an IRA-run bar. Margaret and her husband took him straight back to the bar, repaid his £50 share of the proceeds and made him apologise. 'We came away thinking maybe it was a blessing in disguise, a good warning,' Margaret recalled.

The following Thursday Brian was late for his gardening job so his sister, Linda, offered to drop him off. 'He says "I'm away, Mum", and he just went off,' said Margaret. It was the last time she ever saw him.

Linda dropped him round the corner from where he was working. At 5 o'clock that afternoon, one of Brian's workmates knocked on Margaret's door and handed her his wages. Brian hadn't come to work, he said. Two men had come looking for him. 'Alarm bells started ringing. Brian lived for Thursdays because it was pay day. The fellow just walked away and I knew from the look on his face something was wrong.'

Her husband again contacted a local IRA man, who confirmed the IRA were holding Brian but assured them he'd be all right. Four days passed. The McKinneys could do nothing but wait. 'We couldn't have gone to the police, not with the IRA involved,' said Margaret. The following Wednesday the man came to say that Brian and another local lad named John McClory 'had got put out of the country. They told me not to go near the docks.'

Anticipating that Brian would telephone when he reached
England, Margaret packed a case, raised some money from relatives and waited for the call. She waited, and waited. It never
came. People approached the IRA on the family's behalf, but
were told to stop asking questions. 'That's the way we were
left,' said Margaret, her eyes watering more than twenty years
later. 'We were never told what happened to him. I knew they'd
killed him and I was never going to see him again. I knew in my
heart.'

The weeks turned to months, the months to years. The police
couldn't begin to help in what was – and still is – a virtual no-go
area for them. Margaret was beside herself with grief; she suffered heart attacks. For years she would sleep in Brian's bed and
wrap herself in his coat until one day her husband packed up
Brian's belongings and took them away. Her other son turned to
drink and his marriage broke up.

Margaret would see the men who had abducted Brian on the
streets. She would beg the police to give her a gun so that she
could shoot them. She would follow one of their children to
school and work out ways of stealing him. 'I was sitting crying
from morning to night. I thought blood was coming out of my
eyes, the tears burned me so much.'

There was nobody she could talk to and nothing she could
do. Neighbours believed Brian must have done something wrong
and got what he deserved. 'Nobody ever spoke about it because
it was the Provos that done it,' she said. 'All I ever did for sev-
enteen years was cry and that's the God's truth. I used to be a
happy-go-lucky, singing person . . . It was hell, the darkest, darkest corner of hell.'

Nothing changed until the IRA finally called a ceasefire in
1994. Margaret joined a victims' counselling group called Wave
and discovered she was not alone in her grief. She found that
there were other women whose husbands and sons had 'disappeared'. She received a telephone call from a man who had fallen

out with the IRA and told her he believed Brian and John McClory were buried beneath housing on the nearby Glen Road which was being built when they were killed. He thought McClory had been shot trying to escape, and so they'd had to kill Brian too.

Margaret's suffering was far from over, however. In late 1998 an anonymous caller using an IRA code-word left a message with Wave saying that the two boys were buried beneath the third or fourth steps leading up from the Glen Road to the Glencolin estate. The police started excavating. Margaret began planning the funeral her son had been denied all those years. But after three days' digging, nothing was found. 'I was so sure. I couldn't believe it. I was just devastated,' said Margaret.

There's a large photograph of Brian above a cross on the wall of Margaret's living room, and several smaller photographs of him on the mantelpiece. She took me up to his old room, from which we could see the house of a senior Sinn Fein politician with its several extensions and other obvious signs of wealth. She showed me his mouth organ – about the only one of his possessions she has kept – and told me how she longed for a grave for her son where she could mourn and lay flowers like other bereaved mothers.

Margaret certainly did not regard republican West Belfast as some sort of haven. Nor did she regard the IRA as brave defenders of the community. 'This place is ruled by the Provos,' she said. 'They rule all these estates. They are the ones that rule this area and they are drunken bums.'

Shortly after my visit Margaret had another visitor. She returned from church one Sunday to be told that Gerry Adams would be dropping by that afternoon. He told her and Mrs McClory: 'You're going to get Brian and John back again.' The next day the IRA announced that it had located the unmarked graves of nine of the so-called 'Disappeared'.

Margaret was overjoyed. She bought a plot in Milltown

Cemetery and again began planning Brian's funeral, but still her agony was not over. The IRA refused to identify the sites until the British and Irish Parliaments passed legislation to prevent evidence from the remains being used to prosecute the killers. That took another two months. Margaret then had to endure a further month of torment while the Irish police drained and excavated a remote bog just south of the border in County Monaghan.

She had just about given up hope, and the police were on the point of abandoning the search, when the workmen spotted bones protruding from the earth. Ten more weeks passed while the bones were subjected to DNA testing in Dublin to check that they were really those of Brian and John. Twenty-one years after Brian disappeared, Margaret was finally able to bring his remains home for a proper wake before giving him a decent Christian burial.

The last time I spoke to Margaret on the telephone, she sounded truly happy and contented. She was visiting Brian's grave daily. The galling thing, she said, was that she found herself feeling grateful to those who had put her through such hell.

The Falls is easily left behind. It has a couple of roads that lead straight up and over the hills behind it. I took one some weeks later, when spring had turned to summer, and within minutes the city had vanished and I was driving through that other Northern Ireland of small farms and luscious green fields and roads that double as race tracks – literally.

I'm not joking. I'd gone above six miles and was in the middle of nowhere when I suddenly passed a grandstand covered in Michelin signs to my left, and what was evidently a pitstop to the right. I realised I was on the Dundrod circuit where another of Northern Ireland's road races, the Ulster Grand Prix, takes place.

There was nobody around, so I roared off down the straight as fast as my clapped-out Cavalier would go. Soon I was cruising down towards the village of Glenavy, beyond which lay the blue waters of Lough Neagh, the largest lake in the British Isles, with the humps of the distant Sperrins clearly visible on the far side.

Glenavy had a nice old church at the end of an avenue of lime trees, a pretty three-arched stone bridge across a river, and a war memorial at one end of an attractive main street that listed survivors as well as victims. I consulted Ernest Sandford, and he didn't disappoint me. The village inevitably had a claim to fame. A man called John Ballance was born here in 1839, emigrated to New Zealand, and ended up as its Prime Minister. He died of cancer two years after taking office, but not before he had laid the foundations for two world firsts – women's suffrage and a welfare state.

What I had not expected was to find that members of Mr Ballance's family still live in Glenavy, just as Woodrow Wilson's still live near Strabane, but then people do tend to stay put in Northern Ireland.

The Post Office lady directed me to the farm where Mr Ballance was born and raised. There another John Ballance resides in a bungalow next to the old farmhouse. He was just coming out of the front door when I arrived – a Jack Nicholson look-alike in his early sixties, dressed in blue overalls and a woolly hat. He had a mug of tea in his oil-smeared hand and was in the middle of repairing some piece of machinery, but he stopped for a minute.

The Prime Minister was his grandfather's brother, he told me. The relative lack of intervening generations was explained by the fact that his own father did not marry until he was 60. He himself was only seven when his father died, his mother remarried and he'd never received a proper schooling, so he'd taught himself some engineering. He hadn't visited New Zealand, though he'd been invited to go on the centenary of his great-uncle's death in 1993. The following year James Bolger – New Zealand's then Prime Minister – had visited the farm, and his wife produced a faded newspaper cutting to prove it. As for politics, he had no ambitions himself. 'That takes a little bit of education.'

As I drove on round the south-east corner of Lough Neagh, along tiny lanes flanked by lush pastures and banks of cow parsley, I passed tumbledown farmhouses, old red telephone boxes, a couple of men repairing a boat in a marshy inlet. I momentarily succumbed to the belief that I'd found a pocket of the province untouched by the years of violence, or for that matter by modernity – but it was, of course, an illusion.

I soon found myself driving through the village of Aghalee. The name rang a bell, so when I got home I checked. Sure enough, this was the village where 18-year-old Bernadette Martin, a Catholic, was shot by a loyalist bigot while she slept in her Protestant boyfriend's bed on 15 July 1997 – the day before I arrived in Northern Ireland.

Seven months later the body of a 30-year-old Catholic man called Kevin Conway was found in a derelict farmhouse just outside the village. His hands were tied behind him and he had been shot in the back of the head. On his feet were the slippers he was wearing when abducted. Nobody was ever convicted, but it was widely believed that he had been selling cigarettes and alcohol to children and was killed by the IRA. What shook me was that I'd almost completely forgotten Conway's murder. There have been so many in Northern Ireland that you rapidly forget the victims in all but the most shocking cases.

I was heading for Colebrooke Park, a stately home in Fermanagh, but as I was not due until early evening I decided to meander round the bottom of Lough Neagh to visit the ancient Celtic cross at Ardboe on the western shore.

I had plenty of time. I had dispensed with my map and was simply following my nose. Unfortunately my little lane abruptly ended where the broad River Bann flows into the lough. There used to be a hand-pulled, one-car ferry across but nowadays, I discovered, you have to do an 18-mile detour to reach the other side.

The far side, when I finally reached it, appeared to be one great market garden, a patchwork quilt of black silty fields growing lettuces and strawberries. By now the day had turned positively sultry. I drove on to the village of Maghery where, to my horror, I discovered my way blocked where a second ferry-less river, the Blackwater, entered the lough. With sinking heart I wound down my window and asked a lady taking flowers to the church the quickest way to Ardboe.

'It's not a stone's throw across,' she told me cheerfully, 'but you'll have to drive 13 miles round. They stopped the ferry about 15 years ago. We used to know all the families the other side, but now they're complete strangers.'

It was midday by the time I reached Ardboe's cross. The last few miles lay through meadows full of contented cows and buttercups, then suddenly I saw the tenth-century cross towering ahead of me on the loughshore. In England a cross of such antiquity would be surrounded by walls, car parks and ticket booths. This one is surrounded merely by an old wrought-iron railing and a graveyard containing the remains of two old abbeys, the older one dating from sometime before AD 600.

The cross stands more than 18 feet high, with arms 3'6" wide, and three-quarters of its circle still intact. On the four faces of the sandstone column are 22 carvings depicting biblical scenes from Adam and Eve to the Last Judgement – a sort of petrified *Readers' Digest* version of the bible – though most are now so worn by wind and rain that they are almost impossible to decipher.

In earlier times pilgrims used to come and shuffle around the cross on their knees while saying prayers, but today there was nobody about. However, there was a bungalow up the lane and the old fellow who lived there told me the legend of the cross.

While it was being built a magical cow emerged from the lough and gave the workmen not only lashings of milk, cream and butter for themselves, but surplus milk to mix into the mortar – hence its strength.

My new friend was in no hurry. 'The man who made time made plenty of it,' he told me. He perched on the bonnet of my car in his dirty old work clothes and recalled how there used to be an old wishing tree in the graveyard into which people stuck coins, nails, buttons and other such objects for luck. Unfortunately, in doing so, they poisoned the tree and it died.

He would have talked all day, but there was more I wanted to see before Fermanagh and the afternoon was wearing on. 'I'll not hold yer back,' he told me as I made to go. 'Right yer be. Safe home.'

I sped westwards through the unprepossessing town of Coalisland where there was an ill-fated coal rush during the industrial revolution. All that now remains is a derelict canal built to carry the coal to Lough Neagh.

I skirted the equally unprepossessing town of Dungannon – it has a fine girls' academy and an attractive main street, but the story that sticks in my mind is of a cat blown to bits when some local youths lit a five-inch banger that they'd strapped to the hapless creature.

Soon I was in the green hills of County Tyrone, a place immortalised by Winston Churchill with his post-war reference to its 'dreary steeples'. The great man maligned not only a county of outstanding beauty, but its churches too. There is a particularly fine stone church in the village of Castlecaulfield, just a few miles beyond Dungannon, and one with a story attached.

From 1818 to 1823 it had a shy young curate called the Reverend Charles Wolfe. Around that time the now defunct *Newry Telegraph* published one of his poems anonymously in order to fill some space. It began: 'Not a drum was heard, not a funeral note/As his corse to the rampart we hurried . . .' Other journals reprinted it, and in 1822 Lord Byron declared 'The Burial of Sir John Moore' the finest ode in the English language. Several imposters claimed to have written it before the real poet was identified, but sadly Wolfe died of consumption the very next year.

I was enjoying this meander. I skipped the ancestral cottage of Ulysses Grant near Ballygawley, though I would doubtless have encountered hordes of relatives of America's eighteenth president. Instead I proceeded to the little town of Augher and turned left along a country lane that took me high into remote hills and the Favour Royal forest.

There I found a little car park with a notice instructing visitors to follow the white arrows for a 30-minute woodland stroll to St Patrick's Chair and back. The Chair, it explained, was a huge sandstone boulder carved in the shape of a seat, and wishes made while sitting on it came true provided they were kept secret. There was also a boulder with a hole full of water 'credited with curing many diseases but specialising in warts'. The funny thing about the hole was that it never ran dry.

I set off into the forest, confident that I could gallop round the circuit in a mere 20 minutes. It had turned into a lovely afternoon. I had the place to myself, and the only sound was the cooing of ring-doves, the crackling of twigs beneath my feet and, all of a sudden, the ringing of my mobile phone. It was Katy, my wife; we chatted for a few minutes and then hung up. Unfortunately, it was in those few minutes that I missed the white arrow to my left.

I carried on down the track before me. After a while I began to wonder where the Chair was. Eventually the track ended abruptly at a barrier designed to exclude cars from the forest. I'd clearly missed my way, but as I retraced my steps I spotted another, smaller path leading off in the general direction of the Chair. I took it. After half-a-mile the path was blocked by a

fallen tree. I climbed over it and carried on until the path petered
out altogether.

Katy has no sense of direction. She has been known to turn
the wrong way outside the front door. I've always rather prided
myself on mine, however, so instead of cutting my losses and
turning back I carried on. Soon I was completely lost. For the
better part of an hour I braved bogs and brambles and fought
through vicious undergrowth until finally, cursing and fed up, I
found myself back at the very spot where the wrong path left the
wrong track.

I decided to give up on St Patrick's Chair and set off back.
Barely 200 yards from the car park, I spotted the path I should
have taken. Within five minutes I was sitting on a large chunk of
chair-shaped sandstone and wishing . . . Well, I can't say what I
wished, but it had something to do with signmakers, mobile
phones and wives who call at inopportune moments, and was
not altogether generous.

Just below the Chair, down in a hollow in the forest, was the
boulder with a perfectly round hole in the top. It hadn't rained
here in days, and the ground was perfectly dry, but the hole was
indeed full of water. I refrained from collecting the £2 or so in
coppers and five-pence pieces that people had deposited in the
bottom. You'd have thought if they really wanted their warts
removed they'd have invested at least £1 in the venture. I put
nothing in, which may be why the water singularly failed to
restore hair to my balding forehead.

My 30-minute woodland stroll took me three times that. By
now I was running late, but between here and Colebrooke Park
lay another in Northern Ireland's extensive collection of bizarre
tombs, one to rival that of John Carey outside Toome or the
mini-Taj Mahal near Doagh in County Antrim.

I sped back to Augher, and down the main road to the city of
Clogher. Actually Clogher is a little village with a population of
precisely 550, but I suppose technically it's a city because it has

a cathedral. It was clearly a much more important place back in the fifth century – when St Patrick founded the See of Clogher and appointed his old chum St Macartan as its first bishop – than it is today.

Just beyond Clogher, I spotted what I was looking for on the top of a high hill a few miles to the south: a monument called Brackenridge's Folly. It was not signposted, so I headed towards it along windy little lanes much as a mouse tries to reach the cheese in one of those mazes in children's puzzle books.

I took several wrong turns, but finally I drove up a hill and there it was above me, surrounded by cows and gorse, a square three-storey tower with each storey smaller than the one below and the remains of a railed parapet around the top. This peculiar edifice was in a state of terminal neglect, which may reflect the fact that the locals were never very enamoured of Mr Brackenridge.

He was a self-made nineteenth-century landlord despised by the gentry of the Clogher Valley, that glorious tapestry of small farms and emerald-green fields now stretched out below me. Allegedly he said that if people wouldn't look up to him while he was alive, he'd make certain they did so when he was dead. That is why – a full 30 years before his death – he built his tomb on a hilltop.

He also insisted on being buried not only at 4 a.m., and in the innermost of three coffins, but upside-down. Apparently he believed that when the world ends the poles will be reversed, so he'd be the right way up for the resurrection. It is an interesting theory that I wouldn't presume to question, but unfortunately Mr Brackenridge will not be in a position to prove it. About fifty years after his death in 1879 his tomb was raided, his bones scattered, and his rings and watch-chain pilfered.

I had dawdled enough; it was now early evening and I was already late. I retraced my route to Clogher and continued westwards on the main road to Enniskillen through Fivemiletown which acquired its name because it was exactly five Irish miles from the villages of Clogher, Tempo and Brookeborough. For some reason, Irish miles are 480 yards longer than English ones.

Brookeborough got its name from the local aristocracy, an Anglo-Irish 'plantation' family that came to Ireland in the 1590s and was granted 30,000 acres of land in this lovely corner of County Fermanagh for services rendered during the Catholic uprising of 1641. It was the Brookes who built Colebrooke Park in the 1820s, and the present Viscount and Lady Brookeborough whom I was keeping waiting now.

I turned off the main road just beyond Fivemiletown, as instructed. I drove through some old gates by a fine little church and followed a long drive that took me through lush green pastures where rabbits scurried for cover, and past a cluster of disused farm buildings and an old walled garden with a wonderfully decrepit Victorian greenhouse. Just when I thought I'd taken another wrong turning, I rounded a corner by an impeccably trimmed hedge and found myself staring at a great square barracks of a house with an impressive portico supported by four huge Ionic stone columns. In front of this imposing building, resplendent in the evening sunlight, stretched rolling parkland dotted with ancient oaks and beeches and, off to the left, a colonnaded bridge over a hidden river.

I parked with a satisfying crunch of tyres on gravel. I felt as though I'd driven on to the set of one of those idyllic films about the life of the English upper classes before the First World War, and there was Lady Brookeborough advancing to greet me. 'Sorry I'm so late,' I began, but before I could relate the story of my hapless search for St Patrick's Chair she assured me the other guests had all been delayed at the airport and I was the first to arrive.

A Land Rover arrived from the opposite direction and Lord Brookeborough, a trim fellow in his mid-forties, hopped out. More friendly greetings, and soon he was leading me through a cavernous hall and up a grand staircase featuring a stuffed leopard shot in India by his great-great-grandfather, Sir Victor Brooke, Queen Victoria's godson.

My room was palatial, and replete with a huge four-poster bed, and from my window I had a magnificent view of the estate framed by two of the portico's columns. Already I felt a thousand miles from the grim world of the Falls Road and the Shankill.

Ostensibly I was here to join a weekend fly-fishing course and write a travel article for *The Times* about Colebrooke Park.

Lord Brookeborough inherited this pile following his grandfather's death in 1973. By that stage the 30,000 acres had shrunk to barely 1,000 due to successive Land Acts, most of the 52 rooms were locked up, and the entire contents had to be sold to pay death duties. For the next seven years the house stood empty, and would soon have joined the long list of Ireland's ruined stately homes had not Alan Brookeborough and his new wife, Janet, decided to try and make it pay by hosting shooting weekends in the winter, fishing courses in the summer, and conferences all year round.

They moved into three rooms in July 1980. The place was by then 'like a dirty, peeling mausoleum', Lady Brookeborough told me, and she went round the house removing dead crows and bats from fireplaces. The Queen Mother had complained that it was the coldest house she'd ever stayed in, and that even the bathwater was freezing – and that was *before* it was abandoned.

The Brookeboroughs received their first paying guests – four Germans – that September. With that initial income they began renovating and refurbishing the next room. And so the process continued – with Lady Brookeborough scouring antique shops and making curtains for 15-foot-high windows – until after 20 years the entire house was restored to a state of elegant, tasteful comfort.

The real reason I was here, however, was because families like the Brookeboroughs are just as much a part of Northern Ireland as the paramilitaries and present-day politicians who shape the popular perception of the province. Indeed, for better or worse the family helped to make the place. Lord Brookeborough's father was a member of the Stormont government at the beginning of the Troubles. His grandfather, Basil, was Northern Ireland's Prime Minister for 20 years from 1943. The family's greatest contribution, however, was in the military field, and as the other guests had yet to arrive Lord Brookeborough whisked me back down to the church I'd passed on the way in.

The family built this in 1763 and people joke that it is dedicated to the greater glory not of God but of the 'fighting Brookes'. The walls are covered with plaques commemorating members of the family. Here by the family's personal pews is one to Field Marshal Viscount Alanbrooke, the great strategist of the Second World War. Here is another to James Anson Otho Brooke who won the Victoria Cross in the First World War. Francis Brooke fell 'when gallantly charging the French in the ever memorable battle of Waterloo'. Brigadier General Henry Brooke, killed in 1880, was 'the last to leave the walls of Kandahar and lost his life in the noble endeavour of bringing into safety a wounded brother officer'. The one I felt sorry for was Captain Thomas Brooke, who died rather less heroically in 1838 when two vessels collided in the port of Liverpool.

No fewer than 26 Brookes served in the First World War, and 27 in the Second World War. At least a dozen were killed. My host, however, fought the enemy right here in Fermanagh. He left the 17th/21st Lancers in 1977, returned home to run the Colebrooke estate, and immediately joined the Ulster Defence Regiment. He and his soldiers confronted the IRA for 17 years as it sought to drive Protestants from this border country in a deliberate policy of ethnic cleansing. Lord Brookeborough survived, but 11 of his UDR company did not. They were picked off one by one as they went about their normal lives as farmers, bus drivers and dustbin-men.

Back at the house three of the house-party – a Dutch couple and a London art dealer – had finally arrived. We had drinks in the sunken garden, watched by a pair of peacocks. We dined on salmon and trifle – the first of a string of stupendous meals produced by Lady Brookeborough. Afterwards we sank on to deep sofas in a drawing room littered with books by or about illustrious members of the family. In one, the letters of Sir Victor Brooke, I read how he killed the leopard I'd seen on the staircase in the Nilgiri Hills of Southern India – 'the deadly ball entered that savage eye and crashed through his brain'.

There was no formality; titles were quickly replaced by 'Alan' and 'Janet'. We helped ourselves to drinks. Paying guests or not, we soon felt like part of an Edwardian house-party. Lord Brookeborough and I ended the evening playing 'slosh' – a cross between billiards and snooker – in a billiards room full of stuffed animals and black-and-white photographs of Alanbrooke with Churchill at key moments in the Second World War. My host emitted roars of delight whenever he sank a ball, but I'm happy to report that he lost by a single point.

The fishing was the main business. We were joined by assorted Army officers from Lisburn and Belfast, and several of us were complete beginners, but by mid-morning the next day our lines were happily looping through the air on the lawn. By early afternoon we were actually hooking – though not necessarily landing – our first trout on an open stretch of the Colebrooke River under the benign watch of our instructors-cum-gillies, Patrick Trotter and David Dowery. By the morning of the second day we had become sufficiently expert that we prowled the river bank, searching for challenging pools onto which we dropped our flies with varying degrees of accuracy and stealth.

The Colebrooke, incidentally, is not only a particularly fine trout river. It is also the place where, in 1816, a young girl picked up the only diamond of gemstone quality ever found in

Europe. The 'Brookeborough Diamond' is still owned by the family, and mounted in a ring of Wicklow gold.

But the fishing was only the start of it. Lord Brookeborough is a man blessed by his maker with prodigious energy and enthusiasm, and now that a tentative peace had returned to this remote and gorgeous area after 30 years on the front line of the Troubles he was eager to make the most of it.

At 6.30 the first morning he had knocked on my door, and the room was so huge that it took me a few seconds to spot where he was standing. It was a brilliant sunny day. Within 15 minutes we were crossing the river, looking for otters, and tramping past great banks of purple rhododendrons to the outer reaches of the estate in search of deer.

Late that day we drove down towards the border with County Monaghan through rolling green hills and meadows blanketed with buttercups. Before the famine of 1846 more than 155,000 people lived in County Fermanagh. Today, barely 50,000 do so. Around here the country used to be full of tiny farms – tenants of Colebrooke. Today it is almost empty, much of it owned by the forestry service and littered with abandoned cottages.

With the help of a guide we found the tumbledown, overgrown house in the forest where a family called Murphy had lived until the nocturnal antics of the 'Coonian Ghost' forced them to emigrate to America. Unfortunately, the ghost went with them. Later we met an elderly couple with a stove in their sitting room who said that people around here really believed the story and wouldn't go near the house.

We went to the once thriving Mullaghfad church, now all but abandoned with the forest encroaching on the graveyard. I'd seldom seen anything like it. By the gate was an old stone stable where the curate used to tether his horse. In the graveyard were the graves of two 'B Specials' killed by the IRA in 1920. Inside there were just plain floorboards, hard wooden pews and an ancient pedal organ. Above the pulpit was a single gas lantern, for there was no electricity.

Our presence disturbed a million particles of dust which played in the light slanting through the windows. The bible had been presented in memory of a 17-year-old girl who died in 1890. On one wall hung a faded black-and-white photograph of William Little, the parish clerk who died in 1896. On another was a plaque commemorating 25 men from the parish killed in the First World War. Today there are not that many people even living there.

As we left, I noticed a single chain running down the outside of the church from the bell above. I thought of pulling it, but the sound of chimes ringing through this land of the dead would have been eerie indeed.

On our way home we had another extraordinary encounter. Lord Brookeborough stopped to introduce us to a barrel-chested, wall-eyed farmer of advancing years who was cutting the grass by the side of the lane leading to his home. 'How's the cattle?' my host asked him. 'Oh, shocking bad prices, that's true indeed,' he replied.

His name was John Corscaddan, and he is a dispenser of 'charms' for curing sprained and twisted joints. The afflicted come to him, he puts his hands on the injury and recites an incantation, and – he claims – people leave cured. 'It's handed down from generation to generation,' John said of the incantation. 'I got it from my auntie. Her father gave it to her, and I have to give it to someone of the opposite sex.'

He doesn't charge his patients; he considers the 'charm' a gift to be used for the common good. 'I didn't do it till my auntie died, and she died in 1955. She told me well before she died, right enough, but I never made use of it till she died and people started coming to me. I didn't know if it would work or not, but it did.'

The key thing was that people had to believe. 'Supposing a

person came to me and they said "I have no belief", then the chances are ninety-five per cent sure it would not be any good.' The other strange thing, he said, was that the older the injury the longer it took to cure. If someone twisted their ankle jumping from a tractor and came to him within an hour, he could cure it within an hour.

I soon discovered that John was not a lone dispenser of charms. It seems that County Fermanagh is full of such people, each with their own speciality. They offer charms for bad backs, for ringworm, for haemorrhages. It's like an alternative National Health Service, and evidently produces results or it wouldn't survive.

Some of these people treat humans, others cure animals. John had had a calf with stomach ulcers so chronic that its faeces were black with blood. The vet told him it would be dead by the next morning, so he went to a woman in Enniskillen. 'I gave her a description of the animal and she said, "That's OK, John. I'll do a charm for you." The next morning the calf was sitting up.'

Some days later I spoke to a well-educated man in Enniskillen who told me how any woman who married a man with the same surname gained the ability to cure whooping-cough. He also told me how he himself had been critically ill in hospital with a blood clot on the lung until a young nurse quietly told him she knew someone with a cure. She brought the fellow into the ward, he did his bit, and my man duly recovered.

Lord Brookeborough told me of a woman called Mary back in Clogher who was consulted if his own sheep and cattle fell sick. Clogher was only a few miles back up the road, so when we returned to Colebrooke I telephoned Mary and asked if I could visit. 'Yes,' she said, and put the phone down. I rang back. 'How do I find you?' I asked. 'Ask anyone in Clogher,' she replied.

The woman in Clogher Post Office gave me detailed instructions that took me deep into the country. I had to stop twice more, but everyone did indeed know Mary and I finally found her tumbledown cottage up a rutted farm track. There were kittens playing in the yard, and a sheep scurried away as I approached the front door.

Mary was in her early eighties and rather unsteady on her feet. She sat me down in an elderly armchair. 'I cure all skin diseases of man and beast – dermatitis, ringworm, orph,' she told me. 'I do haemorrhages. I do sprains. I can take the pain out of cancer.'

Her brother had told her the secret prayers or incantations. 'My brother was doing it thirty-five years before he died. I don't know where he got it from. He gave it to me, but I wish to God he never had. I didn't have to do it as long as he was alive, but once he died I was trapped. Your life is not your own. You can't go anywhere. You can't take a holiday. You can't be away a day but there's someone coming looking for you.'

On cue, the telephone rang and Mary answered it. 'Yes,' I heard her say. 'What's the problem?' she asked. 'Take a bottle of olive oil. Rub it on her forehead. Shake some baby powder on it. Don't wash it. What's her name. . . . Teresa.' With that she put the phone down. That was a girl with a rash around her face, she explained. What about the prayer, I asked. 'I've already said it,' Mary replied.

'You can do it over the phone,' she continued. 'It always works – always, always, always. I get calls from all parts and corners of Ireland. I'm known better than a begging ass all over the place.' Some people gave her small gifts – a dozen eggs, a tin of biscuits – but 'I never charge and I never will. I wouldn't count it right to charge on nobody else's illness. I wouldn't count it right.'

The telephone rang again. 'What's the problem, dear?' I heard her say. 'What's his Christian name? I'll do anything I can. Just let me know how he goes now.' Mary returned to her chair. 'That was someone from Ballymena,' she told me. 'He can't get any movement in his leg. I don't know who he is. You never get any peace around here at all.'

Who was Mary going to leave her gift to, I asked? 'Anyone that will take it,' she laughed. She'd offered it to her two daughters and six grandchildren, but none was interested. 'I've got to find someone. I just hope to God I do.'

Could she cure dandruff, I asked as I was leaving?' 'Of course,' she replied. 'That's a skin disease.' She immediately sat me down on a kitchen stool. Then she crossed herself, spat on her hands, rubbed both hands over my hair and murmured to herself. 'Rub in some olive oil once a day but don't wash it for a week,' she told me.

I regret to report that months later I was still using Head and Shoulders.

Back at Colebrooke that evening, we hunted monster pike using whole frogs as bait and searched for crayfish under stones, but the grand finale came on the last night.

Friends and relatives of the Brookeboroughs – the Earl of Belmore from magnificent Castlecoole near Enniskillen, the younger brother of the Duke of Abercorn, the Hon. Christopher Brooke – swelled the party. Twenty-one of us sat down to a dinner of Colebrooke Park lamb. We then piled into a small fleet of Land and Range Rovers and drove up to Jenkin Lough, a magical bowl of water high on the wild, remote, bracken-covered hills dividing Fermanagh from County Monaghan.

Five years ago this was no-go territory, the lair of the Provos, a place Lord Brookeborough could visit only as part of an armed patrol. Today it is as beautiful and unspoiled as any part of the United Kingdom. We ringed the lough as the fish began rising. Lord Brookeborough and his brother, Christopher, began hauling them out with whoops of delight. I had many more bites from midges than I did from trout, but that was a minor price to pay for the privilege of fishing in such a serene spot as the last light faded on this enchanted landscape. Soon we were just disembodied voices laughing and joking in the vast darkness. I was hooked.

This journey was almost but not quite over. I was sent on my way the next morning with a large haunch of frozen Colebrooke venison, and spent much of the day roaming around Enniskillen, another Northern Ireland town whose name will sadly be linked for ever to an atrocity.

In 1987, an IRA bomb killed 11 people attending a Remembrance Day service at the war memorial. The names of the victims have since been added to the monument, along with 11 doves dedicated to the memory of 'our neighbours who died near this spot'. The doves and the inscription were a source of some controversy as several grieving relatives thought them too placatory.

Enniskillen is in fact a delightful place built on an island in a meandering stretch of river linking Upper and Lower Lough Erne. It has a long, hilly high street full of pleasant little shops with their names written in neat gold lettering above their windows, and tantalising glimpses of water down the side streets.

I had lunch and read the local paper, the *Impartial Reporter*, in an amazing old pub called Blakes of the Hollows which has dark panelled walls, private 'snugs' or cubicles, and a brass heating pipe running round the base of the bar to heat customers' feet in winter. The old gas-lamps still stand on the counter and the entire place is listed. The pub has been owned by the Blakes family since 1929, and the current barman's father had served customers there for 53 years before him. It was some lunch, too. My vegetable soup had large, whole boiled potatoes in it.

Enniskillen is also the only town in the British Isles to have raised two regiments bearing its name, and statues of a Royal Inniskilling Dragoon Guard and a Royal Inniskilling Fusilier adorn the town hall's tower. In the lobby there is a plaque to the most famous Dragoon of all – Captain Oates of Scott's ill-fated expedition to the South Pole – inscribed with a verse by John Masefield:

> *Knowing the storm without, the dwindling food,*
> *His failing strength, his comrades' constancy,*
> *This man in hope to save them all, thought it good*
> *To walk alone into the snow to die.*

If the truth be told there is no record of Oates – an Englishman who joined the Dragoons for a bit of adventure – having ever visited Enniskillen, but Oscar Wilde certainly did.

The dramatist was brought up in Dublin, and in 1864 his father sent him to Portora Royal School. I wandered up to this rather imposing Georgian edifice on a hill overlooking both the town and the river where some of the students were out rowing. Robert Northridge, the school's tweed-jacketed, silver-haired vice-principal, kindly showed me round with all the enthusiasm for the institution of a man who had not only taught there for a quarter of a century but been a Portora student himself.

It seems the school cannot quite make up its mind about its most famous old boy who, even at 13, flounced around in scarlet and lilac flannel shirts and spurned all sports. Mr Northridge showed me the honours board in the school hall from which Wilde's name was expunged following his conviction for homosexuality in 1895, only to be restored in about 1930. In the entrance hall he showed me a portrait of Wilde – complete with gloves, cigarette and flower on his lapel – that the school governors rejected in 1944 as 'unsuitable for adolescents', but which was hung in the headmaster's house the following year.

Remarkably Portora produced a second world-famous playwright in Samuel Beckett, the Nobel laureate, and a picture of him in the school's 1923 Cricket XI also hangs in the entrance hall. So does a portrait of a man who would be every school's perfect old boy – nice, wholesome and uncontroversial – the Rev. Henry Francis Lyte who wrote the hymns 'Abide With Me' and 'Praise My Soul the King of Heaven'.

Late in the afternoon I drove down to a tiny place called Carrybridge on the river a few miles below Enniskillen. I'd arranged to meet a couple of friends, Richard and Wendy Buchanan, who moored their boat there. As I arrived the sun came out for the first time that day, and soon we were heading down the river to Upper Lough Erne which, rather confusingly, lies due south of Lower Lough Erne.

I'd never been to the Upper Lough before, but it was quite gorgeous and we had it virtually to ourselves. On a serene, picture-perfect evening we nosed gently through a labyrinth of thickly wooded islands lapped by blue water and backed by distant purple mountains. Bright yellow irises grew in profusion amongst the reeds on the banks. Cows, transported to the islands in flat-bottomed boats called 'cots', grazed in clearings. We saw occasional wild goats, and the odd heron flapped away as we approached. From the shore came the scent of fresh-mown hayfields.

We didn't go far, and we tied up at a wooden jetty on an island called Inishcorkish. We had come to eat at a tiny establishment run by an elderly couple called John and Sheila Reihill, the last inhabitants of any of the myriad islands in Upper Lough Erne except for a Hare Krishna community which has taken over Inish Rath.

You have to warn the Reihills that you're coming, and order in advance. The choice is restricted to salmon, lamb or steak, and while Sheila cooks John chats. He is a large, engaging man with a silver beard and melodious voice. He tells you how his grandfather first came to the island in 1882, how his father and he stayed put as all the lough's other islanders moved back to the mainland, how he hopes to 'live on and die here'. After dinner, he brings out his fiddle and begins to play old Irish airs.

Mellowed by whiskey, good company and the lateness of the hour, we'd just begun to think we'd found that mythical Ireland of yore when Sheila broke the spell. She told us how her son had recently married a girl from North Carolina; they had met and courted through the Internet. There may be no roads or vehicles on Inishcorkish, but it is on the information superhighway.

10

Prods, Poachers
and Pilgrims

It is a fine evening in early July. Belfast's Shankill Road is awash
with flags and bunting. Vast bonfires have been built on patches
of waste ground from wooden pallets, old armchairs, mattresses,
tyres and discarded furniture.

You would be excused for thinking this traditional bastion of
blue-collar loyalism was celebrating a royal coronation. It is
actually preparing for the biggest day of its calendar, 'the
Twelfth' – the anniversary of the Battle of the Boyne in 1690
when William of Orange decisively defeated Catholic King
James II and ensured the survival of the Protestant colony in the
north. In Northern Ireland it sometimes seems that the Battle of
the Boyne happened only last Saturday week, and there is a joke
that pilots flying into Belfast tell their passengers to put their
clocks back to 1690.

Just before closing time I duck into the drab Rex Bar past a
burly, ear-ringed bouncer standing guard beneath a Union Jack
at the door. An ageing crooner with dyed hair and a guitar is tor-
menting the bar's dozen customers, his dire performance
punctuated by ear-splitting electronic screeches from a wonky
microphone. Then comes the moment I had heard about but
never witnessed.

The barman calls last orders. Our homespun Frank Sinatra
begins singing the national anthem. The two dozen customers
jump to their feet and stand ramrod straight. 'God save our gracious Queen,' they bellow. 'No surrender,' squawk a couple of
little old ladies at the end of every line. 'Fuck the Pope!' roars the
assembled company as they finish their rendition.

Nobody leaves. I'm collared by two semi-inebriated men at
one end of the bar, one big and one little. They are caricatures of
loyalists, as full of bigotry, aggression and paranoia as they are of
drink. 'I'm gown tell yew somf'n . . .,' they tell me with a poke of
the finger. 'This is God's own country. Yew talking to bess people
in fuckin' world. We're all arseholes but we're nice fuckin' arseholes. We love people.' This they demonstrate by buying my
pint. 'No, you fuckin' don't,' they snap when I try to return the
favour.

'I'm gown tell yew somf'n,' they continue. 'We have no problem with Catholics, but they fuckin' piss you off, them bastards.'
They recall how a Catholic had once, for some inexplicable
reason, walked into the Rex. He wasn't shot or beaten up, they
point out. The barman simply told him, 'For fuck's sake go
home,' and put him in a taxi. If it had been Gerry Adams it
would have been a different story. 'I'd shoot the bastard,' said the
smaller of my two friends.

For these men, loyalism is a way of defining not what they
are but what they are not. The more they are British, the less
they are Irish. They boasted of being the most loyal of the
Queen's subjects, but in the same breath complained of

betrayal by successive British governments and described the
English as double-crossing bastards who couldn't care less
about Ulster.

'We're a non-existent people,' they protested with a perverse
sort of pride. 'We'd die for Ulster,' they declared. 'There's no one
fucks an Ulsterman about.' Would they kill for Ulster, I asked, in
a roundabout sort of way. The big one held out his hand, palm
down. 'Watch this,' he said, and clenched his fist. As the skin
tightened, jagged white scars appeared right across the back of
his hand. How did that happen, I enquired. 'I fell,' he replied
with a grin and a wink.

I had expected to find a portrait of the Queen on the wall, as
you do in other Shankill bars, but there wasn't one. Instead there
was a portrait of a middle-aged woman with the legend:
'Martha – Simply the Best.' Next to it was the crest of the loyalist paramilitary Ulster Volunteer Force with the inscription: 'For
God and Ulster. All Gave Some and Some Gave All.'

Who was Martha, I asked. The mood changed instantly. 'Why
d'yew want to know?' asked my erstwhile friends. 'Who are yew?
Yew wired up? Got a tape recorder or anything? Don't ask questions about Marfa.'

I judged it was time to leave, and slipped out into the night
through the heavy steel cage that protected the bar's back door.
I never did find out who Martha was.

The next morning I went to see Gusty Spence, a friendly, avun-
cular, pipe-smoking man in his late sixties who lives in a
Housing Executive bungalow at the Shankill's city end. He has
neatly pruned roses and a palm tree in his front garden, and a
small white terrier named Patchy dozed on the sofa as we chatted in his sunny living room. But for the tattoos on both his arms
you would never guess that this man is the very embodiment of
the Shankill's turbulent twentieth-century history.

Raised in its heyday, Gusty helped to propel it into a cata-
strophic vortex of violence and destruction, and has spent the
last third of his life striving to rebuild it. He was a founder
member of the present-day Ulster Volunteer Force, the first loyalist paramilitary to be convicted of murder at the beginning of
the Troubles, and the man who announced the loyalist ceasefire
at the end of them. He is, as a colleague of his once put it, the
'alpha and omega' of loyalist paramilitary violence.

Gusty was born in 1933 in a typically tiny terraced house in
long-demolished Joseph Street, just 100 yards from where he
lives now. It was so small that 'if you had've swung a half-decent
cat you would have beat its brains out on the wall,' he said. He
and three brothers slept in one bedroom, his mother and his two
sisters in the other, and his father and another brother in a box-
room. 'Where my mother and father had sex to produce us I
don't know,' he laughed. The bed-legs stood in tins of paraffin oil
to keep the bugs and lice away.

Gusty's mother's family had lived in the Shankill for generations; she worked where all the women worked – in one of the
half-dozen great linen mills. His father, like most other Shankill
men, signed up first for Edward Carson's original UVF, formed to
fight Irish Home Rule, and then for the First World War. He
fought in the Battle of the Somme, but unlike so many of his
contemporaries he survived.

Of the 760 men from the Shankill who marched off to
France, only 76 returned alive. Gusty pulled out some research
he'd done. Just in his own small parish of St Michael's, 133
men never came back. Three local families lost three sons
each. He remembered as a boy kicking a ball into a woman's
hall and her putting it straight on the fire. 'She doesn't hate
children,' his mother told him later. 'But she's every reason to
question why all you children are playing in the street when
her husband and three sons were killed in the First World
War.'

Gusty's father could not find work after the War, and the family was raised in poverty. It was also raised on a diet of 'blind loyalty to the Crown'. Ireland had not long been partitioned, Ulster's contribution to the War having saved it from Home Rule, and working-class Protestants stoically endured their lot because 'to question was to criticise the government and if the border fell the Jesuits would move in and all hell would break loose. It was a load of crap, but that's what we believed.'

Gusty was a bright boy, but had to leave school at 14 because his family couldn't afford a high school uniform and education was a very low priority in the Shankill. You didn't need it. Provided times were good, Protestants had a monopoly on jobs in the shipyards, Mackie's engineering works and the mills. 'I was destined to go where I was always destined to go and that was the dark, satanic mills,' he said. 'You got your shoes off and kept your head down for 16s. 8d. a week, eight to six and to twelve on Saturday. Every ha'penny was required to maintain the family.'

Sectarianism was already 'endemic, absolutely endemic. Although there were no guns thundering in Ireland there was a war going on. There was always a war going on. We were never a wholesome society.' In those days an 'invisible' peace line divided the Shankill from the Falls. Gusty used to sneak over to go swimming, but had to stick a plaster over the Union Jack tattoo on his arm.

From the mills, Gusty graduated to the Harland and Wolff shipyards. Sometimes there was work, sometimes not, and he spent a few years in the Army. His military experience, plus his reputation as a hard man, was probably why he was approached in 1965 by two Unionist politicians whom he will not name. They asked him to join a new UVF to resist what was perceived in the febrile atmosphere of the time as a growing republican threat and the appeasement of nationalism by Captain Terence O'Neill's Stormont government.

Gusty did not hesitate; he saw himself following in his father's footsteps, fighting to defend his country. Three of his four brothers also went on to join the UVF. 'It appealed to my patriotism,' he said. One night, he and three others from the Shankill were taken to a barn near the town of Pomeroy in County Tyrone where, by the light of hurricane lamps, 40 or 50 men were inducted into the UVF by a former British Army colonel and swore to defend Her Majesty against enemies foreign and domestic.

He became the Shankill's UVF 'active service unit' commander. The plan was to take terror to the IRA. A 77-year-old woman died after her Catholic-owned home in the Shankill was petrol-bombed. A Catholic man was found dead, and buried before anyone realised he'd been shot. At 2 a.m. on 26 June 1966, four young Catholics were attacked as they left a bar in Malvern Street, close to Gusty's home. One, 18-year-old Peter Ward, was killed. Gusty and two others were convicted. He admits he did some 'desperate things' at that time, and was 'up to my neck and ears in paramilitary activity', but insists to this day that he did not kill Ward.

Gusty was one of the first batch of paramilitary prisoners of the Troubles, and idolised by growing ranks of violent young turks on the streets of the Shankill, but prison was his salvation. 'I was 33. I wasn't an extreme person, but found myself serving a life sentence with a recommendation that I served no less than 20 years. I had to find out what historical factors led me to be there. It wasn't just as simple as shooting. I went on a personal quest.'

He began reading voraciously. He studied Irish history. He became convinced of the futility of violence, and that political accommodation was the only solution. 'If you eliminate the mass evacuation or mass extermination of one side or the other, you're only left with accommodation,' he said. As the senior UVF man in the Maze, he introduced compulsory political education

classes for his men, and began teaching them to think for themselves instead of mindlessly doing the dirty work of hard-line
Unionist politicians.

'I presented the stimulus in order to elicit the response,' he
said. 'I saw it as an embryonic peace process.' It was a long,
slow haul, but the UVF ultimately developed its own political
voice, the Progressive Unionist Party, led by David Ervine, Billy
Hutchinson and Gusty's other prison protegés. 'These are fellows
who would have blown the head off you as fast as they would
look at you, but now they're taking a leading role in establishing
peace,' he told me.

Gusty was released from the Maze in 1984 after serving 18
years and seven months. When he had gone inside the Shankill
was still a vibrant, confident community of 75,000 people, but
the Troubles had exacted a terrible toll and the place was now
beleaguered and defensive. Nearly two-thirds of the population
had left; most of the old terraced homes had been demolished.
The 'invisible' peace lines had been replaced by walls of brick
and steel dividing the Shankill from the Falls. The mills were
gone, the good shops had closed and unemployment was rampant.

'The heart was torn from the Shankill. I didn't recognise
where I was. You might as well have dropped me in the middle
of Lapland,' he said. And so, with others, he started trying to
rebuild it. 'Remorse is only words,' he said. 'What you have to do
is through personal example ensure that no one ever again goes
down the road that you went down.'

Gusty made his peace with Peter Ward's ageing mother. He set
up and took charge of an information technology training centre
for the Shankill's young which also became a meeting place for
those who shared his goals. He became an active member of the
Progressive Unionist Party and struggled to persuade the UVF
that violence was counterproductive: 'I don't know how many
rooms I was thrown out of, but I always went back.'

On 13 October 1994, the man who began loyalism's slide into violence nearly thirty years earlier was chosen to announce its ceasefire. He used the occasion to express loyalism's 'abject and true remorse' to the families of its victims. It was, he said, 'the proudest moment of my life'. Four years later he was part of the PUP negotiating team that played a central role in clinching the Good Friday peace accord.

Today the Grand Old Man of the Shankill claims he has 'not a sectarian hair' in his head. Two of his grandchildren go to integrated schools – an idea unthinkable just ten years earlier. Another – to his immense pride – is the first Spence ever to go to university. As for the community, 'There's a renaissance in the Shankill, there's no doubt about it.' It had lived through a nightmare; it had been right down in the abyss, but was now clawing its way back. 'The Shankill is a proud place,' he told me as I prepared to leave. 'It's had the shit kicked out of it, but the pride's still there and they're pulling themselves together by their own bootstraps.'

I spent the rest of the day wandering around the Shankill. But for the bunting it resembled an old war zone where the loyalists had come off much the worst, and where the clean-up work was only just beginning. It had none of the self-confidence or vibrancy of the Falls.

The Shankill Road itself had been reduced to a sorry collection of rather dismal shops with littered pavements and tattered flags on lamp-posts. One shopfront had been taken over by the Shankill Prisoners Aid and Post-Conflict Resettlement Group, two others by hawkers of loyalist paramilitary memorabilia. Outside the Stars and Stripes café a small oval plaque declared: 'This tablet marks the site of Frizzels Fish Shop where at 1.05 am on Saturday 23 October 1993 a terrorist bomb exploded. Nine innocent souls lost their lives and many more were injured.' Only the bars, the bookies and the windowless, well-protected Glasgow Rangers Supporters

Club seemed to be doing much business, and apart from a few young toughs the population appeared to consist largely of the elderly.

The murals off the Falls Road tend to be more cultural in their themes, reflecting growing nationalist confidence, but here they mostly depicted the gunmen in balaclavas who pose as defenders of the community. The graffiti were also aggressive and sectarian – 'Irish Out of Britain', 'Eire – Bring Your Dole Spongers Back Home'. Black granite plaques on gable ends commemorate countless loyalist 'volunteers' killed by the 'enemies of Ulster'. Each had a rank and a company, and beneath their names there were usually a couple of lines of verse that contrived to link these 'soldiers' of the Troubles to the soldiers of the Somme. 'They shall grow not old as we that are left grow old,' read one.

I had a real problem with this depiction of the UVF and UDA – or for that matter the IRA – as 'soldiers'. That may be how people like Gusty Spence saw themselves in the early days of the Troubles, but today the paramilitaries are little more than thugs. One of the hardest interviews I ever did was with a father of three young children called Andrew Peden who had been left with two stumps instead of legs. He lived in the Glencairn estate at the westernmost end of the Shankill. He was grabbed by the UVF one morning, tortured and beaten for ten hours, then taken on to open ground just a couple of hundred yards from his home and shot in both legs. Both limbs had to be amputated, his life and those of his young family were wrecked, and a few months later his 12-year-old son tried to kill himself.

The other thing about the Shankill is that it's literally walled-in. You can't walk more than a few hundred yards to the south without coming to a scrubby patch of no-man's land leading up to a great wall of brick or steel. There are just three roads across to the Falls still open, and even they are closed at times of tension. There has not been a proper bus service linking the two

communities since the early 1970s, and you can hardly blame
the bus company because more than two hundred of their vehicles were burned or wrecked in the first 15 years of the
Troubles.

I stopped to talk to an old lady with curlers in her hair who
was standing in her doorway. She used to work in the mills but
they'd all closed, she told me; she used to go to the pictures in
the Falls, but hadn't been able to do that in 30 years; she used
to know everyone in her street, but not since they'd knocked
the old terraces down and built these modern boxes. Now she
couldn't believe what had happened. The Troubles were a 'lot of
nonsense'. She still doubted she'd see real peace in her lifetime, or the peace walls demolished. 'There's not the trust,' she
said.

I went to see the redoubtable May Blood, one of those big-
hearted, irrepressible, tough-as-nails Belfast women who act as
such a vital counter to the destruction and negativity of
Northern Ireland's male paramilitaries. She was a shop steward
in one of the mills and is now a prominent community activist.
She had a quote from Martin Luther King stuck up on the wall
of her office with the Greater Shankill Partnership: 'The ultimate
measure of a man is not where he stands at moments of comfort
and convenience but where he stands at times of challenge and
controversy.' She is in her sixties, silver-haired and unmarried,
and she has certainly not run away.

May moved to the Shankill at the start of the Troubles, after
her family were driven from another Protestant area of Belfast for
daring to help some Catholic neighbours. She vividly remembers
the last weekend of June 1972, when Catholic families in the
Shankill and Protestant families in the Falls were literally swap-
ping homes, and almost overnight the communities became 'two
ghettoes'.

She was brutally candid about the Shankill. The paramilitaries continued to hold sway, she said; shops and businesses

still had to pay them protection money. There was still plenty of bigotry and sectarianism. The Falls had run rings round the Shankill when it came to attracting investment or winning grants or setting up new businesses – 'they're well organised and fifteen or twenty years ahead of us. We're only playing catch-up, so we are.' Unemployment on the Shankill was rampant, and unlike the Falls the Protestants of the area still attached lamentably little importance to education.

Earlier in the day I'd visited Fernhill House, the Shankill's museum, and been struck by its 'Hall of Fame'. There was one artist, one musician, but no fewer than 16 footballers and boxers. May now took me up to the Mount Gilbert Community College, one of the Shankill's two secondary schools. Parents queued overnight to get their children into the other one, she said, and I could see why. Mount Gilbert was built for 1,700 students but had barely 400. Whole buildings had been abandoned, the place was bleak, dirty and neglected; the teachers looked almost as dispirited as the children. The truancy rate was 27 per cent, and in five years not a single pupil had managed to get five GCSEs of grade C or above. 'It's one of the worst schools in the UK,' said May.

But she, like Gusty Spence, insisted that the Shankill was turning around. She showed me the first smart new private housing to be built in the Shankill in living memory, factory units that had just been let after nearly a decade of standing empty, small business accommodation for which there was now a waiting list, new youth and training centres being built with international funds. The population had bottomed out. The number of children passing the 11-plus each year had finally risen from single figures. The Shankill no longer erupted in violence and riots at the smallest provocation. 'It's done a lot of growing up,' she told me. 'There's just a whole new feeling on the Shankill, but we're only at the beginning.' As for the paramilitaries, 'for many years they've destroyed

the community and now they have a responsibility to rebuild
it.'

In May, I sensed, they'd met their match.

At 3.30 a.m. a few days later I found myself driving back along
the now deserted Shankill Road, up on to the hills beyond, and
along an empty country road to the village of Crumlin, catching
a couple of foxes in my headlights on the way.

Northern Ireland is a long way north. Daylight is a scarce
commodity in winter, but at this time of the year it doesn't get
completely dark until 11 p.m., and the first glimmers of dawn
were already apparent as I pulled up outside Shane Cardwell's
council house.

Shane was waiting on the doorstep – a slight, weatherbeaten
man in his early sixties. He invited me in and introduced his
son, Darren, who was watching motor-racing on television. We
had a quick mug of tea, and then we set off down to the shore of
Lough Neagh for a fishing trip with a difference.

We parked on rough grass by a tiny inlet where they kept
their open boat, and pushed our way out with poles as the sky to
the east turned pink and the birds tuned up for their dawn
chorus. We then started the engine and sped out past Ram's
Island, once the site of an ancient monastery but now wild and
overgrown. Soon we were heading towards the middle of this
great inland sea bordered by five of Northern Ireland's six counties. It was formed when Finn McCool, the same giant who built
the Giant's Causeway, awoke one morning in a particularly vile
temper, picked up a large boulder from the heart of Ulster and
threw it into the Irish Sea. He created the Isle of Man in the
process.

We were searching for a tiny black dot in a vast expanse of
water. Shane and Darren spotted it long before I did: a sealed
plastic container to which they had tied one end of the fishing

line they'd put out the previous afternoon. Father and son put on orange rubber overalls. Shane stuck a sharp knife into a plank of wood laid across the top of a large blue plastic water-drum at the back of the boat. He pushed pieces of black rubber tubing over several of his fingers for protection. Then he sat down behind the drum, legs astride a wooden tray, and began hauling in the line as Darren inched the boat forward through the black water.

For the first minute or two nothing happened, then suddenly there was a splash and a flash of white as Shane flicked something out of the water and into the drum. A few seconds later he did the same thing again, so fast that if you blinked you missed it.

These were not fish, of course. They were eels – great long, slimy creatures with white bellies, grey-green backs and pin-head eyes in pointed heads. They were too slippery to handle. Shane was not even trying to remove the hooks from their mouths. The hooks were at the end of lengths of gut tied to the main line, and he was simply flicking these sidelines across the knife-blade so that the eels plopped into the drum below. 'Sometimes you miss the knife and cut them in two,' Shane chuckled.

Shortly after 5 a.m. a glorious red sun rose above the long, low hills on the lough's eastern shore. I looked around and realised we were not alone. I could see at least half-a-dozen boats working their way across the lough's smooth waters just as we were. We were actually sitting in the middle of Europe's largest wild eel fishery, nearly 160 square miles of temperate, relatively shallow waters that supply about 750 tons of top-quality eels to the gourmets of Holland and Germany each year.

Shane has been an eel fisherman for more than forty years. His father and grandfather were eel fishermen before him, and he briefly interrupted his hauling-in to indicate some of the other boats. They all seemed to belong to cousins. 'The whole lough is related,' he said. 'There are no newcomers. Unless you come from a fishing family you can't get a licence.'

The Lough Neagh Fishermen Cooperative Society issues only about 180 licences a year, and fishing without one is inadvisable. Shane also pointed out one of the four patrol boats that police the lough.

As the sun climbed, so the distant hills turned from grey to green. Above us, overnight planes from America left brilliant white trails across the pale blue sky as they sped towards Manchester, London and Amsterdam. Shane carried on hauling, hand over hand, the line coiling neatly on the tray below him, another doomed eel plopping into the drum every two or three hooks.

Shane and Darren had put out three lines. Each line had 400 hooks, with a stone every ten hooks for weight, and was more than a mile long. This was going to be a long haul, if you'll excuse the pun, but it was a beautiful morning, my colleagues were friendly, talkative people and the time soon passed.

They told me of eel-fishermen getting hooks caught in their noses and falling out of their boats. They wondered why it was that so few fishermen can swim – 'I can swim like a stone – straight to the bottom,' laughed Shane. They explained how they couldn't get insurance because the companies said it was 'too handy if you need a new boat to take the old one out and put a pick through her'. They told me how delicious eels were if cut up and fried in butter, but the funny thing was that nobody around the lough would eat the things. Shane was planning to retire soon. Would he miss it? 'Oh I will, aye,' he replied. 'It's a grand life, a grand life.'

But even this happy, contented pair had not emerged from the Troubles unscathed. Shane remembered a bomb being left in an ice-cream van outside one of Crumlin's pubs. A friend of Darren's had been killed by loyalists. Darren himself had been beaten unconscious and 'left for dead' one night three years earlier. Almost all the eel fishermen are Catholic because, in the old days of rampant discrimination, it was one of the few ways they could earn a living. Nowadays it is Protestants who complain of discrimination because they can't get licences.

It was about 6.30 a.m. by the time we had retrieved more than three miles of line and returned to shore. By that time the blue drum contained a writhing mass of three or four hundred eels for which the Cardwells would receive about £140. We moored in the inlet, drained the drum, and tipped the eels on to a weathered old table with raised sides. The biggest were about two feet long and two or three inches round. Shane and Darren flicked the smallest back into the water.

Could I take a couple home, I asked. 'You can, surely,' said Shane. He picked out four, and used a length of flat wood to push the rest through a funnel at the end of the table and into a landing net. As Darren tied the net to the side of the boat, ready for collection, Shane proceeded to gut the squirming eels he'd set aside. He then decapitated them and peeled their skins down their bodies just as women remove stockings from their legs. The insides of the skins were bright blue, but the really extraordinary thing was that for a couple of minutes the gutted, decapitated and peeled bodies kept on squirming. Then we went off for breakfast just as the rest of the province was waking up.

The day grew warm. About noon a flat-bed lorry with rows of steel water tanks on its back came to collect the eels. I followed it around the lough as it picked up the rest of the morning's catch from the north-eastern shore, and ended up at the cooperative's large new headquarters by the banks of the River Bann in Toomebridge.

I found the chief executive sitting behind a large desk in a spacious but rather spartan office. A short, elderly man with a well-worn face and ring of silver hair around his balding head, he was a far cry from the sort of businessman you might expect to find running a company with an annual turnover of more than £5 million. He was actually a Roman Catholic priest. His name was Father Oliver Kennedy, and over the years he had amply provided for the material as well as the spiritual well-being of his parishioners.

He had become involved back in the early 1960s when a court ruled that the fishermen, whose ancestors had been catching eels in the lough for generations, had to sell their catch to the company that owned the fishing rights, and at a price determined by that company.

The fishermen approached Father Kennedy for help. He didn't know the first thing about eels, but took the view that a situation where a private company controlled the fishing rights over such a vast expanse of water, to the detriment of those who lived on its shores and depended on it for a livelihood, was 'unacceptable and anachronistic'.

In 1963 he helped the fishermen to form a trade union. Two years later the union managed to buy a 20 per cent shareholding in the company. By 1971 it had acquired the whole lot and became a co-operative run for the benefit of the fishermen. Nearly four decades later, Father Kennedy is still in charge. 'I'm long overdue for retirement,' he told me. 'I don't have the energy I used to. I've been trying to extricate myself ever since I started but I've not succeeded.'

Father Kennedy is a hard man to get to see. My phone calls went unanswered. 'Publicity through the press and other media is of no real value to the Co-operative in its efforts to promote the welfare of fishermen,' he finally wrote in response to a letter from me. However, he proved perfectly affable in person, apologising for his elusiveness and explaining how he was having to engage in daily haggling with dealers in Holland.

He took me into a large warehouse behind his office where

that day's catch – a veritable river of more than 60,000 eels – was being sorted by size, covered in ice and packed into cardboard boxes. These, he explained, would be rushed to Aldergrove airport outside Belfast and dispatched on scheduled flights to Holland, Germany and London. The eels we had caught that morning would be collected at Amsterdam's Schipol airport that evening, cleaned, smoked and sold as a Dutch delicacy the following afternoon.

I warmed to Father Kennedy. Perhaps it was reciprocal. As I left, he gave me two packets of frozen smoked eels to add to the fresh ones already in my car boot.

The River Bann is like America's Mississippi. It is a psychological as well as a physical divide. To the east the province is fairly urbane and predominantly Protestant. West of the Bann is more like the American West – wilder, remote, a little lawless and rebellious. It is a region to which the London livery companies, at the behest of King James I, sent thousands of settlers to tame the particularly troublesome natives of Ulster in the early seventeenth century but – unlike America's frontiersmen – they never quite succeeded. There is even gold in the Sperrin Mountains, and long ago people used to pan for it, but at the time of writing the only mine is closed because this is a strong republican area and so for security reasons it cannot use explosives.

It was by now a scorcher of a day – probably the hottest I'd experienced since arriving in Northern Ireland – and I made the mistake of stopping for a lunchtime pint and sandwich in an old thatched pub just beyond Toome. The combination of the heat, the alcohol and an early start proved lethal. As I drove on towards Magherafelt I was overcome by drowsiness. I turned down a side lane, found a suitable field and did what I hadn't done for many years; I lay down on the lush green grass and buttercups and fell sound asleep in the sun for an hour. It was as well I did, for I had another long night ahead of me.

It was mid-afternoon by the time I woke. I carried on into Magherafelt, a bustling little market town built around a large central square by the Salters' Company in the early 1600s.

Bunting festooned the square. A great loyalist arch bearing portraits of those great Protestant reformists John Knox, Martin Luther, Oliver Cromwell and Ian Paisley spanned the main street. This was evidently a settlement that flourished. The fine Anglican church also reflects the town's early prosperity, and it boasts a stained-glass window commemorating a man called Whistler who died in 1657. His family subsequently emigrated to America and spawned James Whistler, one of the greatest of American artists.

From Magherafelt I headed towards the Sperrins, hazy in the heat, and passed through the village of Desertmartin with the smooth green dome of Slieve Gallion as its backdrop. Desertmartin was also decked out with flags and bunting. 'God Save the Queen' read the legend across the loyalist arch that spanned the road. The place looked much as an English village might for some royal celebration. In reality, of course, this seeming festivity was merely another manifestation of the battle for supremacy that began with the 'plantation' of Ulster 400 years earlier. 'Ulster Volunteer Force' read placards tied to the lampposts. 'Ulster – No Surrender'.

Beyond Desertmartin I came to Draperstown, a lovely-looking village of barely 1,000 souls in a bowl of green hills. A broad high street leads away from a central triangle bordered by neat cottages, mature lime trees on trim lawns, a livestock market, a pretty old stone Anglican church and an austere Presbyterian chapel. Draperstown looks a model of Protestant orderliness, but here there were no flags, no bunting – just 'Long Live the Provos' and 'IRA' daubed in white paint across walls.

Draperstown was established, needless to say, by the Drapers' Company – but this is a settlement that has since been recaptured by the natives and today is almost entirely nationalist. Its inhabitants now call it by its old name, Ballinascreen.

I stopped to inspect Draperstown's brand-new visitors' centre with its elaborate audio-visual displays recreating the story of the 'plantation'. It was a splendid, spacious, lavishly appointed building principally financed (once again) by European money. It lacked just one essential commodity – visitors. I was the only one there, and a pleasant young lady called Joanne had to open up the exhibition especially for me. She gave me a personal introduction, sent me on my way, and was there to meet me when I emerged from the other end. I have no objections to such service, you understand, but I did wonder whether the average German or French taxpayer would think this was the best use of their money.

Beyond Draperstown I entered County Tyrone along one of the loveliest roads in Northern Ireland, one that winds through the heart of the Sperrins along the broad valley of the Glenelly River. The verges were alive with purple foxgloves. Clumps of trees marked the streams that tumbled down the verdant hillsides. There were occasional inhabited farmhouses, but many more stone cottages that had been long ago abandoned. In one field I saw a scene from the nineteenth century on the cusp of the twenty-first – a farmer piling hay into ricks. There are even homes in rural westerly County Tyrone that still have no mains water and rely on springs.

Early on I passed some children swimming in the river – but they, the farmer and the sheep on the moors were about the only life I spotted until just before Plumbridge when I saw a cluster of whitewashed buildings on my right that turned out to be the Sperrins Heritage Centre. I stopped, went in, and enjoyed another 30-minute audio-visual exhibition on the history of the Sperrins, courtesy of the European taxpayer. Once again I was the only visitor, and a cursory glance at the visitors' book suggested this was not an untypical day. There had been a group of schoolchildren in a couple of days earlier, however. They were obviously a charming and original bunch of kids. In the comments column they had all written 'Crap', 'Shite' and 'Boring'.

The exhibition talked about poteen-making in the Sperrins, and panning for gold, but it failed to mention another tradition that still flourishes right across this land of lakes and rivers. I am talking of poaching – one-for-the-table-type poaching – and it was, as it happened, a venerable practitioner of this ancient art that I was on my way to see. This was going to be a hands-on exhibition funded not by euros, but by some unwitting landlord.

I'd been put in touch with Mickey by an eminently respectable official at the Northern Ireland Office, and I'd actually met him a few weeks earlier. He had naturally wanted to check me out before inviting me on a foray, and we'd gone for a bit of legal fishing. I'd evidently passed the test because he had readily agreed to this night's little expedition, though I did have to provide £50 for 'petrol money'. The water was low and it was still too early for salmon, he'd warned me on the telephone, but there should be some trout.

I killed a couple of hours in a pub, then headed out to Mickey's modest little council house not a million miles from Plumbridge. He is a short fellow of considerable girth, good humour, native cunning and pride in his profession. He greeted me like an old friend. 'Come you in,' he said, and took me through to a back room where his accomplice, a young fellow named Sam, was already sitting.

The walls were plastered with the clutter of Mickey's misspent life – collapsible fishing rods, various nets, gaffs, photos of him standing proudly before arrays of salmon, trout and other game. In one corner was a small deep-freeze which Mickey opened with evident satisfaction – it was jam-packed with parcels of frozen fish and meat. On the table was an incubator containing dozens of partridge eggs. He picked up one with a crack in the top and you could hear a tiny chick trying to break its way out. In the small yard at the back he kept ferrets, terriers and gun-dogs in a row of cages.

It was too light to go out yet, so we drank tea and talked. Mickey had been poaching since he left school at 15, more than forty years ago. His father did it for 'beer money', he said, but he himself had started because he could earn a tenner a night from selling salmon to hotel chefs compared with £3 a day in a regular job. He'd gradually branched out into other more legitimate activities – exterminating foxes for farmers, breeding dogs, and latterly some gamekeeping. He liked to describe himself as a 'veteran poacher now retired', but he hadn't entirely given up the 'fishing' as he called it.

He had never been caught, though he'd had a lot of close shaves and had to 'take to the water' a few times. In fact he rather objected to being described as a poacher because, he insisted, 'you're not a poacher until you've been convicted'. The key was vigilance – checking the bailiffs' movements, listening for startled cows or waterhens. It was not being greedy – avoiding the best but riskiest pools, taking no more fish than you needed. It was also, of course, 'Lady Luck'.

He had no scruples about what he did. Fish were a 'natural resource – they don't belong to anyone'. Poaching had been 'around since Day One' and there was certainly a romance about it. Nowadays he sold most of his salmon to people he knew, and there was a certain prominent local businessman who 'takes great delight in knowing his salmon have been poached. He says if he had to buy those salmon in a shop he wouldn't enjoy eating them nearly as much.'

Mickey was not completely without scruples. He would never fish out of season unless he'd had a very lean year, he said. He always threw the small ones back, and decried the methods of some modern-day 'cowboy outfits' who wipe out whole rivers with cyanide powder or electrify pools with generators.

By about 10.30 p.m. the light was fading. Mickey picked up a hessian sack and the three of us trooped out of the front door. 'We'll take your car,' he said, not entirely to my surprise. Poachers risk not only a £1,000 fine but the confiscation of any vehicle used in the offence. I had visions not only of headlines in the local papers – '*Times* Correspondent Caught Poaching' – but of my editor's delight on learning that I'd forfeited a company car.

We drove a couple of miles out into the country. 'Take you a left,' said Mickey as we approached an old stone bridge. 'Stop you in that gateway,' he added after we'd travelled just 50 yards down a little lane. 'This is the place.'

The river flowed past the far side of the field to our right. I was a little alarmed. The road over the bridge was not exactly busy, but occasional cars did drive over it. Surely Mickey wasn't suggesting we went poaching right beside it?

That is exactly what he *was* suggesting. Sam would stand on the bridge, he said. We'd net the pools just above and below it. He'd make a noise like a wounded hare if he saw any bailiffs approaching, and duly demonstrated a sort of whimpering noise through pursed lips. I would immediately walk back to the car, pretending I'd been relieving myself, while Mickey would 'melt into the undergrowth' with all the tackle.

With palpitating heart I pulled on my Wellington boots – all I had – while Mickey put on waders. In the gloaming we hurried across the field and dropped down to the river bank below the bridge while Sam took up his position above. It was only then that I realised the walls of the bridge, and the curves of the road on each side, rendered us completely invisible to passing vehicles. Mickey certainly knew the terrain.

He took a bundle about the size of a football from the hessian sack. It was a rolled-up fishing net. He gave me one end to hold, and unfurled the net as he waded across to the other bank, feeling his way with a stick. Along the bottom of the net was a leaded rope, and along the top a line of corks.

There was no moon, just the last glimmers of daylight on the horizon. It was a warm, still, fragrant night. A couple of bats darted through the air above us. Slowly, very slowly, we began working our way down our respective banks, the net drifting along in the cold, black current between us.

Occasionally Mickey whispered brief instructions. When the net snagged on a rock we had to retrace our steps. Once a fish broke the surface with a luminous flash of white. A couple of times the water gurgled over the tops of my boots.

Periodically car headlights sliced through the darkness, illuminating the roadside trees and hedgerows, but I soon ceased to worry about them and began to feel like one of those rather daring characters in a John Buchan novel.

It took 10 minutes to reach the far end of the pool. 'Let go,' whispered Mickey in the darkness. 'Go and join Sam on the bridge.' As he began pulling in the net I squelched back across the field and up the lane feeling, I have to admit, quite exhilarated.

It was a few minutes before Mickey materialised, clutching the dripping net. We climbed over a gate into a field above the bridge. There we unfurled the net on the grass and extracted three small trout, an old tin can and sundry bits of debris from the filament. It was not much of a catch. There had been too little rain, said Mickey. We needed some higher water to bring the trout this far up the river.

Sam returned to his post on the bridge, while Mickey and I made our way about 30 yards upstream to the top of a second pool and repeated the same procedure. This time we carried on down, right under the bridge itself and out at the other side before Mickey gathered up the net again. This haul was almost as meagre as the first, but it did contain one rather fine silver sea trout and represented a significant increase on my haul at Colebrooke.

By now it was midnight. I'd seen the master at work, and had had my little thrill, but the conditions were obviously poor and I'd done more than enough fishing for one day. We agreed to call it a night. We'd not caught much, but then we'd not been caught ourselves. When I dropped Mickey home, he dug into his freezer and produced two hefty trout to supplement our catch and add to the collection of eels in my boot.

I spent the night in a bland modern hotel on the edge of Omagh, the fine old hotel in the town centre having sadly closed a few months earlier. That apart, I like Omagh. It straddles the River Strule, and has a fine main street that climbs up to the neo-classical courthouse and a large twin-spired Catholic church reputedly modelled on Chartres Cathedral.

The town is destined to be remembered, of course, as the scene of the single bloodiest bombing of the Troubles – a veritable slaughter of the innocent that killed 29 people including children, grandparents, tourists and a pair of unborn twins. I prefer to remember Omagh as the home of one remarkable young woman and her equally courageous husband – a couple who embody the indomitable spirit of this battered province and show that good can triumph over evil.

After a late breakfast the next morning, I went to visit them in their new home on a brand-new development just outside the town. Donna Marie McGillion opened the door herself. It was now almost a year since the bomb, but she was still wearing the clear plastic mask she had to put on for 23 hours out of every 24 for 18 months to protect the plastic surgery on her face. She still had pressure bandages over much of her upper body and about twenty areas of raw flesh, and she was returning to hospital the next day for a series of new skin grafts. She was still in pain, had to have her dressings changed every other day, and was still receiving physiotherapy.

Her husband, Garry, was sufficiently recovered to have just returned to work, and was about to start coaching at the local boxing club, but he was still badly scarred around the back of his head and neck. Neither was complaining, however. Both knew they were incredibly fortunate to be alive.

Donna Marie had been out shopping with Garry, his sister Tracey and Tracey's 21-month-old daughter Breda that hot August afternoon in 1998. They had been buying shoes for Breda, who was to be a flower-girl at their wedding the following Saturday. They were about to head home, and were standing a mere car-and-a-half from the maroon Vauxhall Cavalier when it exploded at 3.10 p.m.

Donna Marie, a 22-year-old sales assistant, remembered nothing. Garry, a 24-year-old mechanic, said it felt 'like an electric shock, like I'd stood on an electric cable'. He found himself lying in the middle of the road with his shirt on fire. Amid the dust and debris, he found his fiancée lying apparently lifeless on the pavement, her hand still holding Breda's buggy.

Breda died hours later. Donna Marie was rushed unconscious to the Tyrone County Hospital. Two-thirds of her body including her face was severely burned; she had serious lung damage, and deep lacerations. Her injuries were so bad that her father and brother passed her bed without recognising her, and she was identified only by the sapphire-and-diamond engagement ring on her finger. That night she was flown to Belfast's Royal Victoria Hospital by helicopter, where doctors gave her a mere 20 per cent chance of survival and a priest performed the last rites.

Garry, severely burned down his entire right side, followed by ambulance the same evening, not knowing what had happened to any of his companions. His sister Tracy was also rushed to Belfast in critical condition.

For Donna Marie, surviving those first 48 hours was only the start of a long battle for life. Severe burns destroy patients' natural immunities, exposing them to infections that can cause fatal organ failures. She suffered successive crises – lung infections, pneumonia and septicaemia. Doctors told her parents that they had done all they could, and that whether she lived or died depended on her. 'I thought we had lost her,' her mother, Patricia, confessed later.

As Donna Marie began to recover, she underwent seven major skin graft operations lasting about 25 hours in total. After six weeks she was removed from intensive care, taken off sedation and allowed to regain consciousness. Tony Blair, Hillary Clinton and other dignitaries had come and gone without her knowing. 'I didn't have a clue what had happened to me . . . I thought it was a car accident,' she said. It was a week before her parents told her of the bomb, and another week after that before she asked for a mirror.

Most women would have been devastated by such disfigurement, but not Donna Marie. Having worked with handicapped children, and with the Order of Malta, she had seen others cope with disabilities. She was shocked at first, but soon came to terms with what had happened to her. She felt lucky to be alive, not bitter about her injuries. Unlike others, she had lost neither limbs nor faculties and began telling her doctors what she wanted to do, not the other way round. They even moved one demoralised patient into the next bed for inspiration. Three months later she left the Royal Victoria on Garry's arm with a smile on her face, a heart free of rancour and no trace of self-pity.

I interviewed her at her parents' home a few days after her discharge. 'I'm a strong and determined person. I've always been taught to be positive about things, and I realised that had I laid down and let go the bombers would have won,' she said. 'I could be here from now to Doomsday wondering "Why me?

Why did we have to be there?" But no one knows the answer and no one can tell me. I can't change the past. All I can do is look to the future, and only I can make my future the way I want it.'

I had more response from readers to that story than any other I wrote from Northern Ireland. Donna Marie's family became good friends, and the following March they invited me to her rearranged wedding in the church at the top of Omagh's main street. Hundreds of townsfolk turned out to celebrate after so much grieving, and the priest who had given Donna Marie the last rites helped to officiate at the service.

I hadn't seen Donna Marie or Garry since their wedding. As we sat and drank tea, they told me they had both begun remembering things they had unconsciously blocked from their memory – the smell of burning flesh in Garry's case and, in Donna Marie's, the screams, the sirens and Garry asking where Breda was. But to a remarkable degree they had put the bomb behind them and begun rebuilding their lives.

The wedding 'closed a chapter, but it's not a chapter we'll ever forget', said Donna Marie. Their shared trauma and suffering had brought them closer together, they agreed. It had changed their lives in the sense that every day was now a bonus and they were determined to live it to the full. As for the bombers, they saw no point in bitterness. 'They will get what's coming to them,' said Donna Marie. 'They probably won't get it in this world, but some day they will have to face their Maker.'

There was one small silver lining to all their suffering. Donna Marie and Garry had bought the house we were sitting in with a £53,000 mortgage just three weeks before the bomb. On impulse they had decided to take out a critical injuries insurance policy. They had made just one £5 payment before both were critically injured, and the entire mortgage was paid off. It was a pretty good return on their investment but, as Donna

Marie remarked as I left, they would much rather have spent years scrimping and saving to pay the mortgage than endure what they'd suffered.

Yet again I was late. From Omagh I hurried on through lush green countryside until, 45 minutes later, I reached the shores of Lower Lough Erne.

Lower Lough Erne is not a maze of little islands like Upper Lough Erne. It is a vast expanse of deep, open water, and somewhere in those black depths – probably preserved in pristine condition – lie seven or eight Catalina flying-boats where they were scuttled after the Second World War.

It was the base for several squadrons of flying-boats which hunted Germany's deadly U-boats in the Atlantic. Thanks to a secret agreement with Eamon de Valera's Dublin government, they were allowed to fly directly west over a narrow strip of supposedly neutral Ireland called the 'Donegal Corridor', thereby extending their range by another critical 100 miles. It was a Catalina from Lough Erne – co-piloted by an American secretly sent over from supposedly neutral America to train British pilots – that spotted the *Bismarck* in 1941, enabling the Royal Navy to destroy the mighty German warship one day later.

The nerve centre of this operation was Castle Archdale, an old country estate bordering the lough, and I had a noon appointment there with probably the only man left alive who might know where the Catalinas lie. His name is Bill Waters, a cheery pensioner from Leicester who served at Castle Archdale just after the war and loved the place so much that he eventually retired just up the road.

Bill hopped out of his battered old Ford van as I arrived. Together we walked down to the lough shore through what is now a caravan site. 'We used to call it a holiday camp, but never in a hundred years did I dream it would actually become one,' he laughed.

At the water's edge, now largely obscured by trees and under-growth, he showed me the ghostly old concrete docks and slipways from which the Cats and Sunderlands were serviced. He pointed out where the Nissen huts used to stand, the site of the morgue, the stumps of trees they'd chopped down for fire-wood. Amazingly we found the rusting hulk of a flat-bottomed steel scow that used to ferry bombs and depth-charges to the flying boats, and Bill kept returning to gaze at it with evident nostalgia. It was boat Number 133, he said, and more than half a century ago he was its coxswain.

He vividly remembered scuttling the Catalinas, which were on lend-lease from America but rendered suddenly redundant by the war's end. Some had just arrived from the US and flown fewer than thirty hours in total. Some had brand-new tool kits wrapped in thick greaseproof paper. 'They were fantastic tool kits like only the Americans could provide, but we were told we couldn't steal them.' Instead they had to tow the planes out into the middle of the lough, open their seacocks, chop holes in them with fire axes and blow up those that refused to sink with hand grenades.

The Catalinas were big planes, with 104-foot wingspans, but where they lie Bill simply couldn't say. A few years earlier a London television director had set out to recover one of the wartime flying-boats from the muddy depths. He took Bill out on the lough several times, and spent considerable amounts of time and money scanning the lough floor, but all to no avail. 'They've probably got twenty or thirty feet of silt on top of them by now,' said Bill.

Other eyes which witnessed the sinking of the Catalinas will never reveal their secret. They belong to ancient stone figures who have stood sentinel down the centuries on the shores of the lough.

In the graveyard at Killadeas, just south of Castle Archdale, stands the Bishop's Stone, an upright hunk of granite with a pre-Christian face carved on the front and, on the side, a stooped figure with a crook and bell. In the roofless ruins of a twelfth-century church on White Island, just north of Castle Archdale, stand eight mysterious stone figures dating from somewhere between the seventh and tenth centuries. One appears to be an abbot, another a grotesque female figure, a third a man with a book. Nobody can quite agree on what they all represent, or whether they are Christian or pagan.

My personal favourite, and by far the oldest, is the pre-Christian double-headed 'Janus' statue on the western end of Boa Island which runs along the lough's northern shore. The main road west crosses the island. As that was the way I was going, I stopped to admire the statue one more time. Where a sign said 'Caldragh Cemetery' I turned down a farm track, parked in front of some barns and walked down a grassy path to an ancient little graveyard surrounded by trees, flowering blackberry bushes and an old metal fence.

The gravestones were so old that most were little more than stumps protruding from the uncut grass. In the middle stood this extraordinary Celtic idol, about four feet high and dating from roughly the first century AD. The carvings on the front and back are identical – large triangular faces as inscrutable as the Mona Lisa's, with arms crossed over their chests. There is a hollow on top that may once have been used for sacrificial blood but now contained a few coins left by the superstitious.

As usual, there was nobody else around. I ran my hand over the warm stone, around the eyes and mouths, under the pointed chins carved nearly 2,000 years ago by a pagan artist from another aeon.

I could have carried on westwards to one more stone carving which stands by the remains of the gatehouse of the ruined Castle Caldwell at the western tip of the lough. The Fiddlers

Stone is shaped like a fiddle and inscribed to the memory of Denis McCabe, a fiddler who drowned after he fell out of a barge during a drunken party given by Sir James Caldwell in August 1770. The epitaph admonishes other fiddlers:

> *On firm land only exercise your skill*
> *There you may play and drink your fill.*

That was not the way I was going, however. Just beyond the bridge that connects Boa Island to the shore, I turned sharp right up a country lane that took me to the pretty village of Pettigo. This, too, was festooned with bunting – but for purely decorative reasons. The pubs were brightly painted. There was none of the subliminal tension I'd sensed in the other towns I'd passed through on this journey, and that was because Pettigo was just across the border in County Donegal.

I didn't linger. I was still running late. I drove north on a small lane bordered with fuchsia and montbretia. This took me into a wilderness of hills and moors where the only signs of human activity were the piles of neatly cut turf – next winter's fuel – left to dry next to the peat bog from which they had recently been cut by some old-timer.

After about four miles the lane turned sharply left and there in front of me was Lough Derg – a broad sheet of black water ringed by the wild green hills of Donegal. In the middle stood my final destination – a cluster of institutional grey stone buildings rising sheer from the water and looking for all the world like Alcatraz except for the green copper roof of a basilica. There was another arch across the lane, but this one was not erected by loyalists. It announced the name of this strange place: St Patrick's Purgatory.

I parked where the lane abruptly ended by the water and sprinted down the jetty. It was 3 p.m., and the last boat of the day was about to leave. There was just one other passenger on

board – a raven-haired beauty named Liz from County Kerry
who later admitted that she'd been suffering last-minute doubts
about whether to embark at all.

Liz's equivocation was understandable, for she was about to
start one of the toughest pilgrimages left in Christendom. The
previous summer I had joined 20,000 pilgrims – some barefoot – as they climbed a 2,510-foot County Mayo mountain
called Croagh Patrick to attend dawn Mass in freezing rain at the
summit, but that was relatively easy. This one involved three
days of almost non-stop prayer and barefoot penance with minimal food and sleep. Reservations for what must be the world's
cheapest package holiday at £17 all-in were, for understandable
reasons, unnecessary.

A trim red-haired, blue-eyed man in his early fifties greeted us
as we disembarked on the three-acre island a few minutes later.
This was Monsignor Richard Mohan, a parish priest in Pettigo
who doubles as the island's prior during the 10-week summer
pilgrimage season. Come and eat at 7.30, he told me *sotto voce*,
and off I went to mingle with the scores of pilgrims who
clutched rosary beads and murmured prayers like mantras as
they hobbled, quite literally, round and round in circles.

They were doing their penitential 'stations', explained Seamus
Quinn, one of three priests assisting Father Mohan. He showed
me the ropes:

Kneel at St Patrick's Cross in front of the basilica and say
one Our Father, one Hail Mary and one Creed, he told
me.

Go to St Brigid's Cross, set into the basilica's outside
wall. Stand with your back to the wall, arms outstretched,
and three times declare: 'I renounce the World, the Flesh
and the Devil.'

Walk four times round the basilica, saying seven
decades of the Rosary and one Creed, then go to the

rocky remains of seven ancient monastic penitential beds. Walk three times round each of these beds while saying three Our Fathers, three Hail Marys and one Creed. Repeat the prayers a second time while kneeling at the entrance to the bed. Repeat them a third time while walking round the inside of the bed. Repeat them a fourth time while kneeling at the cross in the centre.

Stand by the water's edge and say five Our Fathers, five Hail Marys and one Creed, then kneel and do the same. Return to St Patrick's Cross, kneel and say one Our Father, one Hail Mary and one Creed. Finish with a final burst of five Our Fathers, five Hail Marys and one Creed inside the basilica.

All that amounts to just one 'station'. Over the three days pilgrims have to perform nine Stations, all in their bare feet. My shaky mathematics makes that a total of 1,981 separate prayers, excluding those the pilgrims say during four separate Masses and various other services in the basilica.

I'd find that challenging in the best of circumstances, but the pilgrims must not sleep until 10 p.m. on the second evening, and apart from the occasional communion wafer are allowed just one meal of dry toast and black tea or coffee per day. Between meals they can drink what has been wryly dubbed 'Lough Derg soup' – hot water flavoured with salt or pepper.

There is little by way of light relief. Cameras, radios and mobile telephones are banned. There is a bookshop on the island, but it does not sell Frederick Forsyths or John le Carrés – just books with irresistible titles like *Praying the Rosary* or *A New Look at Prayer*. The island's setting is stunning, but sit and admire it in the evening sun and you're eaten alive by midges. 'You pray with your whole body,' explained Father Mohan. 'The pilgrims give as much of themselves as they possibly can. They go to the point where it hurts.'

All this is a curious recipe for success, but it seems to work. Pilgrims have been coming to Lough Derg for centuries, and have defied repeated efforts to close the place down.

St Patrick was the marketing genius behind it. While staying in a cave on the island some 1,600 years ago, he claimed to have had a vision of purgatory as a half-way house between this world and the next. By the eleventh and twelfth centuries pilgrims were coming from far and wide to spend nights in the cave. One of them was called 'The Knight Owein', and the tale of his travels through purgatory – past souls being tormented by devils with white-hot nails and cauldrons of boiling metal – became a bestseller throughout medieval Europe and allegedly inspired Dante's *Divine Comedy* with its vision of purgatory, paradise and hell. For the next three or four hundred years, the cave was practically the only Irish landmark to feature on maps of the continent.

In 1632, after the Reformation, the authorities banned the pilgrimage and destroyed the cave and every building on the island. The pilgrims continued coming, however, and in 1680 the place was levelled again. In 1704 Parliament sought to deter the pilgrims with a 10-shilling fine or a public whipping, but that failed too. They continued to come and still do, some 15,000 every summer, from north and south, in cars and minivans and special buses from Dublin and Sligo. Nowadays they wear brightly coloured cagoules and baseball caps, but the rites remain much as they have for the past 400 years.

On this particular day there were about 360 pilgrims – young and old, male and female, men with shaven heads and rings in their eyebrows, company directors, students, a group of young gypsies, a goldsmith from Switzerland and even a 93-year-old woman. Who you are in the outside world really doesn't matter, because removing your shoes and socks instantly destroys social status. It also reveals an amazing array of toes and toenails; it was, as one woman remarked, a 'chiropodist's paradise'.

Why on earth did they come to this 'Catholic concentration camp', as it was once described? I sat on the steps of the basilica, interrupted people as they did their circles and conducted a little survey. Most were friendly souls who seemed to welcome the diversion.

A teacher from Galway had come to pray for her two daughters who were both suffering from ovarian cancer. A frail 75-year-old woman from County Cork was making her thirty-fourth trip to the island, this time to pray for a daughter whose marriage was breaking up. One of the traveller women had buried her husband just three days earlier after he was knocked down by a car. In the 1980s, Una Griffin from Cork promised to make three pilgrimages if God got her a job in a shipping company. The bargain worked, but she's returned another sixteen times because 'it's a wonderful place'.

A student from Coleraine had come to give thanks for passing his exams. A Strabane farmer called it 'squaring the account up' – a way of paying his debts to God each year. Two guilt-stricken women from Donegal had returned because 24 years earlier they had sneaked away without finishing the pilgrimage – 'we were terrified we'd get caught leaving,' said one. A young man from Sligo appeared to have come simply for the challenge. 'There's nowhere else in the world like it,' he said. 'This is the real McCoy. Only the strong survive.'

The pilgrims certainly seemed to get a lot out of it. 'When I finished the last hard thing I had to do today, I sat at the water's edge and started crying. I was at peace,' said Brigid Mikowski from Londonderry's Bogside. 'It feels like hell when you're here, but it feels like heaven when you leave,' commented a young graduate from Tyrone who had come to pray for a job. Tom Hanson, an elementary school teacher from New York, was making his thirty-seventh visit – 'It's always difficult. It never gets any easier, but you get a totally wonderful feeling.'

Shaun McGregor, a teacher from Draperstown, first came after his brother was killed in 1983 and has returned 30 times since. 'It's like a masochistic holiday,' he chuckled. 'Really and truly everyone needs a Lough Derg. It gives you time to think who you are and what you are.'

My particular favourites were a cheery middle-aged male trio from London who called themselves 'The Lough Derg Committee'. Maurice Smith, a police officer, was the secretary; William Henry and Michael O'Shea, both building contractors, were the chairman and transport manager. They'd been coming for 13 years, bringing assorted friends with them. The moment they got home they cooked themselves a slap-up meal of steak, chips, mushrooms and onions and the best red wine. 'We love it, we all love it,' said Maurice.

Not everyone on the island lives in a state of permanent self-denial. The priests are handsomely catered for. After briefly consulting my conscience I decided I was here as an observer, not a pilgrim, and after evening Mass I readily joined them for a dinner of succulent pork kebabs, chips and salad.

Outside the pilgrims hobbled on, dreaming of food and soft beds with clean white sheets. At 9.20 p.m. they gathered in the basilica for night prayers and the gentle singing of hymns, and then began their all-night vigil. Outside the last light faded over the western hills, and the water lapped in the darkness on the rocky shore.

Did I think they were crazy, asked a woman from Portadown? It was the eve of 12 July. All over Northern Ireland loyalists would be guzzling beer, banging their drums and lighting bonfires topped with Irish tricolours. I had a purgatorial vision of black silhouettes against leaping flames not unlike the Knight Owein's. No, I thought. If I were a northern Catholic, I'd think this remote and tranquil island was as good a place as any to be spending this particular night.

Through the small hours the pilgrims prayed or talked or

circled the basilica to keep themselves awake. Those who nodded off were gently prodded by their fellows. Complete strangers enjoyed a camaraderie born of shared adversity. At about 5 a.m., as the hills began to turn from grey to green and dawn tinged the clouds with pink, I found Liz from County Kerry sitting on a bench looking over the lough. 'I'm starving, Jesus I'm ravenous,' she told me. 'I'm thinking of the seafood platter I had before I came. I'm thinking, "Oh my God. I've got a whole day still to do."'

Fortunately, I did not. I had to return to Belfast to cover that day's Orange Order marches. As the bleary-eyed pilgrims re-entered the basilica for 6.30 a.m. Mass, and the sun rose on another beautiful day, a boatman dropped me back at the car park. I sped off home where, some days later, I opened my boot and discovered a mass of putrid, stinking eels and trout.

Epilogue

The Lough Derg pilgrimage was supposed to mark the end of my travels. I had only a couple of weeks left in Northern Ireland before moving on to my next posting in Brussels. But one evening, just before the removal men arrived, the telephone rang. It was my old friend Sean, the one who had taken me to meet Patrick the poteen-maker.

'How'd you like to go cock-fighting?' he asked. It was a question that didn't really require an answer. I'd come to realise that there was an untamed, lawless side to the province – quite apart from its paramilitary activity – without which any portrait of Northern Ireland would be incomplete.

The next evening I drove up to a village in rural County Antrim to be vetted by the man who had offered to take me. Sean had told me to meet him in the village bar, but I never got that far. As I parked in the car park a burly middle-aged, balding fellow drew up alongside me in a battered old Renault and told me to hop in. He asked me various questions. He made sure I understood that cock-fighting was highly illegal. He sought assurances that I would not identify him, take photographs or bring a notebook. I was to tell nobody I was a journalist. He didn't tell me his name, and I still don't know it.

At the end of the week, he called me on my mobile and told me to be in the main street in Moy, a village in County Armagh, at 6.15 the next morning. We were heading for the South Armagh border. 'Bring lots of money,' he added as an after-thought.

I left home at 5.15 a.m. and sped down the empty motor-way feeling distinctly apprehensive. I'm 6'3". I have an unmistakably English accent. I was heading back to 'bandit country' and blending into the background was not going to be easy.

I stood in Moy's picturesque but deserted main street for half-an-hour, watching the previous night's litter wafting in the breeze. My escort finally arrived with two other middle-aged men inside his jalopy, and I climbed into a thick haze of cigarette smoke. They greeted me cordially enough, then car-ried on talking in what might have been Swahili or Singalese but was actually English as spoken in the wilds of County Antrim.

I was at another disadvantage; I had no idea if these other two men knew why I was there. Then I distinctly made out the words 'What do you work as?' coming from the man in the front passenger seat. I said the first thing that came into my head. 'A banker,' I replied, and that prompted a lengthy discourse on how the British pound and the Irish punt were interchangeable at cock-fights despite the wide discrepancy in the exchange rate. I was saved – and forewarned.

We drove through Armagh City and carried on south down

empty roads. Then we turned on to a country lane and drew up outside some farm buildings that were evidently the pre-arranged meeting place. When another half-dozen cars had joined us we were led in convoy a few more miles to an open gateway where three or four men stood sentinel. We bumped over a couple of green fields till we came to a large cow pasture where the superstitious farmer had left a lone fairy thorn standing in the middle.

In the far corner, by a meandering little river, a row of perhaps fifty cars with equal numbers of northern and southern number-plates were parked along a screen of thick, low trees. One man was creating a circle of short grass with a strimmer. Another was roping off the circle to create the pit. The cocks were lustily crowing inside hessian sacks or rough wooden boxes with little round air-holes. There was not a building in sight, and we were completely hidden by the trees and low hills.

'If anyone comes, run two hundred yards in that direction. That's the border,' my new-found friend instructed me, pointing towards the river. 'Don't ask any questions,' he added, and I didn't. In fact I kept quiet, pulled a baseball cap low over my face and found to my relief that nobody paid me any attention.

And so I spent the next few hours watching a succession of cock-fights – at least forty in all, with long gaps in between as the owners laboriously taped two-inch, needle-sharp spurs to their birds' legs.

The cocks were beautiful creatures – deep browns and greens and oranges. Whenever a pair were ready, the couple of hundred spectators gathered round the pit and began placing bets with one another. 'A tenner on McAvoy,' they'd cry until someone took them on. 'Five pound on Turley.'

The handlers then held their birds close enough to take a few pecks at each other, retreated to the opposite sides of the ring and let them loose.

The cocks charged at each other with inexplicable ferocity. There was a flurry of beating wings and slashing talons, of darting beaks and flying feathers. When they became hopelessly entangled the handlers rushed in, separated them and set them loose again.

Some fights were over in seconds, with one bird skewered through the heart or lung or spinal cord. In one contest both birds died simultaneously in their handlers' arms after just one round, their demise heralded by sudden dribbles of blood from their beaks and rattles in their throats.

Other fights became long wars of attrition, the birds suffering broken legs or wings or having their eyes spiked out. Their handlers sought to revive them by blowing into their feathers, licking their combs, or sucking the blood from their gullets to stop them choking. The birds fought on until one or the other simply could or would not continue, by which time their blood was liberally smeared across their handlers' mouths and hands.

After each contest, leathery hands extracted large rolls of notes from grimy pockets to settle debts. The losing bird's handler wrung its neck and chucked it into the ditch behind the cars. The winning bird frequently suffered the same fate because he'd been too maimed to fight again. Three or four fights is the most a cock can expect to survive.

The spectators were certainly not the paramilitary types I'd feared. They were mostly cheerful, good-natured country types with ruddy faces, big bellies and jeans that seemed to reach only half-way up their bottoms. Between fights they ate picnics and quaffed Guinness or whiskey by their cars, joking and bantering much as people might at a race meet or cricket match in England. At one point they passed round a hat for the farmer who had donated the field.

It was another clear blue day, and the sun grew hot. The countryside was bucolic, green and lovely. The field was carpeted in buttercups, daisies and thick green grass, and the river was lazily inviting. Had someone wandered over the brow of a nearby hill, they might at first glance have thought they'd stumbled on some quaint rural summer festival. They would certainly have stumbled on a scene that, for me, rather summed up Northern Ireland.

All the ingredients were there – the beautiful and the ugly, the gentle and the vicious, the charming and the wicked. The spectators looked not outwards but inwards – on one small patch of ground where two innately aggressive males of exactly the same species were engaged in a savage, senseless, essentially territorial fight that neither could hope to win.

I'd had an amazing two years in Northern Ireland. Contrary to expectations, the IRA ceasefire had broadly held. Unionists and republicans had reached an historic accommodation in the Good Friday peace accord, though implementing it was proving highly problematic. The violence had more or less stopped, the troops had largely disappeared from the streets, and a semblance of normality had returned.

Centuries of hatred cannot simply be legislated away, of course, and making predictions about this perverse province is notoriously dangerous – as the author of a previous travelogue about Northern Ireland discovered to his cost. 'To my special joy, I discovered that old bitternesses are waning and that the beauty of Ulster is no longer scarred by old terrors,' Robin Bryans concluded in his book *Ulster: A Journey Through Six Counties* in 1964.

But as my family and I sailed out of Belfast Lough for Liverpool one gorgeous evening in late July, there were certainly grounds for hoping that the fighting was over even if real peace had not yet taken hold, that both sides had realised the futility of violence as a means of settling ancient grievances, that this beautiful but blood-soaked province could finally lift its eyes and begin to enjoy its many assets.

I earnestly hoped so, for I had been quite won over by the place. I would be watching intensely, even though I'd now be far away. I remembered what an American diplomat had once told me. Northern Ireland was like malaria, he said. Once it's in your bloodstream you never get rid of it.

Bibliography

Babington Smith, Constance, *John Masefield: A Life* (1978). Oxford University Press.

Bardon, Jonathan, *A History of Ulster* (1992). The Blackstaff Press.

—, *Belfast: An Illustrated History* (1982). The Blackstaff Press.

Blackwood, Caroline, *Great Granny Webster* (1977). Gerald Duckworth & Co.

Bryans, Robin, *Ulster: A Journey Through the Six Counties* (1964). Faber and Faber.

Evans, Rosemary, *A Visitor's Guide to Northern Ireland* (1998). The Blackstaff Press.

Fay, Marie-Thérèse, Morrisey, Mike and Smyth, Marie, *Northern Ireland's Troubles: The Human Costs* (1999). The Pluto Press.

Fenton, James, *The Hamely Tongue* (1995). The Ulster-Scots Academic Press.

Fitzpatrick, Rory, *God's Frontiersmen: The Scots-Irish Epic* (1989). Weidenfeld and Nicholson.

McCreary, Alf, *An Ulster Journey* (1986). Greystone Books.

MacNeice, Louis, *The Strings Are False – An Unfinished Autobiography* (1965). Faber and Faber.

Moore, John, *Motor Makers in Ireland* (1982). The Blackstaff Press.

Murphy, Dervla, *A Place Apart* (1978). John Murray.

Needham, Richard, *Battling For Peace* (1998). The Blackstaff Press.

Newby, Eric, *The Last Grain Race* (1956). Secker and Warburg.

Newmann, Kate, *Dictionary of Ulster Biography* (1993). The Institute of Irish Studies, Queen's University.

Nicolson, Harold, *Helen's Tower* (1937). Constable and Co.

Reid, James Seaton, *Presbyterian Church in Ireland* (1833). Whittaker and Co.

Sandford, Ernest, *Discover Northern Ireland* (1976). Northern Ireland Tourist Board.

Stallworthy, John, *Louis MacNeice* (1995). Faber and Faber.

Thackeray, William Makepeace, *The Irish Sketch Book* (1896). Smith Elder and Co.

Tucker, Bernard, *Jonathan Swift* (1983). Gill and Macmillan, Dublin.

ALMOST HEAVEN: TRAVELS THROUGH THE BACKWOODS OF AMERICA

Martin Fletcher

'An enthralling addictive book to compare with John Steinbeck's
Travels with Charley or Bill Bryson's *Lost Continent*'
Daily Express

After seven years as Washington correspondent
of *The Times*, Martin Fletcher set off to explore the great
American 'boondocks' – the raw and untamed land that exists
far from the famous cities and national parks. His extraordinary
journey takes him to amazing communities outsiders have never
heard of, to the quintessential America. He encounters snake-
handlers, moonshiners and communities preparing for
Armageddon; goes bear-hunting and gold-prospecting;
meets truckstop preachers and Death Row inmates.
From the eccentric but friendly to the frankly
unhinged, the inhabitants of backwater America
and their preoccupations, prejudices and
traditions are brought vividly to life.

'Surprising, entertaining and original . . . a pleasure to read'
Nigel Williams, *Sunday Times*

'Very appealing . . . I highly recommend this book'
Independent on Sunday

'A triumph of a book'
Economist, Books of the Year

Abacus
0 349 10935 4

£6.99

CARSI CONNLE.

Now you can order superb titles directly from Abacus

☐ Almost Heaven: Travels through
   the Backwoods of America   Martin Fletcher   £6.99
☐ The Land of Miracles: A Journey
   through Modern Cuba   Stephen Smith   £7.99
☐ Our Lady of the Sewers: And
   Other Adventures in Deep Spain   Paul Richardson   £6.99

——————————————— (ABACUS) ———————————————

Please allow for postage and packing: **Free UK delivery.**
Europe: add 25% of retail price; Rest of World: 45% of retail price.

To order any of the above or any other Abacus titles, please call our
credit card orderline or fill in this coupon and send/fax it to:

Abacus, 250 Western Avenue, London, W3 6XZ, UK.
Fax 020 8324 5678   Telephone 020 8324 5517

☐ I enclose a UK bank cheque made payable to Abacus for £ . . . .
☐ Please charge £ . . . . . . to my Access, Visa, Delta, Switch Card No.

Expiry Date ☐☐☐☐   Switch Issue No. ☐☐

NAME (Block letters please) . . . .

ADDRESS . . . .

. . . .

. . . .

Postcode . . . . Telephone . . . .

Signature . . . .

Please allow 28 days for delivery within the UK. Offer subject to price and availability.
Please do not send any further mailings from companies carefully selected by Abacus ☐